CLOSURE

THE UNTOLD STORY OF
THE GROUND ZERO
RECOVERY MISSION

LT. WILLIAM KEEGAN, JR.
WITH BART DAVIS

A Touchstone Book

Published by Simon & Schuster
New York   London   Toronto   Sydney

For the PAPD officers and PA civilians who lost their lives;
For the families who lost their loved ones;
For all those who worked tirelessly in their behalf;
For my mom and dad and my sisters, Kathy and Helen;
For my brother Pat Dundee, gone too soon;
For my beloved family, Karen, Kristine, Tara, and Rory, who are
my heroes.

TOUCHSTONE
Rockefeller Center
1230 Avenue of the Americas
New York, NY 10020

This TOUCHSTONE edition 2007

TOUCHSTONE and colophon are registered trademarks
of Simon & Schuster, Inc.

For information regarding special discounts for bulk purchases,
please contact Simon & Schuster Special Sales at
1-800-456-6798 or business@simonandschuster.com.

Designed by William Ruoto
Diagrams by Paul J. Pugliese

Manufactured in the United States of America

1   3   5   7   9   10   8   6   4   2

The Library of Congress has cataloged the hardcover edition as follows:
Keegan, William, Jr.
Closure : the untold story of the Ground Zero recovery mission /
William Keegan, Jr., with Bart Davis
p. cm.
1. September 11 Terrorist Attacks, 2001. 2. World Trade Center Site
(New York, N.Y.) 3. Keegan, William, Jr. 4. Port Authority of New York
and New Jersey. Police Division. 5. Rescue Work--New York (State)--New
York. I. Davis, Bart, 1950- II. Title.
HV6432.7.K44 2006
974.7'1044--dc22
2006050041

ISBN-13: 978-0-7432-9186-6
ISBN-10:   0-7432-9186-7
ISBN-13: 978-0-7432-9659-5 (pbk.)
ISBN-10:   0-7432-9659-1 (pbk.)

Though they sink through the sea they shall rise again;
Though lovers be lost love shall not;
And death shall have no dominion.

Dylan Thomas

Contents

2 WTC

1 WTC

3 WTC

4 WTC

6 WTC

7 WTC

5 WTC

WEST STREET

CHURCH STREET

VESEY STREET

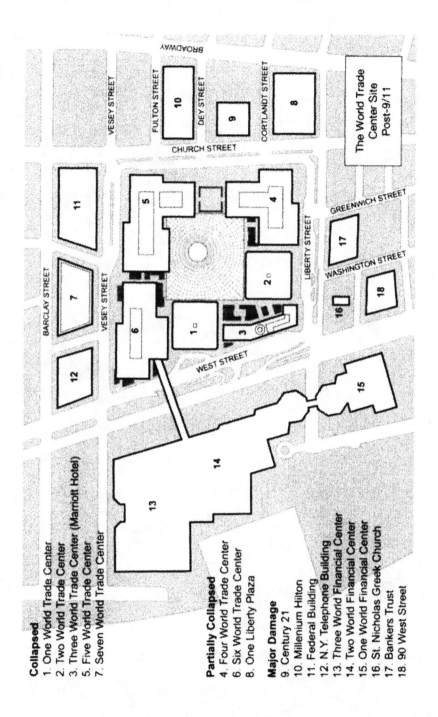

Collapsed
1. One World Trade Center
2. Two World Trade Center
3. Three World Trade Center (Marriott Hotel)
5. Five World Trade Center
7. Seven World Trade Center

Partially Collapsed
4. Four World Trade Center
6. Six World Trade Center
8. One Liberty Plaza

Major Damage
9. Century 21
10. Millenium Hilton
11. Federal Building
12. N.Y. Telephone Building
13. Three World Financial Center
14. Two World Financial Center
15. One World Financial Center
16. St. Nicholas Greek Church
17. Bankers Trust
18. 90 West Street

The World Trade Center Site Post-9/11

Preface

F ive years after the tragic events of 9-11, I still struggle to reconcile the love and compassion I saw at Ground Zero with
the evil that created it. Anyone who lost a loved one that day
knows that some wounds do not heal. For some pain there can be no
closure. Yet the courage, dedication, and patriotism of the police
officers, firefighters, engineers, Urban Search and Recovery teams,
Emergency Service Units, U.S. Marines, ironworkers, operating engineers, Federal Emergency Management Agency teams, truckers,
construction crews, and volunteers I was privileged to work with
will uplift my soul till the day I die.

I was night commander of the World Trade Center rescue and
recovery mission at Ground Zero. I was there from 9-11 to the site's
closing. A lot of what happened has never been talked about. I saw
it all. I got my hands dirty and my lungs scorched every night on
the pile, recovering the fallen in the debris—an unsafe, two-
million-ton mountain of smashed concrete, twisted steel, and
human remains.

Everything we did was condensed to raw effort. Keep moving,
find bodies; steel yourself to carry flag-draped comrades out of the
ruins; learn to lean on each other. We shivered in the same foxholes.
We suffered with the families we served. Our fear and anger were
pure and there was no outside.

In the end, a ragged band of brothers took the hill. For some,
the pain was unbearable. We pulled nineteen thousand pieces of

people out of the rubble. We got used to matching arms and legs like pairs of socks. We didn't feel heroic; we felt sick and afraid. Yet we stayed in sync with a common mission of compassion and self-lessness. For America we changed despair into hope; for the families of the fallen we changed doubt into certainty. In each other's hearts we found courage. In the midst of hell we found the face of God.

Five years later, the vision of Ground Zero has never left me. Surrounded by dark empty buildings, dotted with geysers of thick white smoke, Ground Zero was a pool of harsh light, dust, and fire, a burial ground where no one knew how many were buried. It was a nightmare no one had ever dreamed of . . . and my home for nine months till the day we walked the Last Piece of Steel out on a flatbed truck shrouded in black, and walked away.

Five years have passed since the destruction of the World Trade Center on 9-11. It is a sober anniversary that prompts us to remember the events of that day and the days that followed, with all their hope and gloom, bravery and fear, loss and gain.

Bill Keegan
SEPTEMBER 2006

Chapter One

The day the World Trade Center died was the kind of day it was born for, with the twin landmark towers outlined against a deep blue, cloudless sky. It had cost $1.5 billion, 200,000 tons of steel, 425,000 cubic yards of concrete, and six years to build the North and South Towers. They were designated Building 1 and Building 2 upon completion in 1972, the crown jewels of the sixteen-acre World Trade Center complex that included a twenty-two-story Marriott Hotel (Building 3); two nine-story office buildings (Buildings 4 and 5); the eight-story U.S. Customs House (Building 6); and a forty-seven-story high-rise office building (Building 7) that was home to the new command center of the city's Office of Emergency Management (OEM).

When the attack on 9-11 was over, both of the quarter-mile-high Towers and Building 7 had collapsed. The Marriott Hotel and Buildings 4, 5, and 6 were damaged beyond repair, and ten other buildings had sustained major damage. All that was left of the plazas, parks, and inspired architecture were pickup-stick piles of smashed concrete, jagged steel, and human remains—the landscape of Ground Zero.

I was a lieutenant in the Port Authority Police Department (PAPD), a veteran officer with over fifteen years on the job, assigned to the Special Operations Command. The Port Authority had built the World Trade Center. It was our home. We had a precinct there. We knew it better than anyone. Maybe that's why what was important to me was not how quickly the Towers succumbed, but how long they survived. From the time each was hit by an almost fully fueled hijacked 767 commercial jet, the South Tower stood for fifty-six minutes, and the North Tower stood for one hour and forty minutes. That time enabled the Port Authority Police Department, the New York City Fire Department, and the New York City Police Department—demonstrating bravery above and beyond under the most perilous conditions—to conduct the largest and most successful evacuation in this nation's history, saving thousands.

Under other circumstances, I might have been a small part of the rescue and recovery operation at Ground Zero. Instead, I became the night commander of that mission, charged with recovering the remains of my fellow officers and the thousands of innocent victims killed when the WTC Towers collapsed. This is not my story alone. It is also the story of how the mission at Ground Zero transformed all the men and women who conducted it, and it is the story of how the Port Authority Police Department's profound desire to help the victims' families turned the most overlooked of all the uniformed services at Ground Zero into one of the most important.

The Port Authority of New York and New Jersey was created in 1921 by the two states as an independent agency to oversee the harbors, presiding over a fifteen-hundred-square-mile area with the Statue of Liberty at its center. In 1930 the Port Authority was given control of the newly built Holland Tunnel. Using the tunnel's revenue, the PA went on to build the George Washington Bridge, the Outerbridge Crossing, the Goethals Bridge, the Bayonne Bridge, and the Lincoln Tunnel. In the late 1940s it leased Newark and La-Guardia airports and a small airfield in Queens that became John F. Kennedy International Airport. In the 1950s, '60s, and '70s, it built the Port Authority Bus Terminal; added a second deck to the George Washington Bridge; acquired the Hudson and Manhattan Railroad, which became the PATH rail transit system; and built the World Trade Center, which it owned and operated for almost four decades.

Although the Port Authority Police Department protects almost every major air, sea, and land route in and out of New York and New Jersey; although we are visible at every bridge, tunnel, and airport; and although we have been in existence since 1928, when forty men were hired to guard the new bridges to Staten Island—we are virtually unknown to the public. The PAPD? What is that? The Pennsylvania Police Department? The Perth Amboy Police Department? A standing joke held that this anonymity was why we had "Port Authority Police Department" spelled out on our uniform hats.

However, when the Towers collapsed on 9-11, the Port Authority Police Department suffered the largest loss of law enforcement personnel in United States history—thirty-seven officers. The loss was larger than that sustained by the NYPD and a greater percentage of total force than that lost by the FDNY. The NYPD had 40,000 members, and the FDNY had more than 11,000. The PAPD had only 1,100. Every uniformed service death on 9-11 was tragic, but because of our size, not one single PAPD officer failed to lose someone close to him, including me.

On the morning of 9-11 I was at Children's Specialized Hospital at Mountainside when the call came in to mobilize. My wife, Karen, and I had brought our middle daughter, Tara, to undergo tests. Karen and I had been married for twelve years and had three daughters. Two were healthy. Tara was born with a little-known neurological disorder called Rett Syndrome. It occurs almost exclusively in girls. There is normal development for the first six to eighteen months of life, but then Rett Syndrome leads to severe disability by the age of three. At that moment, she was nine years old.

I tried to get through to our precinct at the World Trade Center on my wife's cell phone. There was no response from any of our desks. By now, every television in the neurology wing had footage of the burning WTC Towers. The newscasters kept talking about the buildings. I kept thinking about the people. How many had gotten out? How many were still trapped? How were we going to rescue them?

I drove Karen and Tara home and packed equipment and clothing for a long stay. I kissed Tara and my wife good-bye. Karen hugged me tightly. She was a cop's wife, and it was a certain kind of kiss. She knew what it meant: I was going into danger and had no idea when I'd be back.

Every highway with access to New York City was closed after the attack. New Jersey state troopers guarded the entrance ramp to the New Jersey Turnpike, and I had to show my Port Authority Police lieutenant's badge to get on. Apart from a convoy of ambulances and army trucks, my big old Mercury Grand Marquis sedan was the only car on the road. I pushed it past eighty miles an hour and headed for the PAPD command post at the World Trade Center.

At that speed the buildings of Jersey City, where I grew up, slid past me like snapshots. I saw the big Medical Center where most of Jersey City was born; Hudson Catholic High School, where from the windows of the third-floor lecture room we watched the Twin Towers being built across the river; the vegetable store on Sip Avenue where I used to see a then-unknown blind sheik named Omar Abdal Rahman holding court, never dreaming our lives would intersect when he tried to bring down the WTC in '93 and on 9-11 when his goal was realized; and I saw the candy store where we tried to figure out how the cranes on top of the towers could ever get down once they were finished building it.

Looking back, I can picture myself driving down the highway in my old Mercury as clearly as if it were a movie. I had the radio on. There were news reports of U.S. war planes in the sky and emergency vehicles arriving at the World Trade Center. Initial reports said there could have been as many as twenty-five thousand people in the Towers, and no one knew how many had been killed or injured. They talked about the attack on the Pentagon as an act of war, and there was constant speculation about the possibility of more attacks. The reports fueled the intensity of my need to get to the Trade Center to start helping. Duty called; I responded. People needed help; that was a cop's job. That morning, it all seemed so clear. Would I have felt the same if I knew the pain of the struggle I would face at Ground Zero?

At that moment I had no idea that the order mobilizing the Port Authority Police to the World Trade Center would mark the start of the longest, most painful, problematic, and rewarding journey of my life. I didn't know I would become the Night Commander of the World Trade Center Rescue and Recovery operation, or that I would spend every day of the next nine months in service to the families of the victims, or that in their service I would make decisions almost unthinkable at any other place and time.

No one at Ground Zero anticipated what the rescue and recovery mission would involve—how it would change us or what we would feel the day it ended, when New Yorkers by the tens of thousands lined the streets to watch the Last Piece of Steel leave the site with hundreds of cops, firefighters, and construction workers marching behind it—and I absolutely did not know what it would cost me to be leading them.

As I drove, I thought a lot about the World Trade Center bombing in 1993. It had injured more than a thousand, killed six, and left a crater two hundred feet wide and six stories deep, but the Towers stood. I was sure they would stand this time too— burned but not broken, like in '93—until I heard on the radio that the South Tower and then the North Tower had fallen and ended all hope. My emotions couldn't accept the Towers in ruins. I had walked through the World Trade Center plaza when I was a kid on my way to Sy Syms to buy clothes. I tried to strike up conversations with the girls walking to work. The WTC was where I took my police tests and physical exams. It was where tourists and schoolkids and workers and people from all over came to sit down and see greatness. The images in my mind were of World War II cities bombed into rubble, except now the city was New York.

I got my first glimpse of the World Trade Center on the Turnpike Extension bridge over Newark Bay and driving down the Jersey side of the Hudson. Across the river there was nothing visible except thick black smoke covering Lower Manhattan like a coat.

I stopped at the Port Authority garage on the Jersey side of the Holland Tunnel, where a patrol car and driver were waiting to take me to the PAPD Command Post at the World Trade Center. In the Holland Tunnel Plaza there were rows of waiting ambulances, and army trucks with camouflage-pattern tops. The PA garage was a big space where we stored snowplows and heavy machines. It had been converted to a hospital. There were rows of white-sheeted cots with IV poles standing next to them. Doctors and nurses talked or made calls or inventoried supplies.

I took my gear over to the command center, which looked more like a store than a police station. I went through the glass doors into a waiting area with plastic chairs. The desk sergeant was sitting behind a Formica counter. He straightened a bit as I approached.

"Lieutenant Keegan? Sergeant Johnson. Your ride's on the way."

"Thanks, Sarge."

The TV on the wall showed nonstop footage of the Towers' collapse. No matter how many times the planes hit or the bodies fell, the sergeant kept turning back to watch it. He just kept shaking his head.

Outside in the plaza, cops and drivers and EMTs all moved at a normal pace. Where was the frantic tempo of an emergency? I expected shock and trauma. Instead the scene was calm and orderly. It was so different from the aftermath of the '93 bombing, when the rescue and relief work went on for days. The rows of ambulances and army trucks lining the plaza looked like bumper-to-bumper traffic except no one was going anywhere.

"Sarge, how long have these units been staged and ready?"

"Since right after the planes hit, Loo, but the Trade Center command hasn't called for a single one. Aren't there any victims?"

Like the rest of us, Sergeant Johnson expected conditions similar to those of the '93 bombing, when more than a thousand victims had needed emergency treatment. That early on 9-11, none of us yet knew how few of the WTC victims would need anything but burial.

"Ride's ready, Lieutenant. Good luck."

A blue and white PAPD patrol car was waiting outside in the plaza. The sergeant's eyes swiveled back to the TV screen.

I was anxious to get to the command post, but the few minutes it took the patrol car to drive through the empty Holland Tunnel were oddly peaceful. The peace disappeared as soon as we drove out of the tunnel into Manhattan. The smell of smoke flooded the car even through closed windows. Everything I could see—parked cars, trees, storefronts—*everything* was covered inches deep in dust as if neglected for decades. There was paper too. Big pieces, scraps, pages of books, ledger paper, graph paper, legal paper—all blasted from 220 stories of offices, banks, law firms, and trading companies by the collapse of the Towers.

We drove to the PAPD mobile command post parked on West Street in front of Borough of Manhattan Community College. I got out of the car and saw Ground Zero close up for the first time. The debris was four stories high across West Street. Returning cops and firefighters were walking back from it like soldiers after battle. Most of my cops were still in rescue gear, talking in small groups by the command post. Every inch of their clothing and gear was coated with cement dust. Their faces were completely white; the only color was the blue or brown of their eyes.

I was worried about them. They talked fast, disjointed—what had happened to them, where they had been when the Towers fell, who else had been there. Some were vacant-eyed; we call it the thousand-yard stare. I had seen victims of violent crime stare like that, never a group of cops. I got to as many as I could, hugged them, talked to them, and comforted each as best I was able.

I went into the Command Post, a mobile unit the size of a bus that was dispatched from the PAPD's Journal Square headquarters in Jersey City. It was white and blue, the same colors as our patrol cars, with "Port Authority Police Department Mobile Command Post" on both sides in big blue letters. Inside, bulletin boards were secured to the walls. There were notices and information sheets tacked all over them. The unit had doors and windows in front and in back, and a center corridor with workstations with phones and computers on both sides. At the very end was the incident Commander's office. It had a special communications area and a conference table with bench seats.

Inside there was so much activity, you had to be an acrobat to get a cup of coffee back to a desk without spilling it. Specially trained technicians were hooking up phones, radios, and computers. Twice the entire command post rocked violently as engineers secured the steel legs that extended from the undercarriage to stabilize it. Inspector Joe Morris and his aide, Lieutenant Preston Fucci, were in discussions with senior officers. At the desks, officers were talking by phone or radio to our people here at the WTC and at other PAPD commands in and around the city.

At one desk, a special officer maintained the log. It was an important job. He logged in PAPD support teams arriving with everything from heavy vehicles to medical supplies, establishing a master list of the resources available to us. It was also the definitive chronology of events—when the FAA ordered us to close the airports, or the Air Force began to do flyovers, or the FDNY declared a particular building unsafe and ordered everybody evacuated.

The PAPD faced serious problems on 9-11. The collapse of Towers 1 and 2 had destroyed our police precinct, our executive offices, our records, and our archives. Also, as a department we were stretched desperately thin. In New York and New Jersey, we were responsible for three airports, two tunnels, four bridges, the PATH subway system, two interstate bus terminals, and seven marine cargo terminals. Closing all the New York and New Jersey airports, all bridge and tunnel crossings into Manhattan, and the interstate highways into New York City was a huge job—and the environment of heightened security only added to it.

I stowed my gear and checked in with Inspector Morris. In our command structure, captains and above—inspectors, deputy chiefs, assistant chiefs, and chiefs—are administration. Lieutenants are the highest rank of Operations. We are the most senior officers on patrol and are actively engaged in what police officers do. In the chaos of 9-11, the administrators were trying to identify the most serious issues. As a lieutenant, I developed plans to deal with those issues. I would determine what resources the plans required and then supervise the sergeants and police officers who executed the plans.

On 9-11 we lost our Superintendent of Police Fred Marrone, our Chief of Police James Romito, Inspector Anthony Infante, Captain Kathy Mazza, and many of our Emergency Service Unit officers. Not knowing the full extent of PAPD losses made it difficult to plan for what initial estimates said could be more than six thousand civilian casualties. It was a relief to everyone in the Command Post when one of our missing cops would radio in his or her location, or report to another PAPD command.

It became apparent to all of us that we had to get people back into position to move forward. I felt the most important thing was for me to get up to speed, to know what was going on. The only way to do that was to reach out to other commanders at the site. So I picked up a phone and started calling them.

Take a step forward, any step; what you don't know, you'll learn. That was how I approached the first few hours. I fielded phone inquiries from agencies wanting information about Port Authority operations at the airports, tunnels, and bridges. NYPD

ESU Captain Yee called us asking to have PAPD officers assigned to his rescue teams to help them get their bearings on the site. The NYPD hadn't quite understood the WTC complex when it was standing. After the collapse they understood it even less. We were the only ones who could show them how to get down to the subways or to different parking lot levels or to where stairways had been located. That knowledge would play a vital role later on when I had to deal with the NYPD, FDNY, and their site commanders.

There were phone calls from upstate trucking companies with materials and equipment to deliver to the site. They had to cross the George Washington Bridge to get here, but it was closed. The only way we let them on the bridge was with a Port Authority Police escort that led them down to the site, or with an NYPD unit that met them at the bridge and brought them down. It was the same at the Holland Tunnel and the Lincoln Tunnel.

My initial intention had been to check in and go right down to the site, but I was too busy. Yet, as I was trying to make some kind of order out of all that confusion, a very small thing happened that showed me how much the wounds inflicted by the events of 9-11 had already changed our most basic perceptions of our lives and ourselves.

I was in charge of dispersing supplies from the staging area Inspector Larry Fields and Officer Barry Pikaard had established in the Borough of Manhattan Community College's big gymnasium to where they were needed. By midafternoon we realized we needed additional space for equipment that had to be instantly accessible to our guys, without request forms or protocol: items like Scott air bottles (the scubalike air tanks that fit into a backpack breathing apparatus), face masks, riggings, body bags, Stokes baskets (the stretchers with low sides used to carry bodies), helmets, and other emergency equipment. Our plan was simple—set up big tents in front of the command post on West Street, which already had site security, including a view from inside via the external video cameras on its roof.

The problem was that West Street was lined with trees, and the tents were too large to fit between them. No one knew what to do. It became a problem. People began to redesign the tents; others looked for new riggings; others made calls to other services to see if they had tents smaller than ours. It became a debate involving nearly everybody—until someone took a chain saw and cut down all the trees.

I had never even considered that. None of us had. Cut down trees to put up tents on a college campus in this city? Not usually, but given the horror we were dealing with, the stakes were simply too high not to do it. It was so small to be so big, but it was my wake-up call. We were operating under new and very different priorities.

A wide set of stairs off West Street led to Borough of Manhattan Community College's gym and the staging area. A conga line ran from the trucks in the street to the gym as people passed box after box of gloves, masks, shirts, flashlights, batteries, and helmets from one person to the next, all the way to where they were stacked and stored. On a walkway outside the gym, I saw my old friend Lieutenant John Kassimatis. I had once worked for John at the Port Authority Bus Terminal in Manhattan. He was big and broad-shouldered, sporting an equally big mustache, and he was famous for his great stories about the "old times" at the Bus Terminal. John was enormously popular; no matter where we went, he always knew someone who greeted him like a best friend. I was with him one time when that included the Greek Orthodox patriarch.

John saw me and waved. He was on his Nextel phone, and I could hear his conversation as I got closer. It sounded like he was talking to his wife. It was the closest thing to normalcy I had heard all day.

"Yeah, I'm down here," he was saying. "You know, we're just getting some supplies . . . Yeah, no, I'm fine . . . I'm just gonna co-ordinate this, I'm not so sure what time I'll be home . . ."

It was the kind of mundane, everyday conversation that he'd had a hundred times about what time he'll be home, what he was doing, how the weather was and everything else. I liked hearing it. Then, in the middle of it, something came over John. His face changed. His voice too. It got deeper and sadder, and it was like there was something he couldn't hold inside any longer. He seemed to crumble a little, and said these words:

"I lost guys."

Those were the words, "I lost guys." *He* lost them. They were working for *him* that day. *He* was the boss. "I lost guys." It just didn't fit the conversation he had been having, so I knew how much he wanted to say it, to tell somebody. He said it once more, and then this big man with his big mustache and great stories bent over the railing and buried his face and his chin into his chest. I walked over to him. He was crying. I put my hand on his shoulder. He didn't react, but at least he knew I was there. That was enough. I stood to the side and waited, speaking, but not really talking, to the people passing.

After a while, John stood up and walked away.

I lost guys.

There was nothing else to say.

In situations like these, who knows why you gravitate to someone in particular? Outside, I found myself standing next to one of my sergeants, a wise old hand at the job, on the corner a little ways away from the others. He had just gotten back from Ground Zero and cleaned up a little and had some water, but he was still covered with ash. For a while we both stared down to the burning ruins of the World Trade Center. Around us, dust fell like snow. I knew from experience you can be in the command post all you want; only the people doing the job on the ground know what's really happening.

After some small talk, I found myself asking what I really

wanted to know. I remember how the dust settling on him made his skin and clothes so white that when he turned his dark eyes to me and opened his mouth to speak, he looked like a photograph with too much contrast.

"How do things look, Sarge?" I asked.

He shook his head. "Not so good, Loo."

"Do we have any missing?"

"Yeah, we do."

"How many?"

"A lot," he said.

"A lot?"

"Yeah."

Every question was mine, repeated again as if I just couldn't get it.

"How many is a lot?"

"We don't know."

"Fifty?"

He shrugged. "Could be."

"More than fifty?

"Could be."

"How about the PATH guys?"

"A lot are missing."

It went on and on. Me asking, repeating his answers as questions.

"Missing? Like who?"

"Bruce Reynolds and Bobby Kaufeurs."

The names stunned me. Old friends. Good friends. I looked at him in disbelief.

"Reynolds and Kaufeurs?"

"Yeah."

Only later did I understand that our conversation evoked in me the same emotional and physical pain as the one I had in Children's Hospital in Philadelphia six years before, when Karen and I were first told about Tara. My daughter sat on my lap while they tested her—find the doll, follow the doll, concentrate on the doll—and even though I saw her fail the most rudimentary tests, I still wasn't ready for what happened to me when the doctor began telling us how she would need a special school. The truth was that as Tara had grown up, we had a growing awareness that something was wrong, but I had desperately avoided the truth. Even now I wanted her to pass the tests so I would not have to face it. I wanted it so much that I barely heard the words when the doctor spoke them.

"Your daughter is retarded," she said, and it broke my heart.

I got the same metallic taste in my mouth as when I was hit so hard on the football field that I got a concussion. The words drove me inside myself. When I didn't react, she said, "You understand, your daughter will never live outside the home."

I started talking just to get myself going, like a boxer punching even when he's out on his feet, punching just to keep on standing because it's all he knows how to do.

"Retarded?"

She nodded. "Yes."

"What do you mean by 'retarded'?"

"Her brain development is arrested."

"Arrested means stopped?"

"Well, there are levels."

"Levels?"

"It can be mild, severe, or profound."

"Which one is she, Doctor?"

"Severe."

"Severe closer to mild?"

"Closer to profound."

I had kept repeating what she said—just as I was doing now on 9-11 talking to the sergeant on the corner, looking down to the site, watching the pile burn.

"*How many?*"

"*A lot.*"

"How many is a lot?"
"We don't know."
"How about the PATH guys?"
"A lot are missing."
"A lot?"
"Yeah, a lot."
It broke my heart all over again.

The first lull in the action came late that afternoon. I had learned a lot about the overall situation from the other commanders, but it was time for me to head for Ground Zero. I needed to see the fallen buildings. I needed to take it all in. I had no specific plan. I'd know what was important when I saw it.

Wanting to see things clearly was a trait I inherited from my father. He was a captain in the Jersey City Fire Department, a man with very strong beliefs but still an independent thinker who analyzed things on their own merits. My father taught me that to make intelligent decisions, you had to "step back, observe, and remain objective." That practice helped me make decisions in the early days of my command at Ground Zero when there weren't any rules to guide us.

I learned something equally important from my mother—the need to "temper justice with mercy." You can't be a really good cop without compassion and understanding. Sometimes you have to look at "extenuating circumstances." My father felt people should take care of their own problems. My mother was a wonderful woman, deeply concerned about the welfare of others and always involved in their lives. Two such different and distinct people had a hard time seeing, much less accepting, each other's point of view.

Maybe because I inherited aspects of each of my parents, I was able to love and appreciate both. I saw good in both. I suppose I was, and am, the fusion of both. Interestingly, living where we did in Jersey City between John F. Kennedy Boulevard and Martin

Luther King Drive, the city's racial border, my parents gave me a real advantage. Even at eight or nine years of age, I could evaluate, appreciate, and communicate with just about everyone I met. Playing so many sports, I had to cross the "border" almost every day and interact with kids from all over the city. I saw that each side knew almost nothing about the other—except fear. I saw how easily fear can become anger, and anger become violence.

It's not easy to be ignorant: you have to be taught. One of my parents' great gifts is that I wasn't.

With the action in the command post at its quietest level since morning, I finished up my work and gave my intended location to the desk sergeant. It was safer to go to the Trade Center site with a team, and I had already seen Colin and Mike Hennessy in the Command Post. Colin, the eldest Hennessy brother, was an NYPD cop. He had just finished his shift. Mike Hennessy was one of my top PAPD cops. I had been especially relieved when he reported in. They were Bronx Irish—fair-haired, good-looking, tough, and athletic. Both were in uniform and had surgical masks hanging around their necks.

I went over and said, "Come on, I'm going down to the site. How about coming along?"

Colin shook his head, "Don't do it, Billy. Those buildings are gonna be coming down soon."

"Maybe they will, maybe they won't," I said. "But I gotta see what's happening."

I grabbed a mask and gloves and hung towels on my belt, like I saw a lot of returning cops do, to cover my face or any other exposed skin if necessary.

Mike had been watching me. He knew I wouldn't order him to go, and I couldn't order Colin because he was NYPD. Mike turned to Colin said something privately to him. Colin nodded and reached for his gear.

"You're not going alone, Billy," Colin told me.

"Hope that's okay, Boss," Mike said, suiting up too.

"It's fine," I said, and we headed out.

Outside, it looked like the moon. The dust on the ground was so thick it came up around our boots. It got even thicker as we moved toward the site. We reached a point where we had to get up on the cement medians along West Street to walk unimpeded.

The closer we got to the site, the more foreboding it felt. The streets were deserted. The evacuated buildings were dark. We couldn't see the sky, and when we reached Building 7, it was on fire. Building 7 had housed the Mayor's Office of Emergency Management along with financial institutions and government agencies like Salomon Smith Barney, American Express Bank International, the U.S. Secret Service, the Immigration and Naturalization Service, the Securities and Exchange Commission, and the Central Intelligence Agency. Now flames were spreading and smoke poured out of vacant windows that had been exploded by the heat.

We spotted a PAPD van abandoned in the street about a hundred yards from the entrance. We were still trying to locate all our people. The van might tell us which cops left it. If they hadn't been accounted for, we'd begin a search for them. I radioed in the number. Colin and Mike threw the van doors open and pulled out two replacement Scott air bottles and a PAPD airport command firefighter's bunker coat with its distinctive silver heat-resistant fabric and *NIA*—Newark International Airport—stenciled on it.

All this was extremely encouraging except for one thing: Building 7 started to collapse next to us.

There was a thundering roar like the sound of a dozen locomotives bearing down that got louder and louder as the forty-seven-story building crumbled only a hundred yards away. It stopped us dead in our tracks, paralyzing us because it seemed to be everywhere. The sound got even louder till it was almost unbearable. A dense black cloud was forming above St. John's University from the smoke pouring into the sky, towering over us. That did it.

Colin yelled, "Run!" and we took off for our lives.

It wasn't until we got maybe half a block away that we looked back. I'll never forget it. Up until that moment, I thought big things didn't move fast, but they did, and we were in trouble. That huge rolling cloud of black smoke and dust and debris from Building 7's collapse was coming straight up West Street at us like it was out to get us.

I heard the Command Post on my radio, "Building Seven is coming down. Building Seven is down." I was running too hard to respond. The only protection was the Command Post trailer ahead of us. The cloud rolled all the way up West Street. The wind reached us first. The three of us got to the Command Post and ducked behind it as the rest of the cloud hit us like a storm.

We were safe for the moment behind the trailer, but hunching there with the wind and dust and pieces of debris hitting all around, I knew Ground Zero was speaking to me personally. It had brought down a building right beside me to make sure I listened to its message: *This isn't going to be like anything you've ever experienced. Be warned. Go back. It won't be like the first bombing. This is the real deal. You could die here . . . and if you're not careful, you will.*

Chapter Two

On 9-11, the Incident Commander of PAPD operations at the World Trade Center was Inspector Joe Morris. Despite the chaos of the first hours, Morris correctly identified a problem that would cripple our effectiveness if not fixed immediately. We were being ignored. The far larger NYPD and FDNY commands left us completely out of the loop. They did not communicate with us, and their radios and cell phones were not accessible to us. We had all kinds of reports that the FDNY and NYPD were conducting operations at Ground Zero; the problem was we had no idea what they were.

We didn't like it.

We were a department with almost a century of experience. The thing we cared about most was trying to rescue as many people as possible. It never occurred to us that it would be an uphill fight. Part of the problem was that we were unprepared to work with the huge and powerful NYPD and FDNY. The Port Authority Police Department didn't belong to the New York City government. We did not report to the mayor. We had only a small relationship with the NYPD and none at all with the FDNY. In those difficult first hours, changes were taking place at lightning speed. Both the FDNY and NYPD were already conducting search operations on the site that had been our home, and where thirty-seven of our cops were buried, and we had no way to access their command.

There was also a competitive atmosphere as the two huge New

York commands fought for dominance. It was new to us. Inspector Morris and the other top commanders realized that for the PAPD to do the work we had come here to do, we had to become equal partners with the FDNY and NYPD. Inspector Morris chose me and PAPD Lieutenant John Ryan to establish that partnership. He gave the day command of the rescue and recovery mission at Ground Zero to Ryan. He gave me the night.

"Billy, find out what the fuck is going on down there. I want to find people. I want to find our cops. Our people are out there on the mountain doing their jobs, but we're still left out of communications. In fact, we're further back—working as hard but not in the loop. I don't like not knowing what's going on. I want you to go down there and find out."

Morris knew I had only limited experience in search and rescue, but that meant less to him than my being tough, aggressive, a quick learner, and impossible to intimidate.

"One more thing, Bill," Morris said firmly. "You have a job to do besides the rescue and recovery. Maybe it's the same job, when I think about it. Either way, you're going to bring this department into parity with those big bastards if you have to carry it on your back."

By virtue of Morris's appointment, I was the PAPD commander at Ground Zero during my tour—a position without authority unless and until the other commands acknowledged it. I wasn't sure I could do the job. There was so much I didn't know. Up until 9-11, I was just a good cop who caught bad guys. For most of my fifteen years on the job, I had worked the graveyard shift in Midtown Manhattan. I saw a lot of damage to people and property during that time. I also comforted a lot of victims. Maybe it qualified me, maybe it didn't. What did it take to go from the graveyard shift at night, to the night shift of a graveyard? I could relate to the families of the victims. They were victims too.

In my head I saw a woman alone in her house wondering if

this was the night the phone would ring and there would be news, wondering if maybe it was all a mistake, if maybe her husband would show up in some hospital with a bump on his head and re-member who he was, who they were. All I could picture was that wife putting the kids to bed, trying not to cry, trying to be strong, praying with them but unable to answer the kids when they asked, *Is Daddy up in heaven? Is he going to be found? It's not like Daddy's dead,* she tells them, *we just don't know where he went.* I could see her walk-ing through a darkened house, where the only light is from the TV. She needs to go to sleep but she waits for the call, exhausted by an-other night of crying, another night in an empty bed.

That was the connection between the night, the families, and me. It was why I couldn't stop. I had to do everything I possibly could to help them. The night might suit me, but it haunted me too. While the rest of the city slept, and my teams and I worked, the families waited without distraction or relief. Alone, all they had was pain.

I was also driven by the need to find my fallen comrades. Every one of them had made the ultimate sacrifice. They had behaved so splendidly that despite the tons of debris that covered them, when I walked on the pile I felt the presence of the most courageous peo-ple I would ever know. I would never forget them putting their Scott air packs on and racing into the Towers and bringing people out, then running right back into the smoke and fire to save more. They smelled burning fuel, saw bodies fall, carried people on their backs—and they kept going back in with no thought of their own safety. I felt tears well up because I knew what had been in their minds: *Let me get my job done . . . I'll be okay . . . I need to make those people okay.*

Then they died, doing their duty.

In 1993 I had gone into WTC Tower 1 on a rescue mission after the first bomb exploded. Thirteen kindergarten kids were trapped in a stalled elevator on the forty-third floor. We got them out. I kept thinking that if I had been doing the same job on 9-11 as I was doing in '93, I would have been buried the same way as my thirty-seven officers and the thousands of others.

Maybe that's why I was still here all these years later—to get them out.

Looking back, I see that I had no idea what "getting them out" would mean. Events on 9-11 and the days that followed taught me my first lesson: nothing I had learned as a Port Authority police officer or in my entire life prepared me for the decisions I would face as night commander of the rescue and recovery operation.

One of the first tests came shortly after 9-11. Fires still raged inside the pile, easiest to see at night and more fearsome, like the eyes of a Halloween jack-o'-lantern. The weather was the worst we'd had so far. Cold winds drove a misty rain that stung our faces and hands. The adrenaline of the first days was wearing off. Fatigue was setting in. Coughing up dust and trying to stay dry while construction machines roared and wheezed all around us shortened everybody's temper and patience.

A recovery operation is about finding needles in haystacks— and that can only be done slowly and carefully. Our goal wasn't to set a speed record; it was to not miss things. To ensure we found every single "needle," we came up with a process we called the "first two looks" and it was mandatory with me.

When a grappler dug into the pile, I wanted a cop or a fireman watching the claw go in, seeing what it closed on, and examining what it pulled out. I also wanted a second look—but this one at the area the grappler opened up. That area was now considered a new site. For illumination at the site we used big Daisy lights mounted on poles with aluminum reflectors behind the halogen bulbs so they were really bright. We focused them down on the area where the grappler had pulled out the debris. I wanted my guys to get right up to it. If that was too dangerous, we set up a viewing platform for them.

Meanwhile, the Operating Engineer turned the grappler

around, put the claw about a foot off the ground, and slowly shook out the debris till everything but the big pieces of steel was sifted out. A cop or firefighter would stand there watching it come out. We got very good at spotting "possibles." So did the Operating Engineers, who sometimes had an even better vantage point perched high up in the grappler's glass air-conditioned control booth. It was not uncommon for an engineer to stop his rig and point down to where he saw something. Unfortunately, most of the time we already knew. When something was uncovered, the smell was overwhelming.

Even if the construction companies had orders from the DDC or the city itself, I refused to allow them to move any debris from the pile directly into a dump truck for removal. It had to be taken first to a "shakeout," where a big grappler pushed the debris into piles for a smaller grappler to sift onto the ground. Later, when enough debris had been removed from the site to give us space, guys would manually rake out the sifted debris to look through it once again. At that point, and only if all the "looks" had been taken, would I clear the load to be trucked to Fresh Kills, where it would be put on conveyor belts and looked at one last time.

When I got to the site at 5 p.m., there was a message for me from the day commander, John Ryan, asking me to respond to the 10/10 Firehouse on Greenwich Street. He was waiting with FDNY Deputy Chief John Norman, a dedicated and well-respected officer with years of experience in rescue and recovery work with the Special Operations Command (SOC).

I notified my sergeants where I was going. The firehouse wasn't far and it was a relief to get out of the rain. Ryan and Norman were upstairs. We all knew each other, so greetings were brief. Ryan filled me in.

"Bill, we've got a body of a cop in a shallow cave thirty feet straight up a sheer wall of debris. The body is in head first. We'll have to cut a lot of steel to get him out."

"How do we know it's a cop?" I asked.

"The boots," Ryan explained. "They're cop boots. We brought one back but there's no way to ID it. I took a scraping from his feet and sent it to the M.E.'s office. We won't know anything more till we get a DNA match from the samples they've collected from the families."

The Medical Examiner had done an amazing job of collecting and categorizing DNA from cell samples taken from victims' toothbrushes, shaving razors, combs, brushes, and other personal items brought in by the victims' families. DNA was a substance that deteriorated rapidly over time, losing its viability as genetic material. Almost overnight new techniques were being invented to prolong its usefulness in identifications.

"Is the location that bad?" I asked.

"It is," Ryan said flatly. "Almost none of the area has been cleared."

John and I were fighting the same fight and there was rarely tension between us. We did things to make our commands mesh more easily, like talking about our tours by phone while either of us was on our way in to the site. That way, we were briefed by the time we arrived.

"How long till it's open?" I asked.

"At least a week. The construction crews and the grapplers ought to get to the site by then," Ryan said.

I didn't like it. "It's too long. He's been found. I want to get him out. Even tonight, if it's possible."

"Lieutenant, we've lost too many people to these nineteen motherfuckers already," Norman said. "Be careful."

"I don't intend to lose anybody, Chief. Who's in charge over there?" I asked.

"John Moran," Ryan said.

NYPD Lieutenant John Moran had the distinction of being a member of the New York Task Force, the combined team of NYPD and FDNY specialists dispatched by the Federal Emergency Management Agency (FEMA) to disasters all over the country. It was obviously a source of pride to John, as he always wore the distinctive red helmet of the New York Task Force.

"You're going to try a recovery?" asked Chief Norman.

"If I think I can get him out, I'm gonna try."

I understood the Chief's concerns. We wanted the same thing and that included our men safe. John Ryan had one of his men take me to the location of the body. On the way, I called Sergeant Kevin Devlin to respond there, along with my main team—a group of PAPD officers from the Port Authority Trans-Hudson (PATH) command. PATH cops were a proud and ballsy group. On 9-11, PATH units accounted for almost a third of all our officers killed. I sent the order for them to suit up and meet me.

The PATH subway system connects Manhattan and the city of Newark—one of New Jersey's poorest communities. During the day, PATH trains carry commuters by the tens of thousands from home to work and back again. At night it's less upscale. Drugs go back and forth; so do guns and gangs. PATH cops deal on a regular basis with homeless people, violent felons, physical assaults, and shootings—what most people consider "real" crime. They are experienced cops working in an environment as dangerous as any in the city, and their attitude is "We don't take a back seat to anybody; never did, never will."

For the record, it was the PATH command officers, men like Paul Nunziato, Paddy Callaghan, Tim Mueller, Gary Griffin, and Mike Hennessy who made it possible for me to do my job. They ably represent a larger group that never once failed the mission or me.

The PATH cops in my crew were in their late thirties with five to ten years on the job. Nunziato was the ringleader. He was a six-foot-one, 210-pound second-generation PAPD cop who talked like a Brooklyn wiseguy and always called me "Boss." Nunziato was an excellent organizer, which was part of what made him the leader. Like all of us, he loved sports; we both played Port Authority football. The only thing Nunziato loved more than sports was practical jokes. If something disgusting fell out of your locker, it was a safe bet Nunziato put it there.

Paddy Callaghan was five foot ten inches tall and had a mustache that curved down to his chin and made him look like a Mexican bandit. He was a big guy when I first met him. By 9-11 he had trimmed down. What hadn't lost its size was his heart. Paddy had a big heart. All of us had some of our closest friends killed, but Paddy attended every single memorial mass the PAPD held. He was a welcome sight pulling up in the old van he drove. That old van was a symbol of Paddy's caring and the place where everybody gathered after the mass to be together. In the back Paddy had built a full bar where we could toast our fallen comrade.

Tim Mueller had learned the job fast. He was street smart and savvy and made a lot of good narcotics arrests, taking large quantities of drugs off the streets. He had broad shoulders and salt-and-pepper hair, and he was such an avid boater and fisherman that anyone who was even considering buying a boat talked to him first.

Gary Griffin grew up in Greenville, same as I did. I had known him since we were kids and played baseball together; he was in center field, I was on third base. We nicknamed Gary "Crime Dog." When it came to crime, he never stopped sniffing. It killed him to think anybody "dirty" was getting by him—that *anything* was getting by him. One night without a collar and he was beside himself. The pile could take all that energy and more.

Maybe because we were all athletes and loved playing sports, we had a natural affinity. Mike Hennessy, who had been with me when Building 7 collapsed, was shortstop for the PA baseball team, quick, agile, a master of distance and timing, Mike was the wiry type who was a lot stronger than he looked and could carry fifty pounds of equipment all day without the slightest strain. He was smart and observant, someone the others knew they could depend on.

Every one of them was dedicated to the mission. They had to be, out on that mountain of debris. They carried their own saws and got their own replacement blades. They were always the first ones out, and the last ones back. They found bodies and body parts and knew exactly what to do with them. Every one was a can-do type. If I said I wanted to move an operation from here to there, it was always "You got it, Boss," and they'd start picking up their stuff. It didn't matter where I sent them; they always did the job.

Nunziato, Callaghan, Mueller, Griffin, and Hennessy responded from our command post to Ground Zero. The recovery site was a part of the pile where the debris towered five stories high over a field of sharp metal at the bottom. I could see why it would be a week before the grapplers could clear it. On one side a sheer cliff rose forty feet straight up to a small plateau, and about ten feet below the plateau was an alcove where the body was located. To get to the plateau we'd have to come in from Liberty Street, climb over the pile down to the plateau, then climb down the cliff face with our backs to the cliff using the steel beams jutting out of the debris.

"You can sure pick 'em, Boss" was Nunziato's only comment.

We stared down to the alcove. The only place to stand level with it was a section of ruined concrete stairway ten feet down. There were lots of pockets between the steel beams, and then a lot of sheet metal where we had to be careful not to cut our legs. We got down to the level of the alcove, but there was nothing on the left or the right of it, so even though it was only five or six feet away, we couldn't jump it. We made our way across the cliff face, around more steel. A couple of times we had to hold on to jagged steel for purchase or to get our balance, and we had to be very careful about our footing.

Chief Norman was right about one thing—this recovery was going to be tough. I was glad to have John Moran's experience to call upon.

"Moran's here," relayed Hennessy from outside the alcove.

It was good news. "Wave him down," I said.

John Moran was six foot one, wore glasses, and cut his dark hair very short. He was intelligent and well-spoken. The temperature was down in the thirties, so he was wearing an NYPD Emergency Service Unit (ESU) thermal jacket and pants, and "lumberjack" boots with steel plates in the soles. John was known to be thrifty, and it was rumored he'd had these particular boots for twenty years. In the windy, misty darkness I followed his red helmet stenciled NY-TF 1 as he made his way down the cliff face to the beam of steel alongside the alcove and then around the projecting steel into the alcove itself. The opening where the body was located was about six feet wide and seven feet high, but the jagged steel overhead made it dangerous to stand up straight; less so for me. John had to stoop a little when he got in.

"Uncomfortable weather tonight, Bill," he said as we shook hands.

"Just a taste of what we'll get in the winter," I said.

He studied the tight confines and nodded. "Then it's incumbent on us to get as much done as we can before that, wouldn't you say?"

I grinned. The way he said it, I knew we had the same spirit—if we can do it, let's do it. "Incumbent as hell, John. I'd like to make this happen tonight if we can."

Tough men are toughest when they speak softly, and that was the way John said, "Bill, as I see it, there's really no reason not to."

"We don't know whose it is, John, yours or mine. Could be a court officer too."

If it was an NYPD cop, the NYPD would take over. The PAPD took charge of the PAPD. Same with the FDNY. It was a matter of respect, of honor: a tradition begun in Oklahoma City when military honors were accorded members of the uniformed service killed there. These were fallen comrades; everyone helped, but ultimately you took care of your own. That was how it was done.

John pushed his red helmet back a bit. "Bill, I hear you work just as hard no matter whose it is."

I said what would become kind of a motto for me. "I'll be

happy for you if he's yours. Just like you'll be happy for me if he's mine."

John clapped me on the back. "That's right."

I had on a pair of black boots given to me by FEMA, and my white helmet. John and I edged out of the cave onto the steel beam that was the only place to stand, and started up. If anybody fell here, it would be onto twisted steel. The drop was at least thirty feet, maybe more, but the ironworkers had said a fall of three stories would kill you. Didn't matter if it was more; after three it was all the same.

Kevin Devlin and John started making plans. They agreed on one thing right away.

"Kevin and I figure it's the steel that's the problem, Bill," John said. "We can cut it but we're going to need a grappler to lift it out of here."

"I don't see how. This alcove is ten feet below the edge of the cliff. How will the operator see what he's grabbing?"

"He won't," Kevin said. "We'll have to relay signals to him by radio, or even by hand if it gets tight. Boss, it's no go without it."

I thought it over. The grappler was a crane-type machine with a four-prong claw on the end of its boom. It could grab pieces of steel and draw them out, clearing the heaviest part of the pile. It would be precarious up on top of the plateau. The operating engineer up in his glassed-in control booth would have to rely on workers on the cliff and in the alcove to give him directions. He would have to keep his grappler balanced on the edge of the cliff while he extended its boom out and down, and people inside the alcove told him when to bring in the claw, when to close it on a piece of steel, and when to draw it back out.

I hadn't come to a decision about all this, but I ordered the resources we were going to need if we went ahead. I requested lights, portable generators, saws to cut debris within the alcove so the grappler could grab it, bottles of water for the guys working down there, and since the mist soaking us showed no sign of letting up, I ordered as many towels as could be found.

The grappler arrived around 7 p.m. John Moran and Kevin Devlin and Mueller and Hennessy were inside the alcove cutting steel. The rest of us managed the setting down of the grappler on the debris so it had a stable foundation. It was still dangerous. The grappler had to lean out over the edge of the cliff to drop its boom level with the entrance to the alcove, then, working by feel alone, extend its claw into the alcove like cupped fingers to pull out the pieces of steel cut by the men trying to free the body.

As soon as we started, the counterbalance weight on the back of the grappler began bouncing up and down, which made the whole machine rock back and forth on its treads. There were a couple of times I thought it was actually going to flip all the way over and fall off the cliff. I wanted to check on the guys in the alcove. I went down that sheer ten feet again and stood outside in the rain.

"How are we doing here?"

"We're doing good. We're getting stuff out," Kevin said.

John backed him. "We're gonna get this body."

"Listen, I got a grappler all set to tip over and lose the operator if he bounces any higher. He's ten feet over your heads. If he goes over he might take this alcove with him or crush everyone inside it. The steel underneath him is shifting. Is he lifting too much weight out of here?"

"No. Just calm him down," John advised. "We're gonna be here for a long time."

Whenever you had a recovery, there was a lot of adrenaline. *Let's get in there, let's dig, let's get it going.* There was a sense of mission. John was right. We were working too fast.

John added, "Believe me, this is no place to get careless."

I went back up the cliff and slowed it all down. The slower pace was better. I pulled out Hennessy and sent in Timmy Mueller. Later I sent in Gary Griffin and Paddy Callaghan. My former partner Tommy McHale assisted in the cutting too. Kevin Devlin and

John Moran continued to remain inside, and we sent supplies down to them. Slowly they removed the steel around the body. There was only room for four in the little alcove, so one person stood on the piece of steel outside the alcove, another on the stairway alongside it, and another on top of the cliff so we could hand down equipment as they needed it.

Some of the steel could be cut by saws. The rest was cut by oxyacetylene torches. Sparks from the torches lit up the alcove and the cliff as they fell in a shower to the bottom, and there was a constant pop and hiss as they hit misty rain and wet steel.

In the eerie light we continued to guide the grappler's boom into the alcove. It would pick up a cut piece of steel, draw it out, and bring it up to the plateau, where it would be released with a heavy metallic thud and then searched for remains.

This went on hour after hour for over thirteen hours. Little by little by little, piece by piece, they were clearing the steel trapping the body. It was going well, and then we almost lost it all.

The grappler claw was directed into the alcove and the command was relayed to close its claw and draw out a piece of steel. It had been cut and was supposed to come out, but it didn't. Either another piece obstructed it or the debris around it had shifted, but it didn't move an inch. The grappler operator had been given the order to pull it out and had no idea it was stuck. He pulled harder. In the darkness, with the rain in our faces, we didn't realize what was happening for a moment, but as the grappler operator applied more and more power, rather than the grappler's drawing the steel up, the steel began to draw the grappler down.

The grappler counterbalance rose up sharply and began to tip the grappler closer to the edge of the cliff. It was like playing tug of war with an immovable object. Sparks were flying out of the alcove. White light flickered in the shadows and the rain. When we finally saw the grappler tipping forward, we started yelling for it to stop pulling and let go of the steel. The noise of its engine drowned us out. Up in his glassed-in control booth the grappler operator was still trying to balance out his machine and maintain the pull, unaware it was sliding toward the edge of the cliff. We had only seconds to get his attention.

I threw a football four or five hundred times a day, every day, when I was a quarterback in high school. I didn't have one at that moment but there was no shortage of debris. I picked up a rock and threw it at the grappler operator's booth. It hit with a sharp crack. I was worried I would shatter the whole thing, but we had to get his attention.

It did. The sharp crack against the glass probably almost gave him a heart attack—he looked around wildly—but he finally saw us frantically signaling. He realized what was happening and let go of the steel—and shot back like a slingshot right off the steel platform and away from the edge.

After some nerve steadying on all our parts, the recovery went on. When enough of the steel was cut away, we were able to see that the body was completely intact and that the radio was Port Authority police issue. A short time later we recovered the gun, badge, and nameplate of thirty-five-year-old PAPD officer Antonio J. Rodrigues, a former New York City police officer who had joined the Port Authority police only two years earlier but was already known for his maturity and sound judgment and was very well liked by all.

Around 6 a.m. some of the day tour guys began to arrive, but none of my guys left. I talked to John Moran and Kevin Devlin on the radio throughout that time. I could hear them: "Listen, if the grappler pulls this piece of steel up and holds it, we may be able to shore, like, this piece of steel under it, and it might hold. And then if that holds, then we can work up underneath there." It was thirteen hours of pick-up sticks with steel beams. If the pile crumbled, everything would be lost.

In the end, the pile held. An hour later I got the word from Kevin Devlin in the alcove.

"Boss, it looks like the body is gonna come out. Should be about fifteen minutes more."

"I'm coming down, Kevin," I told him.

Kevin and John did better than that. I reached the piece of steel outside the alcove in time to see the whole body come out intact. It was amazing to see their reaction. Their faces were glowing. The moment was neither ghoulish nor ghastly; it was a moment of grace. A friend was going home.

We brought down a Stokes basket, a body bag, and a flag and called for a priest. I helped take the body from the alcove, and others passed it on till it reached the top. Kevin Devlin, John Moran, Tommy McHale, and the rest came up. There were about fifty cops from the NYPD and the PAPD waiting to help walk the body out.

We had started the recovery about six thirty the night before. It was now nearly eight in the morning the day after. There was no doubt we had recovered a cop. We had established that around one in the morning, the same time we established he was PAPD. What I thought was key about John Moran, something I will never forget, was that even when John found out the body was a Port Authority cop and not NYPD, he never came out of that alcove. For almost fourteen hours, he stayed on the job, cutting, planning, directing the grappler, all the while risking being crushed if the grappler fell. He stayed because of the mission. It was pure to him.

It was still cold and wet on top of the cliff when John and Kevin made it back up. All of us who'd been in and out of the alcove were covered with mud because the rain wasn't heavy enough to wash it away. It was on our clothes and faces and hands, and as the night wore on, we just got dirtier. When we finally brought the body up, it was a sight to see the night guys covered with brown mud hugging the day tour guys, and the grappler operator was being hugged, and Kevin Devlin, Mike Hennessy, Tommy McHale, Paddy Callaghan, Timmy Mueller, and all the guys who had been down in the alcove were hugging each other too.

"I can't thank you enough," I said to John Moran.

"No need," he said, smiling. "I can't believe we got him out."

"You did some job, John."

"Nah, it was me and him and him . . . ," and he pointed to every guy standing there.

Lieutenant Enzo Sangiorgi came over from the Command Post said: "You guys all look like guys who work in the coal mines. Look at your faces." And he pointed to a bunch from the night tour resting on the tailgate of a beat-up old Ford 150 Port Authority pickup truck that someone had used to bring over supplies. Their helmets were filthy and their faces were grimy and black. They looked just like they had climbed out of a mine. When they cried, the tears made tracks in the dirt on their faces, but no one tried to hide them.

In the early morning rain, covered with mud, we were happy that we had done our job and the family wouldn't have to wait any longer for news. Exhausted and elated, we felt a relief when we accomplished the recovery that was enormous. Antonio's family was going to get a phone call that would end their waiting. Antonio was going home.

The honor guard walked the flag-draped Stokes basket out of the site to a waiting Port Authority ESU truck. The long double line of people stood by while we put the body in back. Nunziato and Griffin jumped in with the body and we closed the doors. It would be taken to the temporary morgue. From there, the truck carrying the body was led by a procession with motorcycles and police cars with lights and sirens on to let people know one of our cops was going home.

The Port Authority Bus Terminal on Eighth Avenue put a line of cops from Fortieth Street to Forty-second Street. As the caravan approached up Eighth Avenue, the cops went to attention and then went to presented arms with the salute. The body went past them very slowly, and once it went by, they would present arms and continue to salute until the truck made the turn onto Forty-second Street to head for Bellevue Hospital.

I'd driven in those trucks on the ride from the WTC to the morgue. People along the way stopped. Some saluted. Most would just stare and think their own thoughts as the long caravan of police cars and motorcycles hit their lights and sirens to defy death, and send the message loud and clear that a hero was going home.

It was time I went home too. I never stopped for coffee or anything. I wanted to get home. I cleaned up, got in my car, and headed for the Holland Tunnel. It always felt like the tunnel took me from one land to another. I liked driving down the highway too, almost empty at that hour. It felt good to be in control of something again, even if it was just my own car.

I got my first and last sight of Ground Zero every day from the bridge on the Turnpike Extension in New Jersey. After a while the smoke became a borderline marking the boundary between Ground Zero and my home in New Jersey. As I headed back, it was the exact point where I felt the pull of Ground Zero fade and the tug of my wife and kids and the life I loved take over, drawing me home. I don't know why, but after a while each time I saw the smoke from the bridge, traveling in either direction, I spoke the words out loud, "There's my smoke."

That morning, as the rain coursed down my windshield, I said, "There's my smoke," and sped onto the highway going home.

I usually got home around 6 or 7 a.m., later on mornings like this one. Most days my nine-month-old daughter Rory was up. I could hear my wife talking to her in the kitchen while she cooked. When I came in, the baby would get so excited Karen would say, "Here comes Daddy," and let her out of her high chair. Rory would take off like a shot for the gate at the top of the stairs, averaging two or three steps before she fell in a heap. Walking wasn't her strong suit but she was a Grand Prix crawler. She scampered across the kitchen floor and waited. Her face lit up when she saw me, and when I scooped her into my arms, something lit up inside me too. I smiled for the first time since I'd left home the day before. I never really smiled at the site—not this kind of involuntary grin wide enough to crack my dry lips. Sometimes I laughed, but laughing is different from smiling.

When the daily working environment is horror you have to joke a lot, so there was always gallows humor. We kidded one of our guys because he was so good at spotting flesh and bones and hair, we swore he was bringing them from home. "We're going to start checking on your in-laws because you can't be this good." Or "Where do you use this talent next?" Jokes like that let you cope with breaking up an argument between two guys where one swears that the hand he found hanging from a piece of steel mesh hadn't been there a minute ago, but it was there now, and he saw it pointing at him, and the other swears it was pointing at *him*. We joked to get past the insanity of moments like that. We were close enough. We could accept it. It was our way of saying, "I know you can put this aside. I know you can get through it."

Karen was smiling. I was home and we were a family again. Whatever she was cooking in the pots on the stove and the pans in the oven, whatever was giving off such rich smells was not just fuel, it was love. It should have been a moment of pure joy, but my first moments home were always the same: I was tired and afraid and had almost no clothes on.

I was tired because we worked at least twelve-hour shifts, every day, seven days a week for the first two months. Then we went to six days a week and maintained that schedule straight through until the end.

I had almost no clothes on because as soon as I shut the front door behind me, I stripped down to my shorts there in the hallway. More than anything in the world I wanted to hug that astoundingly beautiful baby, and inhale her perfect baby smell, and make all the silly noises grown-ups make when a baby smiles. I couldn't.

I was afraid because even though I cleaned up before I left the site, I could still smell Ground Zero on my clothes and in my hair and on my skin. I wanted to be close to Karen and the kids, but I couldn't. I needed to shower first. I wanted to get the site off me, out of me. I tried to wash it off my face and hands, but there was too much still there. I had gotten too familiar with it not to know what it was. It was the smell of death. When I was alone in the shower, the steam excited the olfactory nerves and drained my sinuses, which were full of the dust so I could taste it every time I breathed. The clouds of steam opened the pores in my skin and vaporized the dust in them. I cupped my wet hands over my nose and mouth to filter the air. It felt like the site was inside me, and I couldn't breathe and in that glass shower I had to feel the walls under my hands to re-member I was here in my house, because when that overwhelming smell hit me, it was like I was right back on Vesey and West.

I couldn't let that touch my kids.

So even when I scooped up Rory, I held her at arm's length. Despite that—and I felt it happen every day—when that little nine-month-old face grinned at me and babbled "Daddy," the place I worked was suddenly far away.

What did it say about me that a baby girl laughing and trying to grab my nose or say my name could restore my equilibrium? How could the emotional impact of spending night after night pawing through an unburied graveyard be balanced by an hour or two at home watching her learn to walk and manage one step to-ward me or comforting her when she couldn't manage two? When she lurched forward for *three* whole steps, and the momentum was just too much for her, why was it that the relief of catching her be-fore she hit the coffee table recovered for me some of myself? How was it that keeping the light in her eyes undimmed helped heal a part of *my* heart? It was testimony to our resilience and no small win for the human spirit. It let me keep my head in the game.

The rescue and recovery mission at Ground Zero wasn't the first time my job imposed burdens on our marriage. A cop's life is crazy—the late hours, the physical stress, working a different shift every week, having meals at all different times. One week you're helping the kids with their homework, the next you work from three in the afternoon to eleven at night so they're at school when you leave and asleep when you come home. All the last-minute phone calls telling her you can't make the party or the movie or the dinner because you have to work longer or process an arrest.

The disaster at the World Trade Center amplified the problems associated with my being a cop. It was like the dust blowing out of the site—too fine to see by the time it got to my house in New Jersey but there nonetheless. Dust that fine gets into everything. A marriage is like a hardworking engine: too much dust gets in, it runs rough; it can't handle the burden; it stops running. This wasn't the first time burdens were imposed on Karen and me and our relationship. Ground Zero might have been the worst that work provided, but work wasn't the only source.

The bottom is a very personal place. If you've been there, you recognize it right away. It's riding home after the doctors told us about Tara and trying to find something good to say, trying to find a silver lining and make words like "different" and "special" not such frauds. It's days filled with confusion, anger, and depression. It's a future of overwhelming responsibility and unending work. It's knowing that all the dreams parents dream are never going to happen. It's the bottom.

Nothing prepares you for the bottom; you're just suddenly there. I could not reconcile Tara's illness with God's love. I asked God why. I asked God for a reason not to hate him. He didn't give me one. What he gave me instead was a reason to keep going. That is no small thing because at the bottom there is no reason for anything. At the bottom there is only a choice. It is between hope and despair. I do not know whether God gave me faith or faith gave me God, but I chose hope and suddenly saw it was the only reason I needed; that I could decide to make things better; and that everything in my life, including my daughter's tragic illness, had special meaning.

My surrender and acceptance of that truth enabled me to see

the face of God in Tara's face, his joy in her laughter, and my love in her eyes. I learned her language—a deeper, less complex, more fulfilling communication than I had ever thought possible—and it invigorated me. Tara showed me a different vision of the future than I had ever known, and a reason to dream new dreams.

Looking back, I know that nothing could have prepared me for Ground Zero . . . except what Karen and I went through with Tara. I had been brought to my knees and I had fought my way back. When I went to Ground Zero, I was taken to the bottom again, but this time I knew there was a reason to keep going; this time I knew I had come back once before; this time I had learned to ask for help, and not to get angry, and not to try and control it. So this time, what kept me going in the months after 9-11 was that I chose hope before I felt despair, and armed with that, I could face Ground Zero.

The time I was at Ground Zero was certainly hardest on Karen. She was a cop's wife and we were a cop family and she ran everything virtually alone. Doing chores and fixing things around the house wasn't my strongest suit at the best of times. During the WTC recovery operation, most people expected I would do even less, and I lived up to their expectation. Friends and neighbors knew what I was doing at Ground Zero. The site never left the front page or the TV screen in the first several weeks. That kind of continuous coverage impacts everything, especially relationships.

Our neighbors rose to the occasion and went out of their way to help us. There was Tom and Cathy Coohill, and their son, Tom Jr., who attended college. Tommy was born in Ireland and still had a strong brogue. He moved here when he was fifteen and loved this country so much he joined the Navy during the war in Vietnam. There he saw how important the support of the people back home was to everyone. So when I was "fighting," he showed his support back home for me. So did his wife, Cathy, who worked in a Midtown Manhattan brokerage firm and got home at 7 p.m. but still always offered to watch the kids so Karen could get out, or brought dinner over so she wouldn't have to cook.

There was also the kindness of Nigel and Evette Joseph. They had two children, Ghilene, four, and Brandon, eight. They had boundless energy. In fact, the only people I ever met who were equally energetic were Nigel's parents. At the time of 9-11, Nigel's father was ninety-two and his mom seventy-seven and they were still doing landscaping and yard work.

A person with three kids struggles to do the work of one—two people can do the work of four. Tom and Cathy and Nigel and Evette filled in when Karen needed a partner because I was missing. For the nine months they filled in for me, they were always only a phone call away. They put up the outside lights at Christmas, they fixed the hot water heater when it broke, they babysat Rory and Kristine when Karen had to give special care to Tara, and they picked Karen up when she dropped off the car and drove her back when it was done. Tommy even put up my Christmas tree. They are representative of the many wonderful people who daily showed how much they cared about us.

Equally indispensable to Karen were her older sisters, Barbara and Kathy. Kathy works as an administrator for a school district and is almost as funny as Karen. Barbara is the eldest and generally more serious. When Karen was growing up, the ten-year difference in their ages made her the baby of the family, and for a long time that was pretty much how Barbara and Kathy related to her. Even when Karen and I got married, it was hard for them to see her as an adult.

All that changed when Tara was diagnosed with Rett Syndrome. They saw the depth of Karen's love and maturity as she responded to having a handicapped child, how hard Karen worked to care for her. Barbara and Kathy were always there for Karen and the kids. Perhaps most important, they had no hesitation or boundary where Tara was concerned and along with my family were among the few who would help take care of her.

They took care of Karen too. If she was worried about my safety, or if I hadn't been in touch, Barbara and Kathy gave her the support she needed. They all talked to each other every day on the phone, usually more than once. Her sisters took Karen out when she needed some breathing space. To this day they remain just as close, and Karen and I couldn't have gotten along without them.

Five years later, I believe the only person who has the right to be called a hero is Karen. I may have sustained others, but it was Karen who sustained me. I may have been a good leader at the site, but at home I was selfish, my attention was elsewhere, I put her and the kids in last place, I walked out of the house at will and for as long as I thought necessary, and I had time for anyone who needed me except my wife and kids.

I called this behavior "doing my duty."

For this I was praised and given medals and got to meet the president and was even brought to Kentucky so the attorney general could make me a colonel. Yet I only grudgingly went to a parent-teacher conference and had absolutely no memory or aware- ness of the problem the teacher and Karen were discussing. I spoke up. "Excuse me, Mrs. Brown, I'm sorry, but I've been gone for six months. You're going to have to fill me in."

She looked at Karen a little embarrassed. "Oh, I'm sorry. I didn't realize . . . You two are—"

"No, we're not separated," I said quickly.

Karen said, "He's just not here."

I solved a dozen problems an hour, troubling problems. Walked in the door. Problems. Got to the meeting. Problems. Back to the Command Post. Problems. When Lieutenant Enzo San- giorgi, who was assigned to Ground Zero, was asked by a PAPD sergeant how the group of lieutenants solved a problem, he said,

"It's easy. We all sit down. We all talk about it. Then we ask Keegan what he wants to do."

In short order, I became so exhausted and sick from the toxins and the emotional pressure that I had a car accident. I completely wrecked my car. What was my response to almost going through the windshield? It was to get free and crawl out through the side window, go over and shake everybody's hand and make sure they were all right, call the police, and be driven home.

It was so unimportant to me I never even told Karen until she actually noticed it later that morning.

"Billy, where's the car?"

"I wrecked it last night."

"What do you mean you wrecked it? Where? When? Are you hurt?"

"No. I wrecked it on my ride home. I gotta get another one. Will you call my dad and ask him to drop off one of his tomorrow? I gotta get back to the site."

She looked at me like I was crazy. I didn't think so. It just wasn't worth talking about because it seemed so inconsequential. Okay, the car's gone, I gotta get another one. Don't have wheels— need wheels. There was nothing else attached to it, not the slightest emotional value or concern for my property or me or the fact that the car was dead and I had narrowly missed joining it.

Don't have wheels—need wheels. And I thought she was giving *me* a hard time.

I met Karen in 1984. I had taken the PA police test by that time, but I still had my trucking business and no thought it would change. I was living alone in downtown Jersey City. Mutual friends introduced us, and we went out on a couple of dates. Her brother-in-law, Joe, had been my football coach back in high school. "You're dating Billy Keegan?" he said with a laugh. "Sure, I know him." Fortunately, my record with Joe was okay off the field as well as on, so Karen and I were okay as far as he was concerned.

Karen had a quality a lot of people think they have but few do.

She was funny, genuinely funny. She was someone who always cared about people too. Added together, it meant that within ten minutes after you met Karen, she made you comfortable and at ease. She swept problems aside. I didn't worry about things as much when I was with her. Her laugh made problems seem small by comparison.

We got along right from the beginning. She was good for me. When we first met, Karen was off like a shot: "How are you doing? Oh, yeah? Really? Is that so?" She was a good listener too, and people respond to that. Then she'd make a joke, and they'd laugh, and it went on from there. I tried, but I wasn't in her league. "Billy," she said to me, "do you know what your problem is?"

"Am I going to hear this whether I want to or not, Karen?"

She had this big grin on. "You are."

"Okay, what's my problem?"

"As soon as somebody starts talking to you, they get the message some other time would be better," she laughed.

A lot of good came out of my work at Ground Zero for us, but it wasn't all good. It invaded our family and took over every waking moment. The overwhelming nature of these events was maybe why I didn't see that my daughter Kristine was becoming a casualty of it all. I should have seen that it was all getting to be too much for her. She was eleven, a quiet girl but not overly so, and very bright. I was rarely home, and if I was, I was usually asleep. She saw me on TV and read things about me. I didn't think much about that, so I didn't realize the effect of it on her. On overload, she grew silent and introspective.

One day she came into the den, where I was watching a baseball game. It should have been a nice quiet time, but I was interrupted three times by calls from the site. After the last, she had a funny look on her face. Before 9-11, I had never had a cell phone.

"Dad, do you have to take all those calls?"

I shrugged it off. "You know me."

"Do I?" she asked.

So small a question to be so big. I suddenly got the look on her face. I had become a stranger.

"Do I?" she asked again.

I'm not always great with questions like that so I took a minute to think. Did she know me? I wanted to say, *You bet your ass you know me. I'm the one who feeds you and clothes you* and so on and so on. I'm glad I didn't. I understand now a lot more of what she was feeling. Kids know their parents work, but very few see their parent *at* work. What I was doing was so public, the exposure couldn't be avoided. The one thing we had talked about, the thing I most wanted to limit, was her hearing people say to me, "You're a hero." That's too much for a kid. It's too much for anyone. I had too many flaws to let her be hurt when she saw I was nothing of the kind.

"Kristine," I had said to her, "the hero stuff is for somebody else. It's not heroic. It's work. It's like I got landed with the marines on a beach and there's no running back the other way even if I wanted to. You do what you have to do. It's not a matter of choice."

The hero stuff only got worse till it interfered with my being Dad. Dads are real people, regular guys. Heroes are too big to be either. What happened to horseback riding together? What happened to just hanging out? What happened to doing homework together? That's the stuff that dads do. Dads have flaws and make mistakes. They set the bar at a reasonable height for the kids to try to measure up. But how do you measure up to a hero? Heroes always win. Where does it leave us if the only way to get approval is to be a hero too? It leaves us feeling unworthy of being loved.

Sometimes Kristine got the opposite input. I wasn't a hero. She came to Karen, very upset. "Mom, lots of people say that where Dad works, they're all physically and mentally screwed up. They say they'll never be the same as before." An eleven-year-old doesn't have the experience to process stupidity into anything but fear. You can hear it in the questions. *Why does Daddy go to a place like that? Why is he doing such horrible work? If it's so bad, why is he so excited*

*about doing it, and why does he talk about it all the time? Who are we to
him? How come he could replace us?*

Why is he away all the time?

Why does he sleep so much?

At eleven going on twelve there's a lot of confusion in your life
anyway. This was one more thing she had to go through.

Maybe it was one too many.

Tara changed too. She had always loved hanging out with me.
I could always get her to smile right away. If I rubbed noses with
her or kissed her on the cheeks, she'd start laughing. Tara's laugh is
pure feeling, pure joy. Sometimes I think it's the best laugh in the
world. I think Tara knew only that something was missing. I don't
know if she consciously knew it was me or wondered where I went
or missed my talking to her. She couldn't process information like
that. Looking back, I realize Kristine was afraid. For Tara, I think
there was the vague but familiar feeling that something was missing. She must have felt sad. When I did spend time with her, it
took longer to make her smile.

Every day after breakfast, Tara left on the school bus with her
nurse. Kristine went to school too. Rory napped, and Karen had all
her normal chores plus mine. People used to ask me what I did on
my one day off. Most of the time I was too exhausted to do anything
but sleep or watch TV. My eyes started to close right after breakfast,
when the house was quiet and the next shift was far enough away
not to matter.

The physical distance between my house and Ground Zero
was small, but the emotional distance was immense. Holding the
ghosts of Ground Zero at bay for a time, it let me sleep.

I woke up when it was nearly time to go. After I showered and
changed and ate, I got in the car and headed for the site. At the apex
of the Turnpike Extension bridge, I caught my daily first glimpse of
the smoke rising across the river in Lower Manhattan. I had reached
the boundary line again. In this direction, I felt the pull of my wife

and kids fade and the pull of the smoke take over, drawing me toward it, leading me there.

"There's my smoke," I said, and drove on.

I should have seen what was down the road, but I didn't, or human nature being what it is, maybe I saw it and just didn't care.

It is not enough to say I was doing my duty and I would do it again. There is more to it. Maybe you're not supposed to love a rescue and recovery mission, but I did. Looking back, it seems strange to say it that way, like loving war. The truth is I felt I was doing sacred work that was more perfect for me than any I had ever done. For the first time in my life the entire world and my place in it made absolute and total sense. While I was at Ground Zero, I knew I might never find such meaning again and that I would miss till my dying day the ability to do so much good for so many people.

Five years later, I still don't know how to replace it.

Chapter Three

Leaders are supposed to know something about what it is they are leading. I learned it all on the job, in what was probably the most intense rescue and recovery course ever given. It was taught by some of the most experienced professionals in the world, who gave me their time and knowledge unselfishly. I will always remember the things they taught me during the nine months I worked with them but those memories are problematic. Five years later, there are some I'm still trying to forget.

One of the people who helped me most in the first days was an NYPD lieutenant named Owen McCaffrey. McCaffrey was an Emergency Service Unit team commander with extensive training in search and rescue and the experience to match. He was a muscular man with a warm smile and an easy manner. McCaffrey was also as smart as he was tough. Yet he was the model for interdepartmental cooperation, always responsive to my questions, always willing to give me information. He became my best counsel.

I would never put men at risk by pretending to know something I didn't, so I always called him in to go over what I was planning to do.

"Look, Owen, I wanna do this. How do I get there? What's the risk?"

He'd say, "Dude, can't do it that way. Here's the only way you can do it." That was how he talked. Everyone was Dude or Bro. "Dude, if you do it that way, it's gonna get all fucked up. Here's what you do. We put a couple of your guys with a couple of my guys, put on the Scott airs, and if you think something is down somewhere, we'll work together. We'll bring a lot of guys down there."

"Okay. How *exactly* should this be done?" I'd ask, and McCaffrey would tell me.

Yet first on the list of the things I'd like to forget is the night I met Owen McCaffrey, and the memory of my first partial body recovery.

I was called up to the fire department's east command post, on Church and Dey Street. It was very dark, and the lights strung weren't doing much to alleviate the gloom. There was a very small tent on one side of the street and a large one on the other. Firefighters were resting in the big one, slumped in chairs or sleeping. I responded to the smaller tent as instructed. An FDNY deputy chief named Ron Spadafora was there. A tightly built man with glasses and a thick mustache, he wore a white helmet and heavy bunker gear. There were two NYPD cops standing off to one side. One was Owen McCaffrey; the other was a sergeant named Tim Farrell.

I walked over. "How you doing? I'm Bill Keegan."

"Owen McCaffrey. This is Tim Farrell," McCaffrey said. "They called you about the guy?"

"Yeah, what's up?"

"It looks like the FDNY grabbed a cop."

I frowned because everyone at the site knew recovery protocol was to stop and immediately notify the appropriate uniformed service.

"What did they say happened?" I asked.

"They thought the body they found was a fireman, so they began the recovery. They had already cut it when they realized that it wasn't a firefighter, it was a police officer. They put what they got in a body bag and brought him to their chief, which they say is their protocol. So instead of leaving him where they found him and, calling us, they removed him from the area and took him here."

There was no love lost between Owen McCaffrey and the

FDNY, despite his being a volunteer firefighter in the town he lived in on Long Island. A lot of cops have war stories; as I later learned, Owen McCaffrey had more than most, and one in particular impressed me. In the summer of 1997, Owen commanded the NYPD Emergency Services Unit that raided the Brooklyn apartment where Palestinian terrorists Lafi Khalil and Gazi Ibrahim Abu-Mezer had constructed pipe bombs they planned to detonate in the New York City subway system.

Shortly before dawn, Owen led half a dozen heavily armed ESU cops into the residential building at 248 Fourth Avenue. They entered the darkened apartment quietly. The only light was from the beams of their police flashlights. They wanted the terrorists, but they also wanted the bombs: it was a heavily populated residential section and dozens of people asleep in neighboring apartments had not been evacuated for fear of alerting the terrorists.

Things happened fast. Khalil and Mezer were alerted but ignored the police order to freeze. There was a struggle as one tried to grab a cop's gun and the other tried to get to a black bag that contained a bomb, intending to set it off. The ESU team responded and the terrorist didn't get the chance. Shots were fired. Khalil and Mezer were taken to a Brooklyn hospital under arrest, both in serious condition with multiple gunshot wounds.

For this action, Owen and the team won a "top cop" award as "the best of the best."

Respect was important to McCaffrey. The more he talked about the mistakes in the recovery, the madder he got. What was really aggravating him was the disrespect the FDNY showed by not having done things the right way. The second that they knew they had a cop, they should have stopped and called us.

"I'm gonna find out what happened," I said.

McCaffrey folded his arms across his chest. "You want to talk to them, fine. I got nothing to say."

Spadafora saw me coming. He put down the clipboard he was holding.

"Lieutenant."

"Chief." I pointed to the body bag. "Chief, where did this come from? What's going on?"

"The guys brought it up here. They thought he was one of ours. It was a mistake."

"They had to realize it before they put it in a bag, right?"

"I don't really know."

"Who found the body?" I asked.

"He's not here anymore."

"Can you get ahold of him?"

"I don't know if I can, Lieutenant."

Meanwhile firefighters were coming there with other body bags and placing them on the sidewalk. Spadafora spread his hands.

"Lieutenant, I'm gonna be honest with you. I don't really know what happened. The body was delivered here. It's not one of our people. The guys who found it think it's yours or the NYPD. Like I say, it was a mistake. I was told to wait here with it until you got here. You're here. Whatever you want to do is fine with me."

I went back to McCaffrey and told him what the chief said. I was feeling like maybe what was done was done. The chief hadn't given me a hard time. In the middle of all this insanity I was leaning toward letting it go, but McCaffrey pointed to the body bag at our feet and his anger went up another notch.

"I'm going to tell you this right now, Dude, if this turns out to be one of my guys, I'm going to punch his teeth out."

Sergeant Farrell knelt down and started unzipping the body bag. It looked like a big black garment bag with a zipper down the middle. He only opened the bag an inch, but that was all it took for the smell of the dead body to hit me like a fist. It came rushing out as if it had been growing inside the plastic, bursting at the seams to get out. It jumped out of the bag into my nostrils and took my breath away. I had smelled that smell before, but never as intense or powerful.

The smell got stronger. The sergeant and McCaffrey seemed

unaffected, but it overwhelmed me. I kept trying to recover from it but I felt frozen as the sergeant pulled the front of the bag open. I forced myself to look inside. The body had been so severely burned that there was no form from the waist up. The tendons and the bones had no skin to enclose them. There was a length of wire visible within what had once been a torso. The wire appeared similar to the kind of remote microphones normally worn on a shoulder so the officer could speak directly into it.

McCaffrey and Farrell were putting on gloves and masks. I forced myself to do the same. The wire was all twisted up in the ligaments and tendons and bones. It snaked into the body, through the guts, and all the way around. The sergeant and McCaffrey got down and shoved their gloved hands into the stuff in the bag. You could tell they had done this before. They pulled the wire, hoping it was attached to a radio with the number of a command on it, but it was too mixed up with all those different strings hanging out.

"Gotta turn it over," McCaffrey said.

McCaffrey was down there. The sergeant was down there. I knelt down too. As I helped turn the body over, the skull fell apart. I reached down and put the pieces back together. For some reason, they stuck. We rolled the body over a little more and came to the end of the remote wire. McCaffrey examined it closely. He said he was almost certain the body wasn't NYPD but he couldn't tell if it was PAPD or one of the other departments.

I touched the body. My hands felt pulled into it, and I started to do my job because we had to know the answers to the basic questions—who is this, who does he belong to, how do we get him to his family. I was having a hard time. I concentrated on pushing back the blackness creeping over me. My brain was telling my eyes not to see what they saw, telling me not to feel what I was touching, not to smell what I couldn't stop smelling.

All three of us had our hands in the body, feeling around for something to identify it. McCaffrey found a ring on a finger all charred black. On the chance it was an initial ring, Farrell poured water over it to wash it off. It was just a silver band, but it caught us the way it shined and sparkled against the charred flesh and bone, like we'd never seen anything as bright. We tried to get it off the finger but we couldn't. The morgue would cut it off to check for an inscription on the inside.

That was when McCaffrey blew. "Listen, Bro, if I were you, I'd go over there right now to that fire chief, and I would demand to know what happened here. I'd want his boss, and if he says no, I tell you right now I'll get my boys up here and we'll have it out right now." His hands moved inside the body. I think they were clenching into fists.

"Are you listening? They cut one of ours in half. They dumped him up here like he's fucking nothing and now they're going to tell us that they don't know how he got here, and they don't know who the guy is who got him . . . You know what? Fuck them. Bro, you can't let them get away with this."

I was half listening. There was some water in the body from the FDNY hoses and a lot of mud. The FDNY had done a field amputation to recover what they got—the stuff in the bag. The legs were back in the debris. The skin had been burned away. It was just all burned away. Anything that could burn burned. Most of what was in my head were squishy sounds in the body and burned strings and something that was rubbery like the squid you get in Italian restaurants. I had my hands in it up to midforearm and was tossing it like salad. I wasn't really in the mood for a confrontation.

Farrell helped me clean up. I was still outside myself, unsure if I was ready to come back to earth. Farrell saw it.

"You okay, Lieutenant?"

"Why do you ask?" I was wiping things off my uniform.

McCaffrey was looking at me too. I gave him my confident grin. I think it scared him.

Asking yourself if you've gone nuts is the fastest way to go nuts, so I found the reins of my self-control and snapped them. It brought most of me back.

"Sergeant, can you find the chief for me?" I asked.

Farrell nodded. "Sure, Lieutenant."

"What's up?" McCaffrey asked.

"Owen, we don't know if we've got one of yours or mine or even a civilian. That could be a police radio or a Walkman, we don't know."

"Listen, the way these bodies were treated—"

"That's my point. It's only a matter of time till one of ours is treated that way too." I said. "We should stop that before it happens."

McCaffrey nodded. "Yeah, okay. I buy that."

"So we have here something like the unknown soldier. He stands for all our guys. We fight for him, we fight for them."

"Fair enough. You want me to go with you?"

I pointed to the body. "You organize the honor guard. I'll be back."

I walked over to the command tent and watched the mist creeping over the ground for a while. When Spadafora came over a few minutes later, he looked as tired as I felt, and neither of us had a lot left.

"Look, Chief, I need to know who did the recovery and why he was dumped up here. This isn't the way you'd want your people found, and if it was one of mine, it's not the way I'd want him found."

He looked pained. "Lieutenant, I got firemen coming in from all over this city. You know how many cowboys I have? They're out there on the pile and this is what they bring me." He pointed. At least twenty body bags were piled up on the sidewalk with a chaplain saying prayers over them. "I'm doing the absolute best I can to document who they're bringing in. That's the best I can tell you."

"It's not good enough, Chief.

"Hang on." He looked tired all over again. "Let me see what I can do."

I expected arrogance, but that wasn't what I was getting from Spadafora. It didn't take the fight out of me, but it did take away some of the contentiousness. A couple of minutes later he came back and handed me a phone.

"I have Lieutenant McCormack on the line. He's the one who brought the body in. He's in his car headed home."

I figured I was going to get blown off, but for the second time I didn't get what I expected. When I got on the phone, McCormack's voice was apologetic. He told me he didn't know who authorized the recovery. When he got to the scene it was already under way.

"Think about it, Lieutenant. We thought this was a firefighter. He was treated as one of our own. It wasn't until we put the body in the body bag that we realized it wasn't. We want to recover our own. You want to recover your own. We know that. But the mistake had already been made. We had already recovered him. I followed my protocols and brought him back there."

"Was the location marked?" Later on we used global positioning system (GPS) technology to establish the coordinates of bodies found, but at this stage we could only mark the spot with orange or green spray paint.

"I don't know."

He didn't say what we both knew—that he could have just left the body down there and walked away. If he hadn't taken responsibility, he wouldn't have been in the middle of all this. I was glad he didn't say it. It sounded like he wanted to make it right.

"It's important," I said. "There could be more of mine there."

"I understand that."

I didn't say anything.

"Lieutenant Keegan?"

"Yes?"

"It's been a long day."

He was right about that. I had no ax to grind, and under the circumstances this was the best I was going to get. "All right, Lieutenant."

I handed the phone back to Spadafora. "Chief, this can't ever happen again. I want your guys to know you could find Port Authority officers in uniform and in plain clothes."

The chief looked maybe a little less tired. I was a little less tired too. "Anything I can do to help, Lieutenant, you let me know," he said.

I said I would do that.

I asked Sergeant Farrell to seal up the bag and call the command post for an honor guard.

I shook the sergeant's hand and thanked him. McCaffrey was waiting by the tent with the body. The first thing he said was "Did you straighten that asshole out?"

I said I thought we had achieved an understanding. In a place where reason was in short supply, that was no small thing.

The sun was rising by the time we finished. McCaffrey and I got some coffee and sat on a big spool of cable to watch it come up. One of the things I liked about the night tour was that it ended with the day. I used to think the light was my reward for getting though it.

I looked around the site. Within a few hundred yards there were five long lines of people in bucket brigades moving debris. Recovery teams were higher up on the pile, digging down. A lone Urban Search and Rescue guy was leading a cadaver dog that stopped every few yards and put its nose in the pile looking for the dead.

It was a time of questions and need, and sometimes we weren't able to get help from inside. That's when it had to come from outside. I had never seen such vulnerability as I saw in the workers at Ground Zero. They were strong men and women, all of them. The Towers had been strong too, but they'd had no defense against steel beams twisting like pretzels and fireballs coursing down a hundred stories. That was us—under attack and stripped of defenses, losing the outside shell that gave us form, all completely gone. Like the body tonight, we had no skin. The bad part was the pain would not go away, and there would be more. The good part was we were opened to help. When you're really hurt, you don't have any problem saying, "I need help." We were learning that. People were becoming willing to tell you what was wrong with them, to say, "I'm hurt, mentally, physically, psychologically, emotionally." It was in the eyes of almost everyone you passed. The way they looked at you, with compassion. There was a softness, a real softness. It was always soft.

I said, "That's the first time I ever did that."

"Did what?"

"Dealt with a dead body like that. My hands in it, putting pieces of a head back together."

He shook his head slowly a couple of times and then blew out a long, deep breath.

"Man, I have to tell you something, that's a hell of a body to break your cherry on. There wasn't even skin on it. That might be the worst body I've ever seen in my whole life, my entire career."

"Really?"

McCaffrey made a believe-me-I-know gesture. "Dude, look at it this way. It ain't gonna get any worse than this, so you got your worst out of the way right away. If you could do what you did here tonight, you can do anything."

A grappler crane started up close by, making it hard to talk. The grappler's claw bit into the pile and pulled out a mouthful of steel beams. At a cost of nearly $2.5 million each, there were more than a dozen grapplers at work. Their noise was a constant din, reinforced by the trucks that followed them, waiting to be filled. Big diesel engines revved up and down the scale as the operator in the control booth engaged and disengaged gears, accompanied by the whoosh and sighs of high-pressure hydraulic air brakes and winches and jacks.

McCaffrey and I sat there while cranes reared up like cobras coiling to strike and dump trucks crawled over the rubble to where a dozen grapplers working at a dozen different points throughout the site bit into the pile and pulled out mouthfuls of debris with their hundred-ton hooks.

It was morning at Ground Zero.

One disconcerting characteristic of the work at Ground Zero was how often common, everyday things suddenly felt strange or unfamiliar. Asking someone if he had some gum could elicit a puzzled look. A call from the wife to pick up a carton of milk could leave you baffled. In fact, the more normal the task, the easier it was to feel abnormal—which was why less than an hour after rummaging through a man's insides in my first partial body recovery, it felt strange to go out with McCaffrey for hot dogs.

He had started to walk away after our talk but instead turned back and asked me, "Dude, we're gonna get Gray's hot dogs. You want to go?"

It was so out of the blue it surprised me. You can go to a million meetings with some people and never know them beyond a name on a badge. Food is different. It involves friendship and sharing. It's personal from the get-go. In the middle of all the planning and organizing and learning and doing and using and being used, being asked to go for a hot dog is big. It was a symbol of respect and an offer of friendship. Maybe that's reading a lot into a hot dog, even a Gray's Papaya, but in the soul-abrading conditions at Ground Zero, symbols carried a lot of weight.

"Bro, two of my cops are coming. They're married to each other. Both sharpshooters. You coming?"

"Sure, Owen. Thanks."

It always felt strange to leave the site and enter the city of the living. "Hey, wasn't that it?" I remember saying as we passed the Gray's Papaya a few blocks away on Sixth Avenue and Eighth Street.

"I'm going to the one on Thirty-sixth Street," Owen said.

"Why the fuck are we driving all the way up there?"

"Bro, those dogs are seventy-five cents. The Papaya on Thirty-sixth Street is fifty cents."

I didn't want to be that far from the site. I was okay with Eighth Street. Any farther was too much stress.

"Stop here, Owen. I'm good for the difference."

He turned to me and smiled. "Bro, I ain't stopping."

It was ridiculous. He'd be saving a quarter a hot dog. That could reach almost a whole dollar if he shaved it right. I was getting anxious. It was lunch hour in Manhattan and there were so many people walking around, they overflowed the corners into the street, ignoring traffic lights like a swollen river bursting the dam. It was just too much *life*.

"Dude, stop tapping your foot," McCaffrey said.

I just looked.

"Relax, Bro," he advised. "We're not leaving the country."

If we hadn't been in the twenties already, I might have taken a cab back. Owen parked the cruiser at Gray's Papaya and we got on the line to the counter. There were people everywhere. Maybe ten guys were working between the kitchen pass-through and the counter calling out hot dog codes to each other as they filled orders. The place was packed with people. Their closeness made me uncomfortable. I couldn't connect with them or their world. I was filthy with dust and mud, and I smelled. I didn't want them to touch me. I didn't want to touch anyone else. Mercifully, the line to the counter went fast.

"I'll have two with mustard," I said when it was my turn.

"That's it?" the counter guy asked. "No relish, nothing?"

"Thanks, no."

He looked at me like I had taken all the challenge out of it, but McCaffrey made up for it.

"Bro, three with relish, onions, chili, mustard, everything, and what's the biggest smoothie, extra-large? French fries come with the hot dogs, some kind of special?"

McCaffrey didn't seem to have as much trouble as I did at the register juggling his food to get his money out. It took me a second before I saw why: he had eaten all three hot dogs before he got there. It was maybe six feet from the counter to the register. That's a hot dog every two feet. How do you eat three hot dogs before you even pay for them?

McCaffrey gave me a look. "Not even fucking onions? You are a pussy. I need another drink."

No small appetite; you had to admire that.

"What'd this set you back?" I asked.

"Under five," he said proudly.

I watched him drink another giant papaya smoothie. Most people would have died of a frozen head. Not McCaffrey.

"You eat like a fag," he commented mildly.

I had been around cops and firefighters my whole life. Their ways were not a mystery to me, including the occasions of violence or even death that went with the jobs. The his-and-hers sharp-shooters were new to me.

"You like a lot of salt or a little, asshole?"

"Excuse me?"

McCaffrey was eyeing the big salted pretzels at the counter. "I'm thinking dessert."

"You can still fit dessert?"

"Anybody ever tell you you're very short?"

I laughed. "All the time."

"I'm gonna get one. You want?"

"Nope, I'm good."

"You're a fucking woman," he said, shaking his head.

The crowd was packed a dozen deep at the counter. McCaffrey

sliced through the crowd, moving them aside like the prow of a ship. He sprang for three pretzels, and we got back in the cruiser. He drove with a piece of pretzel sticking out of his mouth like a cigar. Not a crumb was left when we hit Ground Zero.

"Let's do it again sometime, right, Bro?"

"I'll look for McDonald's coupons," I said, and we both laughed.

He drove away munching on a piece of pretzel he must have kept in his pocket.

Normal and abnormal—lots of times it was hard to tell the difference.

It was hours after my tour and I could have gone home but I was drawn back to the Command Post. Emotions there were running high as the effort to establish the extent of our casualties intensified. Every one of us had friends still unaccounted for, and our losses affected every rank. The Port Authority's corporate headquarters had been at the World Trade Center. The World Trade Center had been owned by the Port Authority up until June of 2001, when it was leased to Larry Silverstein, who began operating it. We had employees working there in our medical departments, our aviation and transportation departments, and every Port Authority operation had an office there.

Our top executives were at the World Trade Center. Fifteen floors in the North Tower were dedicated to the Port Authority. As a result of 1993 bombing, the PA moved to make the building safer for evacuation. They painted the handrails and steps in the stairwells so they would be illuminated in the dark. They appointed fire marshals to clear each floor into the stairwells and then search that floor to make sure that everybody had left. These were among the measures that made the evacuation on 9-11 as successful as it was.

Beyond the thirty-seven PAPD officers missing, there were

thirty-eight Port Authority civilian employees missing. Among them were Neil Levin, executive director of the PA, and Superintendent of Police Fred Marone. I had been concentrating on the Port Authority police. The few civilian names I had heard I didn't know. At one point I was handed the newly revised list of the Port Authority people who were missing.

We needed several pages to list the names. On the first page, near the top, I saw the name Andrucki. It took a second for it to hit me. She was somebody so close to me I never called her by her last name. She wasn't Jean *Andrucki*. She was always just Jean. I looked at her name again. I refused to believe it. I asked Bill Barry to find out if this list had been confirmed.

I was looking for any reason, any loophole, to believe her name could be removed from the list. Could these people have been found since? Are there mistakes on this list? Bill went to check. I walked out of the Command Post still holding on to the list.

Jean had worked here at the World Trade Center. She was a fire marshal whose responsibility would have been to get people on each floor up and out and tell them how to get down the stairwells. Then she would have searched the entire floor to make sure that everybody was off and that doors were closed, and she would have made any phone calls that needed to be made. Jean, being who she was, as athletic as she was, as concerned as she was about people— Jean would have taken her responsibilities seriously. She would have been the last person on the floor to go. She would have given everyone the right directions. She would have kept her head. She would have been patient with even the slowest people.

She would have run out of time.

I called my wife. "Karen, Jean Andrucki's name is on the list of missing."

"What?"

"Jean's name is on the list of Port Authority people missing since 9-11."

"Oh my God, Bill. Oh, my God." She started crying.

We went through the same questions all of us ask to give ourselves even the smallest foot in the door of denial.

"How do you know?"

"I'm looking at the list, Karen."

"What do you mean, a list? You know, is the list legitimate? You know, could they be wrong?"

I don't know, I don't know, I don't know, I said. I don't know anything. But I remembered . . .

I met Jean in 1983. She moved into a neighborhood near where I had gone to high school and attended St. Peter's College. At that time I owned a trucking business that I had left college to start. We operated on the New York and New Jersey piers, pulling containers off to deliver them to the customer, then returning the empty containers to the pier.

When my friends and I had turned eighteen in our senior year of high school, we started going to Jack Miller's Pub in Jersey City. It was on Academy Street, just a few blocks from the Journal Square Transportation Center, which was owned by the Port Authority. Most of us lived in the area, so it became a regular thing to get together at Jack Miller's, have a couple of beers, and watch *Monday Night Football*.

Jean had moved to Jersey City from Long Island to work with the Port Authority and lived right down the block from Jack Miller's Pub. Jean was a gifted athlete. She played rugby football, basketball; she was a great softball player. She loved the walls covered with pictures of fighters, baseball players, football players, basketball players, hockey players, and the old Yankees. Boxing champion Emil Griffith's five middleweight and welterweight championship belts also hung there, and once in a while the champ himself came in.

Jean and I enjoyed the bar for the same reason—talking sports with good company. Sometime during the talk and camaraderie, we became friends. She had a great heart, an unquenchable thirst for life. Jean dreamed of going to the Himalayas. She intended to paddle a kayak down South American rivers through the jungle. She had unlimited energy, and sometimes if she couldn't play sports or talk sports, she just jumped on her bike and rode around the city for hours.

Jean was an engineer for the Port Authority. She had two masters degrees and everything going for her, including how pretty she was. Jean was one of the most honest people I ever knew, and as we got to be friends, she made it clear she thought that I was capable of doing a lot more than driving a truck and that I was wasting my time and talent in the trucking business. Her belief in me was so strong that I started to believe in me too. Maybe that made it easier to admit I was never really happy doing trucking.

I was at the point where the economics of the trucking business were changing and profits were harder to come by. It was brutally hard work. In winter, the brakes froze, the engine froze, and we froze. A diesel engine will not start if all forty quarts of oil inside it are frozen solid. The pistons won't chug even if they're cranked until the batteries are dead, and then you just have to recharge your batteries. Winter meant lying on the freezing ground on your back, under the truck. It was so cold the wrench always slipped off the wheel nut and banged your hand, but the cut didn't even bleed because it was so cold.

Early on I thought, *I can handle all this now because at some point, I'll have other people driving for me.* That was wrong. When you have other people driving, you see damn quick that no one takes care of your equipment the way you do. On Friday afternoon, the truck that makes your living is being driven by somebody who wants to get home, so he drives it like a cowboy over the largest bumps and potholes and doesn't care if things are falling off. So you spend your Saturday fixing what he broke on Friday, and there's no pay for that. Your days off, there's no pay. Vacations, there's no pay.

In the back of my mind I could hear my father saying, *You're twenty-five, okay. But do you want to be doing this when you're fifty-five?* Fifty-five? I didn't want to be doing it past thirty, but I couldn't see any way out. I was the son of a fireman, but my father never wanted me to join the department. He felt that if I became a firefighter, we weren't moving forward as a family, generation to generation. It was an unusual stance from someone who had so many friends who were second- and third-generation firefighters from families proud they followed in their father's footsteps. I never thought about being a doctor or lawyer; I was the first one in my family even to get through two years of college. The highest I could reasonably expect myself to aim was maybe wearing a tie in some kind of office.

Certain jobs represented the kind of security and benefits I wished I had. Even though I didn't think the effort would amount to anything, I started taking civil service tests, state government tests, even the Port Authority police test. I still don't know why I did the last; most cops struck me as bullies who liked to bother people for no reason. I sure knew they didn't like truckers very much.

I didn't tell anyone in my family that I took the tests, and the fact is, even though I was ready for a change, it never would have happened without Jean. As physically tough and debilitating as the job was and as insecure as a trucker's life turned out to be, I would have handled it. Even though the business was increasingly dominated by real hard types to the point where every day I was becoming just a little bit harder too, I would have stayed. I had been hit all my life—in the neighborhood, on the football field, out on the Jersey City streets. I could take a hit.

Jean didn't change me. She changed how I saw myself, and *that* changed me. She showed me I did have more to give; maybe I did have talents I had never used; maybe the reason I was unhappy with my life wasn't because the job was tough. Maybe I was unhappy because the job was unfulfilling. Maybe the real issue was I wanted to have a more important role in people's lives than delivering their tomatoes.

I was lucky. I met Jean Andrucki. Jean's special gift was letting people see what she saw in them. I felt her quiet confidence that I could change. I felt the strength of her belief in me, and I began to believe too.

At that time in the mideighties, I was living by myself. On this particular Saturday afternoon I went to the bar to watch college football. It was a little early. No one was there yet. I had grabbed my mail from the box as I left my building, and I was about to sift through it when Jean came in and sat down next to me. I shuffled the envelopes and we launched into the running debate on the Final Four until she noticed a familiar logo on one of the envelopes.

"What did you get from the Port Authority?" she asked me.

"I don't know. I took a test for the police a while back. Maybe it's that."

"Bill, it would be perfect for you. C'mon, let's see how you did."

I opened the letter. It said I passed the test for the Port Authority police with a score of ninety-eight out of a hundred. When Jean saw the score, it was all she needed to close one road and open the other from then on . . .

I came out of my reverie. I was still leaning against the Command Post. I shifted the phone receiver and ran a hand over my tired face. I couldn't continue listening to Karen cry at home, and if I went back into the Command Post, memories of Jean would torment me. I felt my body start to go numb as if it was going to sleep. I didn't tell anyone about Jean, but I began searching for her from that minute on, the entire time I was at Ground Zero.

Even now it's impossible to overstate the importance of each recovery because *every* recovery was a potential identification. Just imagine your wife or husband or child walking out the door one morning and never coming back. What would you give to know what had happened to them? Sure, the families knew the Towers had collapsed, but without a body that's all they'd ever know. Every recovery and identification ended for someone else a lifelong uncertainty.

What would I feel if I did find Jean? What she would look like, and what I would have to do to get her out? I couldn't think about that, so I occupied my mind with the recovery. We knew that the most important sites to locate in the debris field were the crushed banks of elevator shafts, lobbies, and stairwells. Towers 1 and 2 had a total of 198 elevators. Each car held fifty-five passengers, and when the Towers fell, the cars had all contained people.

Thousands of people had used the stairs to try to escape from the burning Towers. Staircases have four components: *plates* are what we step on; *risers* are the back plates; *stringers* are the sides that secure the steps and fasten the staircase to the *landings*. When the Towers' collapse tore the stringers out of the landings, the staircases were left hanging in midair. As the 220 stories of steel staircase hurtled down the stairwell from as high as thirteen hundred feet, long sections of stairs folded together like an accordion.

Staircases were an important find for recovery teams at Ground Zero and also one of the worst things that we had to deal with. A grappler would close its jaws on the topmost step, and if the operating engineer was skilled, the staircase unfolded into a long flat sheet from which we recovered the remains of those who were on it when it fell.

The next most important recovery location was around the entrance and exit doors of the lobbies of the WTC buildings. Crowds had formed at the doors as people pressed together more tightly than anywhere else in the push to get out. There was no protection whatsoever from the falling debris.

That kind of crowding together was brought home to me the morning we recovered what we thought was one PAPD officer in just such a location near Building 1. As we uncovered the body, we realized there was a second body so close they were almost touching. We saw right away it was a second PAPD officer and made preparations to recover both bodies. By now the day tour was coming on, so we worked together to lift the two bodies out—only to discover a third body underneath them that was also PAPD.

As we continued the recovery, we found that underneath the bodies of the three PAPD officers was a fourth body, that of a woman in a steel chair—a rescue device used to carry someone who could not walk. It had handles on the side where it could be gripped. We realized that the officers were carrying the woman out of the building in the steel chair. They had probably stopped to triage her, to address any injuries she had suffered, when the building came down on them. It was only after we recovered the three PAPD officers and the woman that we realized there were two more officers there, a total of five who had died trying to carry the woman out. We commemorated all of them with an honor guard. Both civilians and police officers took part, one of many times civilians were given the honor.

Still trying not to think about Jean, I had begun examining a promising location when there was a sudden rise in the noise level from the grapplers over by Building 2. I got a radio call from one of my team leaders that a firefighter's Halligan bar—a tool with an ax at one end and a pry bar at the other—had just been found in the rubble there. I had told my teams to keep their eyes and ears open. Things happened without warning, and I wanted us to be sufficiently involved to spot them. The PAPD had to be better than the NYPD and FDNY for them to see us as just as good, and I had begun to believe the only way for us to be an equal partner in the search was to lead it.

A bucket brigade immediately formed to search the area where the tool was found. The bucket line extended south back toward Liberty Street. I got on it when I saw they didn't have enough people to pass the buckets far enough back for the debris to be sifted in safety.

A "site" was any area that you couldn't see before. Go into a hole in the debris and clear a space: it's a new site. The hole into the debris where the Halligan tool was found was maybe eight feet high, six feet wide, and seven feet deep. Inside, two big pieces of steel had fallen together forming an A-frame that opened another space about three feet by four feet. We started digging, walking the line into the hole to get the buckets in deeper. No one could stay in that hole for long. When a guy inhaled too much smoke or it got too hot, he fell back and the next in line went in. When the guy in front of me came crawling out gasping for breath, it was my turn.

The deeper I got, the hotter it got. I felt it on my skin. I pressed my goggles against my face to keep the dust out and used my respirator to breathe as we got closer to the fires burning behind the hole. I was filling buckets and passing them back when I looked to my left. There was Chief Joseph Esposito, a NYPD four-star chief of the department. As soon as an NYPD cop was found, Joe Esposito was notified. He responded to every one, every time, and personally carried out his fallen officers. The top officer of the largest police department in the world was down in the dust and debris passing buckets. He pushed back his helmet and I saw his face. He knew what we were about. It was in his eyes.

I moved in deeper and crawled into the A-frame. It was stiflingly hot in there, and the dust clogged my eyes. I kept blinking to get the stuff out but couldn't. I moved in a little closer. That's when I realized Esposito had crawled into the A-frame with me. A molten orange fire glowed in the debris in front of us, only yards away. The steel beams were all that held it back, but the heat was so intense the steel moved as it softened.

Esposito and I worked side by side, both sweating, filthy dirty, blinking from the dust, until we had to leave because we couldn't keep our eyes open to see anything anymore. We crawled, feeling our way back out until the guys outside took our arms and pulled us out. Out of the hole, they used squirt bottles to flush our eyes out. Then we went back in.

We went back into the A-frame until there was nothing else to do in there. We didn't find anything. It was a dead end. So many times we worked toward something but had to back out. In this case, the effort was secondary. It was Esposito who really meant something to me. We had worked side by side. No rank, no title, doing what had to be done. That's a leader. I never forgot it.

I saw Chief Esposito almost a year after 9-11, at the NYPD Thirteenth Precinct on Twenty-first Street and Second Avenue over on the East Side, right across from the Police Academy. The Thirteenth Precinct lost Officer Robert Fazio and Officer Moira Smith. Both were found by PAPD teams, and recovered by the NYPD. A gathering in honor of officers Fazio and Smith was held and we were invited to attend. We humbly accepted memorial plaques.

When Chief Esposito saw me, he came over and grabbed my hand. "How's everything going for you?"

"Fine, Chief, how's things with you?"

"I'm up to here with one thing or another. You know how it is. Listen, you take care of yourself, Lieutenant."

"You too, Chief."

Not a long talk. Nothing complicated. No reminiscing about how you felt or what you thought; what I saw in his eyes was all that mattered.

He still knew what we were all about.

If Chief Esposito was so impressive because he was a great leader, then it was part of the drama of Ground Zero that it was just a simple, good-hearted man who was given a gift from God. Frankie Silecchia, a laborer from Local 73 of the Concrete and Excavation workers was an unlikely candidate for being the genuine article. Frankie was a big man with kind eyes, strong hands, and deep beliefs. The day after 9-11 he walked into Ground Zero, picked up a pair of gloves, wrapped a bandanna around his face, and headed out with an FDNY rescue team to search Building 6, the partially collapsed eight-story U.S. Customs House.

The team began to search the site, working their way deeper down. They only had flashlights to see their way, and in the pitch-black garage, the thick dust made them look like light sabers. Frankie and the team searched the cars. Dust flew up as they opened the doors and the roof lights flared like torches. Frankie hit the headlights and twin beams speared out.

"Hey, Chief," he yelled. "We don't need the flashlights. Turn on the car lights."

One by one, the headlights of every vehicle in the garage came on and the dust danced in the beams. The team worked their way down all six levels, turning on the headlights as they progressed. The basement below Level 6 was inaccessible. The floor had crumbled and the walls were hot from fires still burning. The team had no apparatus to fight fire. This was as far as they could go.

At that point, no one knew what conditions were like in the center of the building, so the team worked its way inward. Building 6 had been eight stories. It was now two. Frankie and the firefighters located three bodies. By dawn the teams had removed all three from the debris, but the job wasn't done yet. The bodies had to be pulled to the top of the pile by rope.

The night of September 13 had been a long one and the men were exhausted from working in the smoke and ash. Frankie volunteered to go to the top and help pull. He followed two of the firefighters back through the garage and up the outer staircase. As they got to the edge of the debris overlooking the recovery site, they saw for the first time that the center of the building was compromised two levels lower, "punched down" in the middle, so the other side of the building was visible across the depression. The debris field curved up like a bowl, and as the full light of morning broke across the area, cradled right in the middle, Frankie saw a twenty-foot-high cross standing straight up in the debris.

What did the sight mean to a near-exhausted man who had been pulling bodies out of the debris for ten hours? Frankie said later that it was like finding someone alive. He stood there for over twenty minutes staring at it in tears. He couldn't tear his eyes away. The cross was a section of crossbeam from the top of the North Tower. Accident or miracle, who can say?

Word of the cross found in the grottolike setting in Building 6 spread through the site. Everyone talked about it. The cross was a sign of hope and faith. I had it in my mind to go see it but hadn't yet. Then I was walking past Building 6 with one of the crane operators, who said, "Bill, have you seen the crosses in there?"

"Not yet, but I want to. How far in are they?"

"Two seconds. Right over that pile."

We walked up to the top of the hill, but I didn't see them until he pointed. Smoke and steam swirled around the big cross, which was as stark and bare as the debris around it, standing perfectly straight with two other crosses lying in the rubble at its base. I just stared. I must have stared for a full five minutes.

It was a beautiful thing and it was heartwarming. It took you back and it took you away. It didn't matter what religion you were: it was all-inclusive. It gave hope to people who were pulling thousands of body parts out of the wreckage and grappling with despair daily. The other feeling everyone had was amazement. We all knew no human being had placed the cross here; no one set it in the ground. It fell out of the sky just the way Frankie found it.

Sometimes at night I'd go over to see the cross just to be in the presence of something that marvelous. It helped me cope with the death and suffering. When Frankie and others began to come together in the hope of preserving the cross as a memorial at Ground Zero, I agreed with them and felt strongly the cross should remain here. But it seemed almost impossible that it would. Frankie had tried for weeks to get someone to champion his cause, but no one had except Father Brian Jordan, a Franciscan priest.

Father Jordan was pressing the mayor's office to preserve the cross. In the weeks that followed Frankie's discovering the cross, there had been no positive response—only rumors that the cross would be moved out of Building 6 to a safe location, and all of them seemed without substance—until the night of October 4.

The group of ironworkers who came to me that night will remain nameless. They had a request: if the cross were to be moved, would I look the other way? They knew I was in charge of the site for the Port Authority and I could stop anything like this from happening, and I had no orders of any kind that allowed for the cross to be moved or to be constructed as a memorial. I agreed that a memorial with the significance of the cross should be embraced, but they were asking me to be an accomplice. The management would know the steel couldn't have been erected on my tour without my knowledge.

I told the ironworkers I believed the cross should remain on the site and they should go ahead and move it and they were welcome to any help I could give.

Moving the cross that night involved the combined efforts of the construction workers who cleared it, the ironworkers who cut it, and the operating engineers who used one of the big cranes to move it. It was welded to a base, and then the base was bolted to the North Bridge abutment. The ironworkers stuck quarters between the plates because steel can't be welded to steel without a space. The ironworkers used about three dollars' worth of commemorative quarters from various states including New York.

Despite the hour, the short notice, and the diversity of religious beliefs at the site, hundreds of us gathered at midnight at Ground Zero to bow our heads in prayer before the cross that was delivered to tell us not to be afraid and not to lose faith.

America woke the next day to almost every newspaper and TV news station across the country calling the cross "inspiring" and the midnight ceremony "an event of national significance." They said the cross was a sign that God had not deserted America and that it was "a monument to give the entire country hope."

After that, no one could take it down.

To this day, no one has.

It has been five years and the cross is still the only memorial to the victims of 9-11 at Ground Zero.

Chapter Four

B y 9-11 I had been a police lieutenant for two years. A lieutenant is an operational supervisor in charge of the people carrying out an assigned mission. For this reason, the promotion from sergeant to lieutenant carries with it an important distinction. It is not unusual for a sergeant to kick a decision up to a lieutenant. A lieutenant almost never calls in a captain to make a decision. Unless the matter is so big or unusual it will ultimately involve the entire Port Authority with the public or press, the lieutenant is where the buck stops.

At this point in the recovery operation the people I had working for me included Port Authority cops, the Passaic County Sheriff's Department, George Washington Bridge painters, workers from the PA construction unit known as SEMAC, Holland Tunnel auto mechanics, Lincoln Tunnel maintenance workers, and the tunnel and bridge agents who responded to emergencies at their respective commands. Officers from New Jersey police departments and Port Authority engineers were also well represented.

Whether by accident or design, the location chosen by Inspector Morris for the PAPD command post, in front of Borough of Manhattan Community College on West Street, put us further north—uptown—than any other WTC police or firefighter command. The choice had an interesting and unforeseen result. We were the first recognizable authority people encountered as they walked downtown to volunteer at Ground Zero. This was an obvious asset for a service as small as ours, because it added to our ranks scores of retired cops, merchant marines, military officers, union workers, and Port Authority civilian staff.

By the end of the first week, I was supervising over three hundred people in addition to our own PAPD cops. I organized them into teams, assigned supervisors, and deployed them in the nightmare landscape of Ground Zero. Our force didn't compare to the hundreds of NYPD cops and even more FDNY firefighters, but it gave us a presence and we fought to maintain it as the numbers at Ground Zero swelled. Adding the forty-person Urban Search and Rescue (USAR) contingents arriving from all over the country, the construction workers, the retired servicemen, and the FEMA and OEM teams, there were thousands of people combing through or moving out the debris at Ground Zero.

Every one of these dedicated souls added immeasurably to the initial rescue and recovery effort. People who would be of special importance to me later on were the members of Team Romeo. "Romeo" is the word that designates the letter R in radio communications, like "alpha" is used for A. In this case, it stood for "retired." Every member of Team Romeo was a retired PAPD officer. They banded together and came to the site to help in any way they could. Recovering a body held by red-hot steel beams heated by a fifteen-hundred-degree fire burning just yards away was precise work that required explicit directions and tight communication. The guys from Team Romeo had been through a lot in life, and their age and maturity was an important balance to the youth and inexperience of many of my guys at the site.

The guys of Team Romeo were legends in the department, bigger-than-life stars of another era. They had been assigned to the Port Authority Bus Terminal command on Manhattan's West Side during the early eighties, when the city struck down its loitering laws, handcuffing cops charged with keeping order in public places like the terminal. What was the result of being unable to remove people if they wanted to stay, no matter how offensive or bizarre their behavior? At one time it was estimated that as many as six to seven hundred people were living in the stairwells, ceilings, boiler rooms, and wash closets of the Port Authority Bus Terminal and having babies in the bathrooms.

The Team Romeo cops were tough, effective, and fearless but had maintained their humanity and their sense of humor. They also provided the answer to the most-asked question at Ground Zero during the nine months I was there, one that everyone came to sooner or later. Was Ground Zero worse than Vietnam? A lot of us asked because the intensity of its ugliness and the damage it inflicted on American citizens seemed equal. Others asked it because these were simply the two worst things that had ever happened to us.

The members of Team Romeo were old enough to have been in Vietnam, in combat.

"Hands down," Billy Haubert said, gesturing like an umpire. "This is worse."

"Why?" I asked. "Beyond the obvious that this is our home."

"We went through boot camp. We were taught how to kill, when to kill, how to get used to killing. That's what boot camp was—a complete stripping of what was normal in your environment, and then rebuilding you into something else.

"No one who served at Ground Zero went to boot camp. None of us were trained. Our emotions were stripped by buildings falling down. All that was normal was death. No one prepared us for that, and no one told us how to deal with it. And no one was training us on what to do once it was over.

"We were not trained to suffer. The experience was the training—and that meant we had no defense, we weren't prepared. Somebody decided we were going to learn how to swim—and threw us overboard. Not only were we thrown overboard, we had to look for other people thrown overboard, and the boat was pulling away and there were no life preservers and no rules and no land in sight."

My being able to use volunteers out on the pile had another

benefit. It freed up cops for special operations. Joint USAR/PAPD teams went into the PATH subway tunnels to try to find people who might be still alive in WTC basements and stairwells. The WTC PATH station platform was undamaged, so we figured people might have started walking through the tunnels to get to New Jersey, as they had after the '93 bombing.

We knew from the '93 experience that a lot of people tried the stairwells and exit doorways along the way. But when we got down there after 9-11, we learned that the tunnels were flooded, especially at the downgrade midriver where water collected. The NYPD planted listening devices deep underground, hoping they would lead to a rescue, but no one was ever found.

By now, the NYPD was becoming somewhat more accessible. They stationed an NYPD liaison officer at our Command Post; we had a PAPD liaison officer at theirs. We exchanged PAPD and NYPD radios for more effective communications. As we worked together, relationships formed and people opened up. It became routine to share information—which could be anything from "Hey, I heard this was happening on-site, what did you hear?" or "What's the word on so-and-so?" to formal briefings on special operations. The "good word" on us was sent back to the NYPD command post.

As the PAPD got more involved, word spread about our special knowledge of the WTC. This first became clear when an NYPD captain, John Yee, asked us to help one of his teams that had come to a dead end in the lowest level of a collapsed section. Did we know of a way around it, or over it, or maybe an elevator or a stairway? PAPD officers led the team to their destination. It made me realize the strength of what would prove to be one of our key assets: my men had the blueprint of the site in their brains.

That "blueprint" showed me that the huge number of cops, firefighters, engineers, and rescue teams working in the same place without central guidance presented huge problems. Emergency Service Units swarmed over the pile working any area that looked good rather than doing an organized grid search. With emotions clouding vision, hundreds of volunteers crawled through the tangle of girders and debris looking for a place to dig—*any* place—where somebody else wasn't already digging. They had the best of intentions, but looking back now, I see that in the beginning all anybody knew was that on top of the pile, you dug your way down; underneath it, you worked your way up; outside, you carved your way in.

All of us thought we'd rescue a lot of people. I remember feelign that it was impossible there was no one left alive at Ground Zero after only two days, but no one had been found alive in the past twenty-four hours. On September 13 that changed with a suddenness that rocked us. We were besieged by phone calls from people all over the city who were waiting at home for word of their loved ones and had just gotten a phone call from them.

"Baby, I'm okay. I'm with about twenty-five people and you know, it's crazy but don't worry about it. I'll be home soon."

"Honey, I'm with a bunch of people in the subway. We're okay. See you soon."

People receiving these messages called to tell us their husband or wife was alive and gave us the location. Some calls were taken by answering machines, so the date and time they were received was clear. The problem was that rescue teams had been in or near many of these locations and hadn't found anyone. We thought it possible these were crank calls. (One twisted mind had actually been leaving messages like "It's me. I'm here. Please come get me.") But these calls were genuine. Entire families confirmed the person speaking was the wife or husband or parent.

The calls had to be followed up. I gathered my team leaders. "Start getting a route together, because we have a message saying as many as twenty-five are trapped and we're going to go in and get them."

The teams left for the pile with renewed hope. *There are still people alive. Whatever it takes, we are going to get into the location and find them. This is a rescue mission. We are going to bring them out.*

Some hours later they radioed back to me in the Command Post. They had gotten to the location but there was no one to rescue. There was no one there at all.

Another call we followed up came from a man who said he was safe in a storage room in one of the basements. We mounted a rescue operation. The storage room was one of ours. It was located under Tower 2. We called it the Vault because it had thick doors and security glass. The PA stored sensitive information there—records of the swipe cards used to go through the turnstiles, and tapes from the security cameras. We needed to get those to show us where patrol cars and fire engines had parked so we could identify where the cops and firefighters entered the buildings and might be waiting for rescue.

Officer John Stella, who knew every inch of the World Trade Center, led a joint mission with a Port Authority Emergency Service Unit and an Urban Search and Rescue team. It took them two hours to reach the location. There wasn't anything left of the Vault. It was crushed under the debris. The records, tapes, and cameras were pulverized. No one in it could have survived. They would have been killed immediately. So if no one could be alive, who made the call?

The call that hit me hardest went to a young girl from her father, whose office was in Tower 1. It came three days after 9-11 telling her where he was, that he was okay, even calling her by her pet name.

"Only my father calls me that," she insisted distraught and in tears. "It has to be him. You have to find him."

We sent in search teams. They made it to the location—a bar in the lower atrium that served breakfast. The bar was undamaged, but there was no one in it. I didn't know what was worse—the idea that everybody was dead or that they were still alive and calling for help except that we couldn't find a trace of them. We couldn't explain what was going on and it was driving us crazy.

I went on the rescue mission to find the girl's father. All of us hoped he was in the bar, drinking beer while he waited for us, and when we got there he'd say, "What took you so long?" and we'd all have a drink together and make a toast and bring him home to his daughter and they would hug each other and cry.

We found no trace of him. He had left this place and been killed when the building came down, or he was never in it. The irony was that if he had been here, he would have survived. Everything was coated with dust. The tables were still set and some had plates of food; the chairs were standing; liquor bottles all the color of dust still stocked the shelves behind the bar.

None of us guessed the truth. It was the number of calls. So many people made calls on their cell phones in the interval between the planes' striking the Towers and the towers' falling, the communications satellite couldn't transmit them all. The overload activated safety programs that stored what could not be sent. It took days for the system to "drain" and recover its capacity to handle traffic freely. As soon as it went back on line, the program sent the stored messages.

At Ground Zero, the dead spoke for themselves. In the bar, it was the bottles that spoke to us. We decided to break them.

A lot of people were having a hard time. The last thing we needed was anyone grabbing a bottle and going off alone to get drunk and do something stupid, or get hurt, or hurt others. Still, it seemed such a small and petty thing to do. We talked about it. Someone said maybe the bottles were contaminated and would make people sick. It didn't matter. It was as good a reason as any. We couldn't leave them here, and it was too much work to carry them out.

It felt bizarre adding to the destruction. Throwing bottles—after a while it was a heated thing: the sound of glass shattering, shards sparkling on the floor, the smell of beer and liquor, the bonds of destruction. It was a release partly, like when kids throw rocks at windows. But it was a guilty thing too, and we all felt it.

It was a sin to break anything that had survived here.

• • •

This period was one of the hardest times for me. I didn't have emergency service training, so I was going on instinct and gut. Anytime something was needed, I just took a step forward and tried to get it done. I was put in charge of all PAPD on-site resources to allocate them to our teams in the field. The experience turned out to be an important asset later on. Not only did I get to know every resource we had, I also learned where it came from, who had more of it, and how and where everything was being used at the site.

I was quickly becoming someone who knew where everyone and everything was—and how to get things done. All well and good, but this was New York City, and the biggest problem turned out to be one I knew nothing about—the conflict between the NYPD and the FDNY that had raged for decades.

Budget cutbacks by successive New York mayors had created a fierce competition between the departments for money and jobs. Except in their most basic roles—law enforcement and firefighting—each was intent on outdoing the other. The police department had a scuba team; so did the fire department. The fire department had rescue units; so did the police department. When it came to Ground Zero, the dust hadn't settled before they were fighting over which one would control the site.

The NYPD claimed jurisdiction because the city charter gave the police control of all crime scenes. The WTC site was, in fact, the largest crime scene in this country's history. The crime was murder; the weapons just happened to be Boeing 767 jetliners. It meant the Manhattan district attorney's office had to conduct an investigation. So did the medical examiner's office in order to determine if autopsies—possibly thousands—were required by law. But a crime scene closes when the criminal investigation is closed. There was no question of the cause or means of death at the WTC, and those who had carried out the crime were dead. Further investigation would not reveal more than was already known. The DA's office closed its investigation. Despite the NYPD's protests, the WTC ceased to be a crime scene.

Attempting to outflank the NYPD and the FDNY was the mayor's Office of Emergency Management. The OEM director reported directly to the mayor. OEM's stated mission was "to plan, prepare for, and mitigate emergencies . . . and to coordinate and support responses to and recovery from emergencies." Wanting to eliminate "conflict among responding agencies with overlapping expertise"—exactly what was occuring between the NYPD and FDNY—Mayor Giuliani put the OEM in charge of all disaster sites by designating it permanent "on-scene interagency coordinator." In 1999 he had also built OEM a $13 million Emergency Operations Center. Unfortunately, he built it on the twenty-seventh floor of World Trade Center Building 7. Fourteen minutes after the first plane crashed into the North Tower, city officials activated OEM's Emergency Operations Center. It was destroyed three minutes later.

Regardless, the FDNY had no intention of giving up operational control to the OEM or anyone else to manage a site it claimed by right of its huge death toll—the loss of 343 firefighters. The same city charter that defines the NYPD's jurisdiction also defines the FDNY's. It is in charge of all collapsed buildings and all buildings on fire. It was no contest. On September 12 the FDNY took over Ground Zero, establishing what it believed was its rightful control of the site.

Immediately the FDNY and the New York City Department of Design and Construction (DDC) divided Ground Zero into four quadrants and assigned one construction company to do the work in each quadrant. The construction companies moved swiftly. They all knew how to do business in New York. They had done a lot of it. They began to move heavy machinery into the site to replace the bucket brigades. They also hired the union workers who would operate them. The mayor's office told them to complete work before the mayor left office, just a few months away.

From that moment on, there would be those of us who saw

Ground Zero as a rescue and recovery site and our job as being to find fallen heroes for their loved ones, and those who saw it as a construction site and their job as being just to clean it up.

All this wrangling took place without PAPD participation. We woke up to find the FDNY was in complete charge and we didn't have a damn thing to say about it. This was a setback for us. The FDNY was unreceptive to us from the start. We obviously wanted to have a larger role at the site, but everything needed to be approved by them, and they weren't quick to approve much. They liked working with their own. They trusted their own. Their radio communications were accessible only to their own.

The PAPD had never experienced anything like the WTC disaster on 9-11. Even the '93 bombing paled by comparison. We had never had relationships like this with city departments before either. We weren't a city agency. We didn't report to the mayor. The politics of New York City were alien to us. I had been a Port Authority cop in Midtown for fourteen years. I had interacted with a number of NYPD cops during that time, but almost never with FDNY firefighters. The FDNY was a closed culture, almost impossible for an outsider to penetrate.

Three events made me realize I had to deal with the situation head-on. The first was the rescue of PAPD sergeant John McLoughlin and PAPD officer Will Jimeno, the only people pulled out of the pile alive—the last rescue.

A volunteer found them by chance, a former Marine Corps sergeant who kept walking back and forth through the dust and debris calling out all day, "U.S. Marine Corps. If you hear me, holler. U.S. Marine Corps, if you hear me, holler . . ."

Near midnight on 9-11, a voice came from the rubble, "Yes, I'm here. Find me."

The sergeant went for help. He located some NYPD Emergency Service Unit people. One was named Paddy McGee. Paddy got some more lighting and went back with the volunteer to the rescue site. McGee looked down, heard what the ex-marine heard, and radioed for support.

McLoughlin, Jimeno, and three other officers had been carrying medical equipment to treat people across one of the World Trade Center's underground concourses that connected the two Towers. They were heading toward the North Tower when the South Tower came down.

One of the unsettling things about the disaster was that a person standing twenty feet to the left of something could walk out without a scratch, while another standing twenty feet to the right was pulverized. That was what happened here. Will and John were buried by rubble but still alive; two other officers standing just yards away were killed instantly. The last, Dominic Pezzulo, was unharmed.

Dominic tried removing debris to get to John and Will, but it was impossible. At that moment, Dominic could have gotten out. He could have left and reached safety. He didn't. He stayed and started talking to John and Will, trying to comfort them, telling them they'd be okay. He would get help . . . just hang on. He tried to get through to us on his radio. He wasn't sure how to tell us where they were if someone answered, or even how to describe the location, but he kept trying as he talked to John and Will to keep their spirits up.

Will and John could barely see Dominic through the dust and debris, but they could hear him. They also heard a terrible sound begin again, as terrible as when the first building collapsed. It was the roar of the second tower falling.

Will tried to warn him. "Dominic, something big, man, something big's happening. Something's happening."

"All right, man," Dominic began.

Then Will saw him hit by something very big falling down.

"I've been hit," Dominic said. "I'm dying."

"Hold on, Dom. Hang on. It'll be all right."

There was only silence.

"Dominic's gone," Will said to John.

"He's in a better place now," John said.

Port Authority Police Officer Will Jimeno was rescued at 11 p.m. on the night of September 11 by a team of PA police and NYC ESU cops and firefighters, and a retired marine. The body of Officer Dominic Pezzulo was recovered shortly after. Officer John McLoughlin was pulled out of the rubble eight hours later, at around 7 a.m. on the morning of September 12.

Sadly, we found no one else to rescue. We were there to help. We wanted to find people, but there wasn't anyone. That feeling was so empty. We all thought we were going to be rescuing people. We could certainly find ten here, twenty-five there, then maybe thirty or fifty more. We got nothing but an eerie silence in response to our calls.

The single rescue we made should have given us hope. So why was I dissatisfied? It was because we weren't there to help our own guys be rescued. The FDNY responded. The NYPD responded. The PAPD wasn't even called until the rescue was well under way.

The second event was that five bodies were sent to the morgue without PAPD presence or approval. They just put them in bags and shipped them off the site. Maybe some of them were my cops. Some of my guys were wearing plain clothes when they responded. Now I might not know for months, until they were identified, if they had been found.

I vented my anger outside the Command Post. It cleared the area quicker than a backhoe, except for an NYPD chief named Bruce Smolka, who set me straight. I had first met him years ago when my partner and I responded to a fight call and found Smolka on the ground struggling with the guy he was arresting. We unhinged the guy from Smolka and helped him up. He brushed himself off and looked at us curiously.

"Port Authority cops? Jesus. Where the fuck did you guys come from?" He stuck out his hand. "Thanks. I guess I owe you one."

That night at Ground Zero, Smolka paid me back. When he saw I was angry, he asked why, and I told him.

"I should have been called," I said, still hot. "The FDNY has a guy in the morgue. He could have called me."

Smolka shook his head like no one should have had to explain something this simple to me.

"Bill, it don't matter what *they* have. You need a guy of your own at the morgue. You can't expect them or me or anyone else to care about your guys: *you* have to. Sure, I'll help one out if I see he's in trouble, but bottom line, he's *your* family. Are you a provider or not? Nobody waits for an invitation to this party. You invite yourself in."

The lesson wasn't lost on me. From that night to the end, I posted guys at the morgue.

The final element that changed my thinking and made me realize I had to elbow in deeper was the fact that my guys were coming back to me just too many times from the FDNY assignment area having sat around for hours till they were sent back without ever getting onto the pile. Waiting was a killer. We were all anxious. We had to get in and get our hands dirty, be doing something. Maybe it's productive, maybe it's not; at least you're doing something. You're involved.

The situation was difficult enough for us; being marginalized made it almost impossible. The Command Post was the biggest hub of the PAPD, but in the larger world around us it didn't mean a thing. Up to this point we had tried to play by the rules. It was getting us nowhere. I wanted to grab the FDNY people in charge by the neck and say, "Look, *my* friends are in there too. Our ESU teams have the same training you have. We know the site in ways you never can. We're going in."

Inspector Morris expected me to get out in the middle of the action and leverage the PAPD into a position of strength, respect, and effectiveness—carrying it on my back if necessary. I didn't want to dwell on the fact that I had no idea at that particular moment how I was supposed to do that.

I went over to the FDNY Command Post to talk directly to Chief Frank Fellini, who was in charge of all four quadrants of the site. He was tough and smart, so my approach was simple and direct: *Chief, where can I get my people in? What are the protocols and sign-in procedures? All you have to do is tell me the system, and we'll fit into it.* I didn't mention I was going to send my people into areas that weren't being searched, with or without his permission.

As far as I was concerned, I hadn't come here to work for the FDNY or the NYPD or even the Port Authority. My cops and I worked for the families of the people buried here. I knew how valuable the PAPD would be to that effort, and I was damn well going to see us become part of it. When I met Fellini, however, I saved that lecture. I needed to have a good relationship with the FDNY. Getting this chief on my side could open things up and let me show everybody what the PAPD had to offer.

I told him, "I'm not trying to go around you, Chief. I tried to work within the structure, but I can't anymore. Your people tell me they need guys over there. The guys go over there. They end up sitting in a tent on Church and Liberty. A few hours ago your deputy told me to send them over. My guys are still sitting there. That's not why we came here. We came to work."

"Cool down, Lieutenant," he said, and got on the phone with the deputy. He talked for a minute or two, then held the phone away from his head so I could hear.

". . . conditions are unstable, Chief. We're looking at a possible building collapse. I pulled our guys out too."

Fellini hung up. "Lieutenant, everybody was pulled out. Not just your cops."

"That's not what *my* guys are telling me, Chief. They tell me your guys are still working out there."

Fellini shrugged. He wasn't going to go against what his own guy told him on my say-so. I wouldn't, in his position. No commander would.

"Look, Lieutenant. It's a whole new landscape out there. We'll have it all figured out soon."

I might have said something argumentative but a thought hit me when he said that, and it stopped me. The WTC wasn't new to us, no matter what its condition. The FDNY might have the territory, but we had the map. We were the experts in WTC locations. We knew the buildings so well, some of the guys could stand on top of six stories of debris and say, "Below here was *this* store. That was where *that* stairwell was. There was an elevator bank *there*. Here's where the trains came in. Here's where the hall was . . ."

The FDNY covered the city, all five boroughs. We had found that a lot of firefighters from the Bronx, Brooklyn, Queens, and Staten Island who were put in charge of operations at the World Trade Center had never been *in* the World Trade Center. Half the time, they didn't know what they were looking at, couldn't visualize what any area had been before it was ruins. They were getting lost and getting frustrated.

It was the same thing when the Urban Search and Rescue teams got to the site. They were from all over the country and had never seen anything but pictures of the WTC. They had even less of an idea than the FDNY how it had been constructed or what had been in it. They also had far less of an attitude about working with other commands.

I used to tell my people what I learned in Jersey City to get to baseball practice or to get home: you can't negotiate while you're walking backwards. We had to take advantage of our strength. When one of the USAR guys told me he thought he might be able to get to an emergency entrance that could be under a certain portion of the pile, I brought PAPD officer John Stella over to help him. John closed his eyes and listened as the USAR guy described that part of the pile, and then John told him where in the building it had been located and several ways to get there.

The USAR guy was amazed. "Do you have any *more* guys like that?" he asked.

"Every one of my guys is like that," I said.

We began advising the USAR teams on a regular basis. I made sure it was always in the presence of the FDNY. Eventually, when the FDNY saw there were questions only we could answer, they came over to us for help too, and things began to snowball.

A few days later I was on my way to relieve Day Commander John Ryan and ran into FDNY Chief Fellini. He was in a huddle with Ryan, and a civilian, in front of the FDNY operations tent. The engine noise of the grapplers and trucks and the throb of a dozen separate Daisy light generators were punctuated by blasts of the FDNY's big air horns warning workers on the pile whenever there was the possibility of a section collapse. I had to lean close and cup my ear to hear the conversation. They were trying to figure out how to move trucks and equipment to and from Staten Island a lot faster.

I said hello to John Ryan, nodded to the chief.

"Lieutenant," Fellini acknowledged curtly.

I was about to introduce myself to the civilian when he saw my name tag and lit up like a Christmas tree. "Wait, I know you. Keegan, right? The quarterback. From Jersey City, right?" He stuck out his hand. "I'm Peter Vincent. I used to watch you play back in high school. My father owned the haircutting place in Greenville."

It was a nice surprise. "I lived in Greenville," I said as we shook hands. "I used to get my haircuts there. That was your place?"

"My old man's." He turned to Fellini. "Chief, do you know what we got here? Keegan was like the quarterback for all Jersey City."

Fellini didn't fall off his chair. No big deal.

"What do you do here, Peter?" I asked.

"Bill, any truck rolls in or out of here, it's me who has to know about it." He said it with a confidence that told me he could probably get things done and wasn't afraid to shake the trees a little to do them.

"Our trucks carry some of the most expensive steel in the world. Being World Trade Center Steel makes it even more valuable. Some loads are upwards of fifty thousand pounds. One truck tried to transport a steel box beam so heavy its axles collapsed when it hit a pothole on the highway."

Peter brushed his dark hair off his forehead and smiled like a salesman. "Listen, Bill. You know me, I know you. We're both from Greenville. We can help each other, right?"

"Anytime, Peter," I assured him.

They went back to their discussion and asked me join it. The problem involved routing the trucks to Staten Island. There was too much traffic taking the Brooklyn-Battery Tunnel and the Verrazano Bridge to the Fresh Kills landfill, so the turnaround time was too long. The route wasn't working, and we didn't have enough trucks to make it work.

"Billy," Vincent prodded me, "you got anything here?"

"What about using the Holland Tunnel?" I said. "It's closed to the public, but that wouldn't stop us opening a dedicated lane for our own trucks. After that, they head up to Bayonne and take the Bayonne Bridge to Staten Island. The Bayonne Bridge has zero traffic compared to the other bridges, the Goethals and the Verrazano."

"No traffic at all if Peter coordinates the timing," John said.

Peter gave an "easy as pie" wave of his hand.

Fellini said, "Who do we need to talk to?"

The bridge and tunnel were both Port Authority commands, so the PA Surface Transit Division representative at the site would have to approve it. John called him to come over.

The rep arrived a few minutes later. You didn't have to be Freud to read the I-didn't-ask-to-be-here expression on his face or the fact that he was unhappy having to deal with whatever it was we wanted. When he heard what it was, his expression was even less encouraging.

"I have to check," he said, and walked off to use his cell phone in private. He came back a few minutes later.

"Okay, you can bring the trucks through the tunnel and over the bridge, but you have to wash them before you do, to get asbestos or any other byproduct of the collapse off them. We don't want to be fined if EPA inspectors come into the tunnel and find this material." That had us scratching our heads. Who could think of that at this moment?

"Water?" Fellini made kind of a snort. "I got plenty of fucking water. We can have a fire engine wash them before they go in the tunnel or over the bridge."

It seemed like a good answer, but the Port Authority rep looked unsure. He walked away to make another phone call, returning maybe five minutes later.

"Where," he asked, "is the water going to go that comes off the trucks? It also contains contaminants, and the Port Authority would be responsible for the runoff."

Fellini was a burly guy with a big voice. He leaned into the PA guy's face and used all of it. "Let me get this straight," he boomed. "Let me get this *absolutely* straight. We just had two hundred twenty floors collapse here. There's a cloud of asbestos and everything else you could possibly worry about, passing Arizona on its way to Mexico by now—and you're worried about a trickle of water off a truck that might have some dust on it, a mile away? Is that what you're telling me? Is that what's holding this whole thing up?"

It was.

The rep looked at his watch. "Gentlemen?"

I said, "We could keep the fire engine right here at the site to wash the trucks before they leave. The runoff stays on-site."

"They can also wet the trucks down so nothing goes flying," Ryan added.

The PA rep thought it over. "We can probably accommodate that," he said, and left without another word.

It was a done deal sooner than I think anyone expected.

"Good fucking idea, guys," said Fellini.

I didn't fall off my chair either.

John and I needed to talk about some mutual issues. We turned to leave, but Fellini stopped me.

"Lieutenant Keegan."

"Yeah, Chief?"

"Why don't you go up to the ten-ten firehouse and tell them I said for you to grab a radio. Call me if you need anything."

I was more than surprised. The FDNY, NYPD, and PAPD systems were all separate and there was no way to integrate them. The radio would link us to the FDNY's command and network so we could talk to them directly. I already had the NYPD radio. Soon I carried all three—two hooked into remote microphone speakers on my collar and the third in my pocket turned way up. The radios were a badge of rank for me; they said I operated on the same level as three- and four-star chiefs, that I was another leader of the site.

Morris had told me to find out what the fuck was going on out here.

No problem.

We were now in the loop.

There is an interesting footnote to that day. It wasn't long before trucking debris all the way to the Staten Island landfill was supplanted by a far better idea. Somebody very bright realized we were on an island and could run the trucks barely a mile from the World Trade Center to Pier 25 on the Hudson River, where the debris could be loaded onto a barge and towed right to the site at Fresh Kills.

The route was far faster, avoided traffic, and cut the turn-around time for the trucks to a fraction. I liked it because although the loads we sent out from Ground Zero were supposed to contain only steel and dirt, nothing was perfect and I always worried we might miss something. There had been instances when the workers looking down from the high scaffolds of the wet-down stations, as they hosed off the trucks to keep the dust in, spotted what appeared to be body parts—what we called "possibles." Now I could have the debris screened one more time—right at Pier 25. The debris-filled trucks themselves became the sorting devices. A driver slowly moved his truck along the pier while gradually elevating the bed. The debris slid out onto the ground behind the truck maybe a foot high, and construction workers took a last look.

Then, on the night of October 12, I received an urgent radio transmission from Lieutenant Ed Moss down at Pier 25. Ed had received a phone call from the operating engineer at the pier that while scraping up a load of debris, a construction worker had noticed an object in the rubble that resembled the black boxes that everybody was looking for so intently. Before 9-11 had ended, the FBI were all over the site combing the wreckage for the black boxes from the Boeing 767s that crashed into the Twin Towers. In those first days, there was almost nothing more important than the recovery of the black boxes, as they might have provided critical information at a time when we had none. Posters with photos of them were plastered everywhere so workers would recognize them if they turned up in the debris. The photos showed us that black boxes were not actually black; they were bright orange with white stripes. Each plane carried two—a flight data recorder and a cockpit voice recorder. Each of those types was depicted in the posters, which were so numerous the site looked like a neighborhood where someone had lost a beloved dog or cat.

They were in every Command Post. They were taped to anything that could be taped, stapled to anything that could be stapled, nailed to anything that could be nailed. The posters worked. Moss was calling me that day to tell me an operating engineer thought he had recognized an object the same shape as a black box, but it was too blackened and charred for him to tell the original color.

No one wants to make a call like that and end up identifying a toilet bowl or a video camera, so it was clear the engineer thought seriously enough of what he saw to stop operations at the pier and get an opinion from the crane operator. The crane operator agreed that it looked like a black box and should be reported. The Port Authority Police Department was running the security posts at all checkpoints that allowed access in and out of the site. Pier 25 was one of those points, so the engineer's call about the find was routed to the officer in charge of security, Lieutenant Moss, at our Command Post. Hearing their description and the excitement in their voices, he went to Pier 25 to see for himself.

Lieutenant Moss advised me that he and Lieutenant Bill Doubrawski were responding to Pier 25 and he would call me when he formed an opinion. Twenty minutes later I got a radio transmission from him.

"Billy, I saw the object. Could you three-nine me?" Three-nine was code for a secure call. He didn't use any other description because our radio could easily be monitored.

As soon as I reached him by secure phone from the Command Post, I heard the excitement in his voice.

"Billy, I think we found one of these things. I'm looking at the diagram. I think this is it."

"Doubrawski agree?"

"Absolutely."

"What is it like?"

"Hard as a rock, not orange. Looks like it was torched, all blackened."

"Okay, I'd like to take a look at it."

"Billy, if this is one, it's some find. This is incredible."

"Did you get all the guys' names over at the pier?"

"Sure. Be right there."

Moss and Doubrawski were the third and fourth people to decide the object matched the pictures in the poster. I was the fifth person. I compared the object to the FBI photos. After my comparison, I agreed with Lieutenant Moss and Lieutenant Doubrawski and the operating engineer and construction worker. The object found on the pier was absolutely close enough to the pictures available to us to notify the FBI without delay. With the FBI on-site, we had no trouble getting through to them through our EOC. We asked for agents to respond to our Command Post, telling them we had an item of interest for them. Obviously, it was a fantastic find—if it was verified. In that case we'd make sure that the guys down at Pier 25 were rewarded by at least the knowledge that they had made such an outstanding recovery. We wanted our supervisors to know that we were involved in the recovery of a black box. Obviously, everybody right down the line wanted to know whether or not it *was* a black box.

Twenty minutes to a half hour later, two FBI agents came to the Command Post. They took a look at the object, they took a look at the diagram, and they both said words to the effect of, "Wow, this looks like it" and "It's the same shape." We gave them the names of the men who had found it, names that were also recorded in our daily operating log at the Command Post—the ongoing chronology of significant events.

However, after looking at the object for several more minutes, one of the agents said, "We don't think it's a black box."

"So it's okay to throw it back on the barge?" I asked. "You're clearing it?"

The other said quickly, "No, no, we're going to take it with us."

The agents left with the object, and we went back to more pressing business. But we never forgot about the find at Pier 25, nor did we ever receive any information on what it was, or wasn't. Nor were we so surprised when the official 9/11 Commission Report came out and stated unequivocally that none of the black boxes from either of the jetliners hijacked on 9-11 had ever been recovered.

Chapter Five

Amonth after 9-11, Ground Zero was still an earthquake landscape with hills of wreckage and valleys of collapsed steel where lines of dust-covered men with buckets snaked out of smoking holes. Leashed dogs wandered over the pile, stopped and sniffed . . . stopped and sniffed. All over the harshly twisted landscape, machines tore out debris for trucks that rocked on their springs crawling to receive it.

We were conscious of America watching. No one talked about it, but we were. Was Ground Zero a sign of hope? No, it was an open wound. Were we brave soldiers and conquering heroes? No, fear was everywhere. Continuous TV coverage on the news stations and every opinion in the world on the opinion shows didn't help either.

When I looked at the mountain of debris, it seemed as if we had barely made a dent in it and I tried to convince myself we would be able to remove it. We were still struggling just to get our feet under us. The pain was new; for some it was unbearable, and we had not yet learned how to help each other.

We were all afraid, although it wasn't something we talked about. We all knew the greatest danger in the first days at Ground Zero was that the buildings surrounding the site could collapse just as the towers had. We were trying to deal with the terrain, catching on to the sudden shifts of debris and the traps of fire and steam, but what would we do if one of the big buildings came down on us? We wanted to get people down to the site to search for bodies, but we had no way to judge the accuracy of reports that the forty-story-plus Millenium Hotel, the Deutsche Bank, and One Liberty were all near collapse.

Then we were told we all might drown.

I was working off Liberty Street when I noticed an engineer using a device that shoots a laser against buildings to check their movement over time. I asked him about the danger of the buildings falling.

He shook his head. "Your problem isn't whether or not these buildings will fall. Your problem is whether or not the tub wall is going to break."

I went cold. "What are you talking about?"

"If that wall goes, the whole site will be undermined. Everything west of it will go. Everyone will drown. All of Lower Manhattan underwater."

A little history is in order here. The idea behind the World Trade Center was to give Lower Manhattan, the oldest part of the city, the kind of growth that Rockefeller Center had given Midtown. The Port Authority was the agency chosen to study the issue. It determined the project was feasible—but only if several major problems could be solved.

Half of the sixteen-acre site was composed of landfill that had extended Manhattan Island seven hundred feet into the Hudson River. Over a million cubic yards of that fill would have to be cleared for the foundation of the Twin Towers to be laid on bedrock. The tools to do the excavation were readily available. The problem was how to keep the Hudson River from pouring into the hole—seven hundred feet long and sixty feet deep—created by the excavation.

The solution was to build a "bathtub." Excavating machines dug a three-foot-wide and seventy-foot-deep trench down to the bedrock below. The trench was divided into twenty-two-foot-wide sections and a slurry of water and expansive clay was pumped in to seal the dirt sides. Cranes lowered a twenty-five-ton, seven-story-high cage of reinforced steel into each section, and concrete was poured in to each of the 152 such sections needed to encircle the site. The resulting wall, which came to be known as the "bathtub," kept the river out when the fill was removed from inside.

After the collapse of the buildings on 9-11, the construction companies abruptly realized that the slurry wall alone wasn't strong enough to keep the river at bay; it needed the internal support of what had been the WTC buildings' basements and garages. Now, the *debris* of those buildings and basements supported it—and as workers removed that debris, they were also removing the slurry wall's support. In addition, the companies had moved some of the biggest cranes in the country—capable of lifting up to a thousand tons—as close as possible to the slurry wall. Now they saw that these machines were only adding to the pressure on the wall. The situation was critical. If the wall broke, the Hudson River would flood the site, the subway system, and Lower Manhattan—a disaster of even greater proportion than the WTC collapse itself.

The operation to secure the slurry wall lasted nine months, and meanwhile every day at Ground Zero we faced the possibility we could drown if the wall collapsed. It was another reason why security was so tight. We all feared a second terrorist attack. If terrorists breached the slurry wall, they would finish the job they started on 9-11 and destroy New York City itself.

The only choice for the construction companies and engineers was to replace what they were taking out. For us on the recovery mission, it was the most serious issue to date. Trucks were coming in with dirt and backfilling places we were trying to excavate. The fill was not only obscuring the bodies, it was burying them anew.

Yet dirt was better than water. A shored-up wall was better than a flood that would wipe out everything, my mission included. For us the logical compromise was to work with the construction companies. If the walls went, so did the recovery. The engineers decided to install close to thousand tiebacks to secure the "bathtub" walls. They drilled through the slurry wall and inserted pipes into the bedrock. Then cables were sent through the pipes beyond the wall, expanding and securing them like molly bolts. It was the first major realization that we had to depend on the construction companies, and they had to work with us.

As a commander, I learned a vital lesson from the slurry wall. More than any other element, judgment—not merely facts—was the critical factor in making decisions, as I saw twice more before my own moment of decision came . . .

On the morning of 9-11, Inspector Joe Morris had made one of the great gut calls of all time and prevented the deaths of everyone in the PAPD Command Post.

The Command Post had been dispatched from Jersey City to the WTC as soon as word reached there that the Towers had been hit. It arrived at 9:30 a.m. The North and South Towers had already been hit and were on fire. Initial orders were to set up shop on the corner of West and Vesey, next to WTC Building 6, which stood in the shadow of the North Tower. Setting up the Command Post so close to the action was standard procedure. The post quickly filled with command personnel and technicians. Inspector Morris, the most senior officer, became incident commander as PAPD officers, NYPD officers, and FDNY firefighters evacuated nearly twenty thousand people. Morris had a million things to do at that moment, calls to make, men to dispatch, orders to give.

The order he gave was "Move the Command Post."

The collective groan was the kind people make when they find out a trip supposed to take five hours is going to take ten. Weren't things chaotic enough? People were in motion; the Command Post was almost operational; no one wanted to disconnect everything and start all over. Morris checked a city map and pointed, "Move it there."

The Command Post relocated to a new site at ten o'clock in the morning. Twenty-eight minutes later, the North Tower collapsed and crushed Building 6, covering the exact spot where the Command Post had stood with tons of debris.

At almost the same time as PA Inspector Morris gave the order to move the Command Post, one of the highest-ranking NYPD commanders was about to make a similar kind of decision and save a lot of lives. The difference is it was the wrong decision, so it isn't talked about as much—except by the cops whose lives it saved.

The Special Operations Division of the New York City Police Department supervises five special units; the Harbor Unit, the Aviation Unit, the Taxi Unit, the Anti-Graffiti Unit, and the Emergency Service Unit (ESU). ESU teams respond to situations requiring the most specialized training, such as hostage taking and water rescue, and employ the most advanced equipment. All ESU members are EMTs or paramedics; they are certified public safety divers, firefighters, specialists in high-angle and confined-space rescue and in vehicle extrication, and they are deployed as both SWAT teams and rescue squads. The saying among cops is "When civilians need help, they call the police. When the police need help, they call the ESU."

On 9-11 the commanding officer of the ESU was NYPD Inspector Ronald Wasson, a studious-looking man who spoke more like a college professor than a cop. Wasson was worried that with all his personnel inside the buildings, he had no way to protect the cops, firefighters, or civilians from the kind of low-intensity warfare—snipers, automatic weapons, car bombs, hostage situations—he was sure would follow the attack. Burning buildings were the FDNY's responsibility. The NYPD had to prepare for what they thought would come next—armed terrorists or "insurgents" attacking the first responders to the WTC.

The order was given by the ESU command staff to "go tactical."

The order meant that ESU members had to respond from the Towers to the SWAT vans and suit up in the now-familiar BDU suits and flak jackets, with heavy weapons, assault rifles, Kevlar helmets. ESU members received the command and came out of the burning buildings—and so survived the collapse of the Towers only minutes later.

The order was wrong. There was no reason to go tactical. There were no attacks. Of the twenty-three NYPD officers who died that day, fourteen belonged to the ESU, but every ESU member knows that a far greater number of them are still here because Wasson's order pulled them out of the Towers and saved their lives.

I had heard these stories and thought about what I might have done in similar circumstances, what I might do in others. I never anticipated the kind of judgment call I *did* have to make—or the events set into motion one cold night in October when I received a call in the Command Post from NYPD Deputy Commissioner Jack Dunn. Dunn told me the FDNY had located two bodies deep in the debris over by Tower 1 and began to recover them till they realized they were cops. The firefighters called Dunn, who had dispatched an NYPD ESU team to the location and was now calling me. He asked me to respond to Tobin Plaza, where he would be waiting.

I took Officers Nunziato, Callaghan, Griffin, and Hennessy with me and responded from the Command Post. I was grateful to Dunn but angry at the FDNY. To me, this was more of their disrespectful attitude toward the PAPD. The FDNY hadn't called us directly; they had called Dunn. We were fortunate *he* respected us enough to bring us in.

The night was pitch-black, and at Ground Zero there was so much dust in the air that the stadiumlike Daisy lights mounted on poles on top of their own generators were just a glow behind it, creating pools of darkness and shadow. At Tobin Plaza small knots of NYPD Emergency Service Unit members stood around a cleared space in the debris talking with uniformed officers, construction workers, and firefighters. Commissioner Dunn was waiting alone beside a makeshift table—just a sheet of plywood across two police sawhorses.

Dunn was a tall, thin man who favored work clothes over fancy suits. It didn't lessen the intensity of his presence. He might look like a common worker; you still knew he was somebody. Dunn had been at the site quite a bit, walking with a pronounced limp from recent surgery on both knees. I had a lot of respect for him. He dragged himself down to the site every day despite the obvious pain, and he was still here at this late hour even after an all-day tour.

Dunn was holding a white bucket, one of those large painter's buckets, cradling it as if there was something sacred inside. To his left were piles of pontoons—big wooden beams twice as thick as railroad ties that were set down to support the six-hundred-ton crane anchored there. The crane was a big help because there were no roads in and no roads out of that area. Before the crane arrived, we had to walk debris out in buckets. The crane, which could boom out all the way to the middle of the Tobin Plaza debris pile, enabled us to move debris in twenty-yard containers. It extended its long neck into the debris like some gigantic bird feeding, picked up cables attached to the container with a hook attached to the end of its boom, and pulled it out.

On Dunn's right side was WTC Building 5, the L-shaped building that had held our PAPD precinct but was far better known for the Borders bookstore on its corner at Church and Vesey. Sticking out of its north side was a huge piece of steel that had fallen off Building 2.

We greeted each other but instead of shaking hands, Dunn held out the white bucket. "Lieutenant, we have two guns in here. Firemen took them off the two cops."

It was the wrong thing to do. I knew it and so did Dunn. Guns had serial numbers which were as individual as a driver's license. Not knowing which gun was found with which body removed one important way to identify the remains.

"Do we have any numbers off them?" I asked Dunn.

"Lieutenant, nothing has been done with these guns. They haven't left my sight or my possession since I took them from the firefighters. I'm about to run the serial numbers. I was waiting for you. I wanted us both to be here at the same moment when we found out who they were."

"Okay, Commissioner."

Dunn took out one of the guns. It was a Smith & Wesson 9mm semiautomatic with a fifteen-shot clip, silver, with a black handle. It was the kind of gun the PAPD used but not exclusively. We took some water and washed away the mud and the debris. When Dunn turned it over, I noticed a number above the trigger. It had four digits preceded by the letters *PA*. The gun Dunn was holding belonged to one of my police officers.

"That's mine," I told him. "It's one of mine."

"How can you tell it's yours?"

I pointed. "That's our PA identification number. It's a number on the gun besides the manufacturer's serial number. It identifies Port Authority police guns."

He was angry but not with me, with himself. "How come I don't know that? I should know that. *We* should know that." He turned to one of his aides. "Make sure all of our people know that Port Authority guns have the letters *PA* before a four-digit number." To me, he said, "All right, Lieutenant, how do you want to handle this?"

"Let me run the number and find out whose gun it is."

He handed me the gun. I called headquarters on my Nextel. We had gun numbers for all our missing officers. A few minutes later, I was told the computers recognized the gun as belonging to thirty-two-year-old WTC Command officer Uhuru Houston, who had seven years on the job. I did not say his name out loud, and I told the teletype officer who gave it to me not to say anything either. I didn't know if I could get his body out. At that moment, all I had was his gun.

I told Dunn I was going to keep the name to myself for a

while. He didn't object. He showed me the second gun. As soon as he started to wipe the dirt off it, I saw another PA number.

"Commissioner, that's one of mine too."

I called in the number on the second gun. It belonged to thirty-nine-year-old WTC Command Officer Clifton Davis Clifton, who had fourteen years of service. Dunn couldn't help but be disappointed—the NYPD at this point had not made a single recovery of its twenty-three missing police officers—but it didn't stop him from saying, "I'm glad you got two of your guys, Lieutenant. How can we help?"

"You sent an ESU team to the location?"

He nodded. "My guy Owen McCaffrey is in charge. He and the others are making their way back out now."

"I know Owen pretty well," I said. "What does he report?"

"It's going to be a very tough recovery. He says you got bodies pinned almost shoulder to shoulder under unstable steel beams that are less than ten feet from internal fires." Dunn went on to say that if the bodies couldn't be pulled out, they might have to be cut out. He called it a "field amputation," the first time I ever heard the words.

"Lieutenant, you might only be able to recover pieces. It's a tough call. I think you better speak to Owen," he concluded. "One of my men will take you and your guys down there."

"I appreciate that, Commissioner."

"Listen, whatever we have, you have." Dunn shook my hand. "Good luck."

I was feeling my inexperience. Cut a body in half? Could I really order someone to do that? As we made our way through the debris, I tried to think things through. I couldn't. I was relieved that Owen and his team were coming out of the "entrance" into the pile where the path to the bodies started, a hole barely large enough to admit them into what looked like a bowl of spaghetti.

They were all wearing Scott air packs (scubalike air tanks for breathing) and Tyvek suits (protective plastic clothing that encapsulated the entire body and zipped up the front like a big garment bag). McCaffrey was bathed in sweat, drinking water one bottle after another as he pulled off his equipment.

"Dude, it is hot as hell in there," he said.

"Owen, what are my options?"

He frowned. "Not many. Captain Yee just told me we're not going back in."

"What do you mean you're not going back in?"

"Besides the heat, everything is moving. It's unstable. We've been told we're out."

I started to protest, but he cut me off. "Dude, you wanna put the shit on and go in there, you go right ahead. My guys aren't going back in."

I didn't know whether he was angry at me or angry at whoever told him he couldn't go back in even if he wanted to. "Take it easy, Owen. I'm just asking a question. I got no ESU training."

He poured water over his head. "You're a quick learner."

"One of these guys gets hurt, I don't wanna have to tell it was because I was learning. I wanna be a hundred percent sure, which is why I need you to tell me."

He let out a long, tired breath. "Dude, you might be able to get the one body out. I'm not sure. You ain't getting the second one out unless you amputate what you got in there. The only other thing is to try to dig in from the top down."

"But if I leave the bodies there . . ."

He shrugged. "Right. Those bodies are so close to the fire, you stand a good chance of not getting anything. Maybe you could tie them off. Get some ropes inside there and tie them off so that if the steel does move, they don't fall into the fire."

I shook my head. "Rope burns too. Owen, I gotta get them outta there."

"Bro, I'd do the same thing. I'm just explaining. It's bad in there. Maybe try one of those task forces. If anybody can get them out, they can get them out." He hesitated. "They have surgeons with them."

I thanked him and put in a call to the task force headquarters to ask for a team. Then I went over to my guys.

"Listen, here's what's happening," I told them. "We got two cops in there. One might come out whole. The other one doesn't look like he will. I may have to authorize a field amputation to get one or both out. I want to know what you guys think, because right now in my head, I just don't know which way to go yet on this. I want you to think about it. The alternative to a field amputation is tying them off and waiting for the steel to shift, which could just as easily drop them into the fire, or trying to dig in from the top, which has an even greater chance of losing them in the fire. In either case, we won't recover anything. If you were the family, what would you want?"

"That's not an easy answer, Loo," said Callaghan.

"Talk it over," I said.

By this time, Task Force 8 of the San Diego team was arriving and I left to confer with its operations chief, Ken Matsumoto.

We shook hands. "I hear you've got a couple of guys down there. Can we be of any help?" he asked.

"I hope so." I explained the situation.

Matsumoto listed my options, including the one I most wanted to avoid. Matsumoto saw that. "Lieutenant, we have a surgeon with our group. If there does have to be a field amputation, she can do it the best possible way by cutting surgically, rather than using a chain saw."

It was when he said those words, "cutting surgically" or "using a chain saw," that the image really came home to me. Using a chain saw on a body, on a friend, on a human being . . . somebody's loved one . . . It all started to get jammed up in my head.

Matsumoto put a hand on my shoulder. "Let me get my team together, Lieutenant. You think about what you want to do. We'll be back in a little while."

I thanked him and went back to my team. Nunziato spoke for the group.

"Boss, let's go in there. Let's see if we can't get them out."

I nodded. "You gotta do it fast and clean. It's too hot to spend any more time in there than you have to."

"Nobody faster or cleaner, Boss," said Callaghan.

"Okay. Get ready."

All the guys who had walked out of the pile had been drinking water in megadoses, bottle after bottle. I ordered more water moved down to the area, also supplies and lights, and gasoline for the generators. We also brought down K-saws, chain saws, and radio equipment the men would need in the debris.

While the San Diego team and my guys got themselves together, I walked out of Tobin Plaza and sat on a curb at Church Street. A few hundred yards away was the antenna from the top of Building 1 on the ground where it had fallen. It was still pointing to the sky.

Just beyond was the gold globe from the World Trade Center fountains at Tobin Plaza, where people had gathered to eat their lunch. Jazz and pop concerts had been held here, some even put on by the Port Authority itself, with all kinds of gymnasts and acrobats. People came to watch and listen on their lunch breaks. Under PA management, the WTC became a global headquarters for international trade as well as a meeting place known all over the world.

Hanging from a building across Church Street was a blackened sign from a Century 21 store. It was the twenty-first century and I was possibly going to cut a body in half. It was barbaric— cutting people, taking pieces, leaving pieces. I wondered if it was against the deceased's religion, a desecration of the body. Would his family want only half of him?

What would it be like for my cops to go back in that hellhole of fire and dust and watch it done? I was putting the living in harm's way to recover the dead. Was I right to do that?

There was a word for people who did field amputations. With a sort of black humor, they were called "ghouls." *You need someone cut? We'll send a ghoul in to cut him.* Was I a ghoul for doing this? The idea started to consume me. How did I get here? I thought about the home where I grew up. All the mistakes I had made in my life. All the good things I had done. It was like watching a slide show. The different turns, the hills and valleys—

"Lieutenant Keegan? Bill?"

The voice belonged to Father Dave Baratelli, chaplain of the Port Authority Police Department. He was wearing protective clothing and a helmet.

"Hello, Father."

"Are you all right, Bill?"

"I don't know." Saying that was a big deal for me. I never said anything but "I'm fine." I never asked for help.

He sat down next to me and I explained to him what was going on. He listened, then put his hand on the back of my neck and looked straight at me.

"Bill, I think that it's important that you get what you can out. The family will understand that. To return a man's heart and a man's head to their family, that will be the important thing, especially that you returned his heart."

I didn't know whether to laugh or cry.

"Father, I really appreciate that. But that's not the half I'm getting."

The body was facing *into* the debris. The torso was trapped under the steel; only the legs were sticking out. We've seen plenty of people in wheelchairs without legs. It was hard to envision legs without people.

He just looked at me, stunned. I never saw a priest so completely at a loss. Father Baratelli looked anxious to leave.

"My son, whatever decision you make, I know God will be supportive." He was gone ten seconds later.

I was still hoping that I wouldn't have to make it when I got word on my Nextel phone that my team and the task force were ready.

All the thinking in the world wasn't going to get those bodies. I gave the order to go in.

●　●　●

For the second time that night I waited at the makeshift Command Post in Tobin Plaza for word from the teams inside the debris. It seemed like forever, but it was probably not more than forty minutes till Devlin advised me on the Nextel in a voice filled with relief.

"Boss, we have the one body. Intact."

"That's beautiful, Sarge. Just great. Congratulations. Which one is it."

"Boss, it's Uhuru Houston."

"You're certain?"

There was no question. Devlin told me they had found his wallet. He was in a T-shirt and jeans because he had been in Manhattan court that day and responded from there to the World Trade Center when he heard that the building had been struck by planes. Along with his brother officers, he had strapped on a Scott air pack and gone in to save lives.

We decided that rather than trying to carry his body across the debris pile, we would have the big crane boom all the way out to the middle of the debris field. We would put the body on a Stokes basket, and the crane would bring it back. My team and the task force began crawling and pulling the body through the debris pile to reach an open space where the crane could lower its hook down to them.

No one outside the pile knew the names of the officers we went in to recover. There were close relationships among the guys, made even closer by the small size of the PAPD and the magnitude of our loss. One of my sergeants, Ray Bryan, was a very close friend of Uhuru Houston. I knew that Uhuru Houston's wife had asked Ray to bring her husband home.

I walked through the crowd that had begun to gather at the Command Post as word spread through the site that we were bringing a body out. I found Sergeant Bryan.

"Ray, I want to talk to you for a second."

He gave me a thumbs-up. "I heard the good news, Loo. How can I help?"

"Ray, we got the body coming back. I want you to go out on the crane and meet it."

He looked puzzled. "Don't you want me to stick around? We got that other body. Maybe I could help do something with that."

I just looked at him. I started to get emotional because I knew what I was about to do: I was going to send him out to meet one of his closest friends. Ray would be the one to take Uhuru out of this field of hell. He was going to give his friend peace and tell Uhuru's wife and two kids that her husband and their father was coming home.

"Ray, they're bringing back Uhuru. Go bring your friend home."

It hit Ray, and his eyes went flat, then shiny with tears. He started to walk away and then came back and hugged me.

"Thanks, Boss," was all he could manage.

The crane operator brought the basket down and Ray got in. The crane lifted him up and boomed him out to the middle of the debris field. I picked up the binoculars. I could see the team members starting to emerge from the mountain of debris. They put the body bag on a Stokes basket, laid the flag over it, and walked it out to where Ray Bryan and a guy from the San Diego task force waited beside the boom.

Ray pulled the body into the container and got in beside it, and three or four others got in beside Ray. Almost impossibly slowly—the memory of it still amazes everyone who was there— the boom came up without the slightest swing or sway, so slow that at times it looked motionless. The crane operator handled the boom like he carried the most precious cargo in the world. Those of us on the ground tracked the flatbed container across the sky, backlit by the fuzzy glow of the stadium lights. The crane operator lowered the basket so slowly and steadily it seemed to be part of the sky itself.

By this time almost everybody on-site had gathered around. It wasn't morbid curiosity. There might have been problems with the guys who went inside; people could be needed right away if there was a subsequent collapse, or if someone was overcome by heat or smoke. They were all staring up at the boom as it brought the body to us.

We came to attention and saluted. We were a horseshoe curve of PAPD, NYPD, construction workers, FDNY, ambulance drivers, people from the medical examiner's office, all standing at attention as the crane operator put the body down right smack in the middle of the horseshoe.

We took the body out of the container and called for a priest, who said prayers over it. One of our lost heroes had come home. It was a victory, but we still had to go back in for the second body, and the chances of success there were far smaller.

I came to a decision and radioed Devlin. "You're going back in. If I have to cut, I'm gonna cut. Get ready."

I had to get the second body out, however much I could get. If somebody had a problem with that, so be it. I was going to authorize the field amputation because the only thing I couldn't live with was losing the body completely and having nothing for that family. If it wasn't what somebody else would do in my place, there was nothing I could do about that.

The San Diego task force was too exhausted by the recovery of the first body to go in again. I had no trouble with that and was pleased when the South Florida task force from Miami volunteered to take their place.

I asked the team's surgeon if we could speak privately.

"How can I help, Lieutenant?" he asked.

"Do everything you can to get as much of the body as possible. I want to know that we got as much as we could."

"I understand how important that is to you, Lieutenant."

"It's not only about my guy. There are families involved."

"They'll be my first consideration."

"Thank you for understanding, Doc," I said.

"I'll do everything I can."

I rechecked my Nextel link to the task force leader, Chief Dan Thornhill, who would relay any decisions I might have to make. Both teams went into the debris. I waited. It seemed like forever but was probably about an hour before Devlin reported to me that they had reached the body. Then another voice replaced Devlin's.

"Eight-zero, Hennessy here." Eight-zero was radio code designating the rank of lieutenant. "Devlin had to go over to the surgeon. He said to tell you the doc doesn't know whether he will be able to get as much as he thought. He might not get the pelvis. He might only get the legs. He wants you to confirm."

"Tell him the order is confirmed. Let's get what we can."

I waited, and to this day I cannot say how long it was till the Nextel came alive with Devlin's voice. I tried to identify the tone. The only word that came close was "astonished."

"Boss, there might be some good news."

"What?"

"Hold on, Boss."

I could barely stand it, but only a minute or two later Devlin's voice came over the Nextel again.

"Boss, you're not going to believe this, but I think they're gonna get the body out."

"The legs *and* the pelvis?"

"No, I think they're gonna get the whole body."

It was overwhelming. This was a miracle. It was something I had never anticipated. It was as if God had heard my prayers. Maybe Father Dave had been right that God would support me in whatever decision I made! He had. Kevin Devlin's voice came back on the Nextel, filled with excitement.

"Loo, we got him . . . all."

"Are you telling me we got the body intact?"

"Boss, it was incredible. The surgeon began to maneuver the body just above the waist, and the minute he applied pressure to the skin, there was this *whoosh* sound and a lot of gas and fluids came out, and the body just kind of deflated. Listen, we not only got the whole body, we even got a Scott air pack strapped on its back. No one even saw it till the body slid out."

The task force liaison, Chief Virgil Fernandez, came out of the Command Post beaming. "I swear I've never felt like this in my life, Lieutenant."

I shook my head. "I know."

In this place and time we were operating under different rules. Here, this was what success meant. We understood the pain. We took comfort in being able to alleviate it. We felt the suffering. We took solace by ending the suffering of others. The work at Ground Zero was a cause, a righteous cause. There are not many of them anymore. One more person was leaving this place and going home to family, friends, and loved ones, for whatever closure that gave. He was a dead cop, and a dead friend, but those of us at Ground Zero began to glimpse another truth as we worked, one that touched even the hardest cop or operating engineer or firefighter. Could the selfless devotion of so many change part of the evil caused by the worst of us into something reflecting a part of the best of us?

I picked up the binoculars and watched as the body was carried out of the pile, and put into a Stokes basket draped with an American flag. The crane operator boomed all the way out and lowered his basket. The body was secured and Kevin Devlin got in beside it with a couple of the Task Force members, and once again there that same booming up into the smoke and the fuzzy white light, moving so slowly it looked like somebody was holding it. Once again the crane set it down right in the middle of us. We stood at attention and saluted. This time, the crane operator came out of his booth and stood with us, his hand over his heart.

I went over to him, "What you did tonight was incredible. My guys and I appreciate it, and I know his family appreciates it, too."

We shook hands and he said, "Lieutenant, it's been my honor to bring one of yours back. I can't tell you what it means to me to be here."

From all over the site, the emergency services, the uniformed services, civilians, ironworkers, laborers, and crane operators came and formed two lines that stretched from the body through the debris and wound all the way back to the ambulance.

Callahan pointed with his chin. "Boss, how come the Task Force guys are taking off?"

"Nice call, Paddy." I ran and caught them. "Hey, where are you guys going?"

"The job's done," the leader said quietly. "You got your guy. God bless you."

I put my hand on his shoulder. "Chief, you're part of this."

I felt another surge of gratitude when I saw the surgeon standing a little ways away. His Tyvek suit was covered with blood, biological waste, and hazardous materials. He said honestly, "I never imagined it would go the way it did."

"We're in your debt."

"Glad I could help, Lieutenant."

Six of my guys carried the flag-draped basket, followed by the honor guard made up of the South Florida task force, the San Diego task force, clergymen, and members of the FDNY and NYPD. They joined the line of PAPD officers as we walked slowly from Tobin Plaza up to street level, where an ambulance waited to receive the body.

I watched the ambulance leave. So many things had happened. I wished I could sort them all out, but that would have to wait for a time when there *was* time. Instead I chose to take the night's events as a sign that maybe things could work out okay, even here.

Chapter Six

My plan for promoting the PAPD was great except for one thing. It wasn't working. We were increasingly mobilized but the PAPD still wasn't an important factor in the success of the overall recovery mission.

One incident, having nothing to do with either the NYPD or FDNY, especially hurt. The Tishman Company decided to do something nice for all the workers. They unfurled a huge banner at least five or six stories long from the front windows of the Verizon building that faced West Street. "Thanks to Our Workers!" it read, and listed everybody—the NYPD, the FDNY, the ironworkers, the operating engineers, even the Department of Sanitation. The banner was painful to us. We were not on it.

They were very nice when we called. They sincerely apologized for the error. Several days later the PAPD appeared on the banner with everybody else. But I remember the crestfallen faces of our people after working so hard; not to mention how bad they felt that our thirty-seven lost officers were overlooked too. The memory hurts to this day.

I tried to figure out where I had failed. I had set out to work with the leaders of the site; now I could call them freely. I didn't know anything about rescue and recovery when I arrived; I had learned the job. I wasn't quite a bridge over troubled waters for the NYPD and the FDNY, but they seemed to have less animosity for me and the PAPD than they did for each other. What wasn't I seeing?

I was tired and I was mad. For all the politics that had taken place since the Towers fell, there was still only one thing I wanted—to work. I didn't care about hats and badges or who did what to whom, or the mayor or the budget or celebrities or photo ops. I was here to work; the PAPD was here to work; and so far we seemed to be among the few who thought that this wasn't about money or buildings or jobs or old enemies: it was about the families of the fallen.

We might have been new to city politics, but we knew who we were working for. We might be the smallest contender, but so was the racehorse Seabiscuit and he beat them all. The reason he won was his immense heart. We were a small force that never had to compete before. The entire Port Authority Police Department fit into two or three NYPD precincts; the FDNY was over ten times our size—and maybe they both had more of almost everything than we did, but they couldn't have more heart. I knew that because there were times it was all we had.

Standing out in the rubble, I sent a kind of mental declaration of war out over the site.

I tried to be a gentleman, but it didn't work. You're not going to like the alternative, because I came here with only one other thing besides heart—a nasty, thick, stubborn, winner-takes-all Irish temper—and it is up.

They could beat us up, but they couldn't beat us—not if we stayed with the mission and the reason for it: finding the fallen for their families and loved ones.

The most significant change at the site in the early days was the arrival of the big grapplers brought in by the construction companies. They cleared debris faster and more efficiently than bucket brigades. They picked up the steel beams that were the impediment to searching the pile. An ironworker on the ground directed the grappler's operator—the operating engineer—in the machine's glass control booth. The ironworker selected which pieces of steel should be pulled out and which beams were too big to manage. These larger ones would be cut by other ironworkers under his supervision. The ironworker was also responsible for the grappler's safety, keeping it from moving onto anything that couldn't support it. The arrival of the grapplers marked the ascendance of the construction companies. It was a new era—the era of the machines. The grapplers started eating debris so it could be put into trucks and taken away. Construction supervisors made their appearance like western cattle barons intent on keeping the territory under their control.

The cranes couldn't handle the steel—it was too big for their buckets—and they seemed almost gentle compared to the grapplers. The grapplers started to chew their way into the site, ripping out the largest pieces of debris. But the problem was that the site was a burial ground. We found skin and body parts even in remote areas. Unless the grapplers were used with extreme care, in support of the mission, the big jaws closing on the debris could destroy what we were looking for.

However, the advent of the grapplers steered the site in a new direction. The power of the machines decreased the recovery effort's influence. The city announced that volunteers were no longer needed and would no longer be allowed onto the site. In addition, people like the PA auto mechanics and bridge painters who had come down and built whatever we needed—from recovery platforms to an on-site Command Center—and who augmented my recovery units were either sent home or could no longer be used on the pile. The construction companies said the change was in the interest of safety, but the real reason was that searching for bodies slowed down the grapplers.

At sea you can sense a storm coming by a change in the wind. All of a sudden, the wind blowing over the site changed. The recovery mission at Ground Zero was going to be endangered by the construction cleanup. From that moment on, the difficulty of our job was increased tenfold by the frustration of having to fight to keep the recovery a priority.

Interestingly, the arrival of the grapplers also marked the moment the PAPD would emerge as an equal partner in the mission at Ground Zero, rendering service to the victims and their families without hindrance from the other commands and to the full extent of our abilities.

Part of the help we needed came from my ex-partner, PAPD Detective Tommy McHale. Tom had a talent for networking. Give Tommy any group of people, and he would either amaze them with war stories or throw out enough names to find several mutual friends. I partnered with Tom in 1988, and we patrolled Manhattan South during the height of a crime spike in New York.

Both Tom and I enjoyed working and our talents complemented each other. He rushed in; I held back. If we responded to a radio call that there was a robbery in progress in a PATH station, Tommy would jump out of the car and run down the stairs. I would interview people at the entrance. Sometimes Tommy would catch the bad guys at the scene; other times I had enough information to catch them on the street.

Tommy's father had been an ironworker in Jersey City for over forty years, and Tom was following in his footsteps. Most of the time, I would continue the arrest process after our eight-hour shift while Tom reported to the ironworkers union hall on Newark Avenue in Jersey City hoping to be sent out to a construction site.

At this point in PAPD operations at Ground Zero, my major problem was to get my cops working. It was no good their waiting to work and my having no place to assign them. Waiting took its own toll. They had to get to work, get involved, so they weren't sitting around staring at the destruction and thinking about the friends who were dead in it.

I had moved some teams to an area by the South Bridge from the World Trade Center to the World Financial Center. The only way to get there was to walk through the World Financial Center, so there was only a single grappler operating there with an iron-worker directing it. One day, while waiting for me to get free, Tommy noticed the grappler and struck up a conversation with the ironworker directing it.

The ironworker's name was Tim Carroll, a tall, thin guy wearing a bandana under his helmet and dark glasses; he was very tan, as most ironworkers were who were outdoors all day. Tommy asked him what was going on as far as construction workers were concerned, and then brought him over to meet me.

It turned out Tim knew me from when he was working on a project on the Outerbridge Crossing and I had instituted certain procedures to eliminate safety hazards. I had issued violations to one of the supervisors who refused to clear up the situation. Tim and I also shared a sadder bond. His daughter was very ill. She had a disease for which the doctors seemed to have few answers, and he was bringing her to a hospital in Chicago to see their specialists.

"Half the time I'm just working to take my mind off it," he told me.

We talked for a while. At that moment it was the most I could do for him. I just talked to him about being a father. Ironworkers or cops, doctors or dockworkers—you want to protect your kids and you hate feeling helpless. Fathers should never feel helpless when it comes to their little girls. I also told him that when he got back, I would make some calls to the support people and groups that he could talk to, and he was very appreciative.

Tim asked if he could be of any help to me, and he, Tom, and I began to work out the logistics of how we could use the grappler he was working with in this area to get my men working. "Tim, when you go in and pull things out, I'd like to send my men in. It's better for us to look at what you take out right there where you took it from."

Instead of trucks coming in and big loads going out, what was happening was the grapplers were going in and pulling debris out and leaving it in a pile. The trucks couldn't get to it, so when we were done searching it, the grapplers had to pick it up, swing around, and came back out to dump it into the trucks. In reality, there was very little material from the pile of debris actually being taken anywhere.

I wanted an area where we could establish our presence once and for all. Tim suggested we go to the location where the grappler he was directing was working, in the area on Liberty and West. It was perfect. I took over that section of the site and put a number of my teams to work there. I already had some of my men working at locations off Church Street by the plaza and over where Building 1 and Building 2 had come down, but this was the first time we had a location that "belonged" solely to the PAPD.

That location over by Liberty and West enabled us to establish our first forward Command Post. We put up a small tent over on West Street on one side of a concrete wall maybe two feet high. On the other side we put a makeshift area for supplies. We brought down cases of water and food. We brought down saws and buckets and whatever else we were going to need. Now we had a Command Post at the site to respond to and from each area where I had stationed a team of my men.

Soon I had the entire PAPD force working at Ground Zero. The PAPD teams would report to their locations. If there was an FDNY chief in the area, I told them they should walk over and say, "Chief, Port Authority. I'm Sergeant so and so, team leader. I'm going to take six men in here. I'm responsible for them. I'll let you know if we need anything. If you need anything, you let me know."

We controlled our areas without interference or questions. As the days passed, we developed into an undeniable presence. We maintained it. We instituted what is called in police work a "key to key" operation, which meant nobody left the area until they were relieved. If John Ryan had twenty-five guys down there working with him, I would send him twenty-five guys to relieve them. I made sure that the day tour did it the same way, and we kept security on the tent to watch our equipment and supplies. John Ryan didn't leave the site till I relieved him, and I didn't leave until John relieved me.

We were now working at 100 percent capacity. I had the confidence of my own men. As interactions increased, I began to have the confidence of the FDNY chiefs, NYPD lieutenants, and the construction supervisors. It was only a few blocks from the new Command Post at Liberty Street and West Street back to the one at Borough of Manhattan Community College, but it was a long way for us to go and it said that we were here to stay.

For me, the story of Ground Zero would not be complete without one particular incident involving the PATH cops several weeks before the top brass would send Nunziato and Paddy Callaghan and Griffin and Riley and all the rest back to their commands. Knowing them as I did, and do, in a very personal way, I can say it was their finest hour.

On-site security demanded that civilians be identified before being allowed onto the site. To lessen the administrative headache, each command was told to issue IDs to their own civilians. NYPD would issue its own IDs, the FDNY theirs, the PA ours, and so on. On the day we were issuing the IDs, unbeknownst to me, the PATH guys all went to Port Authority Police Department Headquarters in New Jersey, where the staff was handing out the new ID cards. It is important to note that the police ID and the civilian ID were both stamped "Port Authority Police Department," but the civilian ID didn't have "Police Officer" stamped on it. It was a blank slate waiting to be written upon.

We'll never know if the PATH crew asked a friend to look

the other way or if some sleight of hand was involved, but the guys wound up getting ID cards issued to them about ten ranks above what they were. Police Officer Paul Nunziato became Chief of Detectives Paul Nunziato. Police Officer Paddy Callaghan became chief of operations of the Port Authority Police Department.

The PATH guys wanted to get the job done, and they were ballsy enough to become chiefs. If they weren't chiefs, they were detective captains. If they weren't captains, they were inspectors. They also had no problem telling people what to do. Suddenly, the FDNY and the NYPD were dealing with nothing but chiefs of the Port Authority Police Department.

I didn't find out about the ID cards until the day an FDNY deputy chief came over to me as I was walking the site. He was coming back from where the PATH guys were working. I had my lieutenant bar on my lapel, as always, and thought I might be needed.

I said, "Chief, you got a problem with my guys over there?"

"No, no, no," he said. "No, they're fine. I just talked to your chief. He said they are going to be working in that area, they're going to be throwing stuff into that container over there, and the chief told me that everything was okay."

"Really? A Port Authority chief or one of your chiefs?"

"A Port Authority chief. There are a couple of them right over there."

Not only was this confusing—because I knew that there wasn't one single chief from my job down there—but so was the fact that we were working in that spot and it seemed he had no problem with it. A chief stopping to talk to my guys *always* had a problem: "It's an unsafe area, so I'm going to pull you out," or "You gotta move because that building's going to come down," or "Our guy says this floor is going to collapse, so pack it up." It was always something.

"You're sure there's no problem?" I asked, surprised.

"No, no, no, the chief over there has a good handle on every-thing. He's taking care of it. He's going to work that area, they're going to be throwing things in—"

"Where are these chiefs exactly?"

He gave me a how-come-you-don't-know-your-own-chief look. "Right over there, Lieutenant."

He pointed in the direction of the PATH cops. A few of them looked over their shoulders, following me and the fire chief walking toward them.

"Which one is the chief?" I asked him.

"Right there, Lieutenant."

He was pointing to Paul Nunziato, who turned around and threw me a salute.

"How are you, Lieutenant Keegan? It's a fine day, isn't it? Things going well?"

He had a half smile on his face and could barely keep it to-gether. I looked at his ID card as I returned his salute. It said "Chief Paul Nunziato."

"Fine, Chief Nunziato," I said. "And how are you?"

"Good, good," he said expansively. "I was just telling this fire chief here that we're going to be working this area, we're going to be doing this and that, and throwing things in there and—"

"Okay, Chief," I said, "that sounds good to me."

At that point, Paddy Callaghan and some others walked over. I just looked at Callaghan. He was captain of detectives. Some of the guys with him only had five or six years on the job. I look over at one and sure enough, chief of operations.

I said, "Well, Chief, looks like you have everything under con-trol here. I'm going to head back."

"Fine idea. Carry on, Lieutenant."

I walked away with the FDNY chief and just laughed to my-self. These guys were something else. I kind of hoped one day the fire chief would walk into a bar and see Nunziato and the guys and give a big hello to the chief of operations and the captain of detectives he liked so much.

Of course, once the FDNY chief was gone, I went back for the ID cards.

"No problem, Lieutenant," said Gary Griffin, handing his over with a grin. "One of the sergeants was giving out ID cards. We thought they might be advantageous to us here."

"I can see how you would," I said.

I almost let them keep the cards till they were sent back to their command. That would happen a few weeks later when their replacements began to arrive. We still had demands for heightened security. The top brass wanted the PATH cops back with their command to perform their patrol functions again.

The PATH cops made me feel like I was Joe Torre, coach of a team of all-stars. All I ever needed to do was keep everybody out of their way. They were very important to me at the most difficult time, the beginning. They never forgot why we were there. Even their slight larceny was for the cause.

They served with all their hearts.

They made me proud.

Chapter Seven

The wreckage at Ground Zero contained 220 stories of objects from two of the most important office buildings in the world. As the recovery mission searched for the remains of the fallen, it was inevitable the debris would yield up some of the contents of the million square feet of space those buildings contained. In November a grappler reached into the rubble and pulled out one of five laundry carts filled with $14 million that had been delivered to a bank loading platform on 9-11 and buried there when the buildings fell. We found plastic bags of drugs from the evidence locker in the U.S. Customs House, Secret Service shotguns, bags of PATH tokens, safes, and even paper currency shrunk to the size of Monopoly money by the intense heat.

Of greater importance than anyone realized at the time was what PAPD officer Wayne Piccone found one morning in mid-October buried under WTC Building 4 at Ground Zero.

Officer Piccone had almost twenty years on the job, most of it in the PATH command. Wayne worked midnights, and he was always awake and poking around curiously. Five or six years before 9-11, he had been assigned to the PATH post at the World Trade Center Command for a time. There was no better place on earth for a guy like Wayne. At the WTC he had an almost unlimited number of basements, corridors, passageways, and storage areas to wander into.

One night on the job, he was partnered with a WTC Command cop. The course of their patrol took them deep under Building 4. In a labyrinth of corridors they came upon a roll-up metal garage-type door leading to a large chamber with a red steel door set into the far wall. Wayne wanted to know what was there. The WTC cop told him it was a vault belonging to Scotiabank, a Canadian financial institution and WTC tenant. Wayne was lucky the other cop knew even that much. There were no outward signs to indicate it was a bank vault. The red vault door was nothing like the stainless steel marvels in the movies—just a featureless metal door covered with faded red paint. Few people besides the bank officers knew of the vault's existence, let alone its location.

The two cops kidded about what would be kept in such a shabby vault and moved on, but Wayne always remembered it.

Wayne will tell you his head is full of useless information like that. It made him a likable team member in the harsh conditions of Ground Zero, a kind of absentminded professor. That mid-October night he was responding to a medical emergency and suddenly recognized the area as the one he'd been in years before. So when he came across the roll-up metal garage-type door—and beyond it the vault, exactly the same as when he saw it years before, with the same faded red door, all unaffected by the devastation on the surface—Wayne marked it with spray paint, finished his mission, and reported the vault to me as soon as he came back.

The bank vault was news to me. I had never known it was down there. We knew that currency vaults owned by Citibank and Chase had been badly damaged or burned as fires raged after the attack. The Scotiabank vault, built inside the old Hudson-Manhattan terminal under Building 4, appeared undamaged. I filed Wayne's report with the Port Authority, which made proper notification to Scotiabank that their vault area had been located and was accessible. For the time being, it would be guarded by my PAPD cops, on a rotating basis, twenty-four hours a day, using three officers with shotguns in the area of the vault—one in front of

the vault door, one at the stairwell access, one on the loading platform.

I went to see the vault after Wayne found it. There were no
entry marks on it, so I concluded that no one had ever attempted to
break in. I had the guards there within hours of Wayne's finding the
vault, but none of the cops or recovery workers even knew what was
in the vault; no one on the site did except the bank's officers.

What piqued my curiosity was that no bulletin was ever put
out on the vault, no directive to search for it. I looked up Scotiabank on the Web and found it supplied retail, commercial, corporate, investment, and international banking services; had millions
of customers; had branches and offices in fifty countries and em-
ployed forty-eight thousand people. They were no mom-and-pop
candy store, but they had never asked for a special search, and if
Wayne hadn't noticed the vault, it and whatever it contained would
have just stayed there.

I wondered what they would do now that they knew the vault
was accessible. If you went into Building 5, you could walk down a
set of stairs to the first-level basement, then make a right turn
across where the mall concourse was, and when you got to the loading docks, there was a door to a stairwell that led all the way down
to the vault level. There were markings all over the place too.
USAR teams, Port Authority ESU, and FDNY markings saying
that the area had been searched, and searched quite a few times. But
we were searching for bodies and recoveries, not bank vaults.

The vault didn't cross my mind again for almost two weeks; I
was too involved in the recovery operation. But on the morning of
October 29, I was called in at ten o'clock in the morning, nine
hours earlier than my normal start time, and sent to a meeting in
the Park Avenue offices of Kroll Associates. Kroll is an independent
risk consulting company that operates all over the world. Their
"experts in security, protection, engineering, business, and emergency management help clients prevent, prepare for, and respond

to the many threats they face at home and abroad." I hadn't changed from my work clothes and boots, and I can't say I felt totally at ease with antique desks, sculpture, and other art, but realistically, what's a risk consultant except a well-dressed cop?

The conference room I was taken to had a polished oval table that had to be twenty feet long. The seats were occupied by men in such perfectly tailored suits that in the whole group there wasn't a crease above the waist. Other people stood behind them, also in suits, also expensive. The grooming and clothing and the way they sat at the table so comfortably and still all said one word to me—power.

The center of attention was the man, seated at the head of the table, who was running the meeting. His name was Peter Harris. I couldn't put into words why Harris dwarfed the others, I just knew he did. I learned later he was a partner at Kroll who had merged his own security business into the company. Harris was the only one who had no one standing behind him. Everybody was in front of him. He was the king. He was holding court.

Harris was in his late forties, trim, energetic, and well dressed. His hair was black and cut above his collar. Movie stars and great politicians have that kind of hair. I listened to Harris talking in low tones to the man to his right, a plump, brown-haired man with sharp eyes and a well-fed belly swelling the vest of his gray pin-striped suit. I felt that Harris was lobbying the other man for his support, and he seemed to get it. Then he turned to those assembled and called the meeting to order—and I found out what this was all about.

"Gentlemen," Harris addressed the group, "you know by now that in the bowels of the World Trade Center complex is a multi-story vault belonging to Scotiabank that is a repository for silver and gold and other precious metals, and coins, and records. This vault has been uncovered and it is intact. It is no ordinary vault: it contains half a billion dollars in gold and silver, nearly one-tenth of this country's gold reserves. It must be moved to a secure location.

We have been retained by Scotiabank to determine when and how that should done.

"The urgency of the situation is that the construction supervisors at Ground Zero intend to collapse Buildings Four, Five, and Six because they are a danger to the workers. This will bury the vault. We will not be able to get to the gold for months. When it becomes public knowledge that ten percent of the U.S. gold reserve is inaccessible to the COMEX market, it will upset the commodities markets and negatively impact the world economy. I want to move it before that happens.

"We no longer have the luxury of ignoring the problem. It will not go away. Obviously, we are here because the cat is already partway out of the bag. We will face a crisis if we do not act. We have a limited time. I see no other choice but to move the gold without delay."

They discussed whether it should be done, and how best to do it. What were the ramifications if they did it; what were the ramifications if they didn't do it? Would it even be possible? Then the logistics: how do you move that much in so short a period of time? It made me wonder, if Wayne Piccone hadn't found the vault, would they have just left the gold there?

I stood there shedding dust like dandruff and trying not to get it on the suit of the guy next to me. They were talking about half a billion dollars. They were talking about the world economy. It was staggering.

Harris laid it all out. He said he'd had conversations with the mayor, and they had had conversations with the governor. There were four days when they might be able to take out the gold and silver. He outlined a broad structure as to how that would happen. Some of those listening had obviously been pondering the problem for a while. Some began to nod. Others tapped their pens against the table impatiently.

One thing was clear to me. If they were going to mount an operation to move half a billion dollars in gold and silver, they were probably going to do it when population and traffic density was lowest, and security least problematic. That meant starting at night, and that would make it mine.

It was also clear they were going to need a lot of people to run this operation, so I knew what was coming when Harris looked out over the room and asked, "Who is here from the Port Authority Police Department?"

I raised my hand. It felt like I was in school.

"You are . . . ? " asked Harris.

"Lieutenant Bill Keegan. Port Authority night commander."

"Can you provide us with manpower, Lieutenant Keegan?"

There was another PAPD lieutenant there, and he cut in, "Well, it would depend how many people you need. We'll have to go back to our headquarters for that."

I hadn't come this far to ask for permission. I said, so everyone could hear, "We can do that."

Harris looked me over. I looked him over right back.

He nodded. "That's it then."

"That's it," I said.

We had joined the mission.

On the afternoon of October 29 a meeting was held at Pier 92 to make final plans. The Brink's people were there and the people from Kroll and from Scotiabank. Kroll would be running the operation.

A Scotiabank employee named Joe Gilhooley actually ran the vault and was responsible for all the gold and silver in it. Gilhooley was an interesting man. He had begun his career over thirty years before as a junior accountant and joined Scotiabank in 1997 when his previous employer, the British Standard Chartered Bank, ceased to operate in Canada and its metals services were retained by Scotiabank. The vault itself was one of the largest gold depositories in North America, with over ten thousand square feet of floor space.

One of the purposes of the vault was to be the backup for Wall Street, where large amounts of money are moved between brokerage houses and banks. At any one time traders are executing stock transfers worth millions of dollars. These stock transfers are backed up by gold until the actual transfer of funds. Say Merrill Lynch has just bought $80 million worth of a stock from Goldman Sachs. Gilhooley moves that much gold from Merrill Lynch's locker in the vault into Goldman Sachs's locker in the vault. He physically moves it. Later on, I saw all of the lockers with the names of all the brokerage houses and banks. Each of them had ingots of gold in their locker, and Gilhooley was the guy who put five ingots in or took four out, and so on.

Gilhooley didn't think we should move the gold to another location. Why risk it? After all, the vault wall hadn't been breached even by the towers' collapsing on 9-11. Maybe we should just leave it alone. Gilhooley's argument was one of the things that got me more involved, because any discussion about the physical movement of the gold or its security ultimately involved me and the PAPD.

"Lieutenant Keegan, what advice can you give us?" Harris asked.

"I don't know if it's advice exactly. Mr. Gilhooley believes the gold shouldn't be moved. Mr. Harris, you believe it should be moved. That's for you to decide. What I know is that it *can* be moved and how to move it."

I told them what preparations needed to be made and how we'd secure the area. How we would make sure it was just police and Brink's personnel and vault personnel involved. We would spot-weld all of the doors at all of the access points down to that level, so that there would be only one way in and one way out. For security I would provide cops with shotguns and heavy armor vests at all of the access points to that area. We would enter the vault first, with our own air monitors and our own special weapons people, and we would stand by until the power went on and lighting was put into the vault so the removal work could be conducted by the vault staff. No one else would enter the vault until it was cleared by the Port Authority Police Department Emergency Service Units under my command.

Three operational theaters were established. The PAPD was in charge of the operation underground. We mapped out the vault area and decided on a special spot where we knew we could load the Brink's trucks securely. In the middle of the loading platform was a special bay enclosed with cinder-block walls and secured by an entry gate. The gold would come up the elevator to the loading platform and be moved to the special bay, then loaded into the truck parked within the bay walls, and no would see what we were loading or get any clue as to where it was going.

In fact, the gold was going from the vault under Building 4 to a Brink's Security Company secure facility at the Brooklyn Navy Yard. The PAPD would be responsible for the recovery of the silver and gold from the vault to the Brink's trucks. We would provide security for the entry points, tunnel, loading dock, the loaded Brink's trucks, and those waiting to load, and escort the trucks up to the Barclay Street exit, where they would be met by the NYPD.

John Moran and the NYPD would be in charge of the movement of the Brink's trucks from the WTC to the Brooklyn Navy Yard. The NYPD would provide security for the trucks en route, including armored trucks, heavy weapons, and security people inside mapping the route.

The job inside the vault itself belonged to Joe Gilhooley. To move that much gold and silver up to the loading dock, we would have to use an elevator that was inside the vault, but it had no power. Nothing in the WTC did. We needed lights, same problem. The air quality could be a problem too.

Harris and his people at Kroll wasted no time. The plan was approved Monday October 29, and the preliminary measures for the operation began hours later. PAPD teams moved through the vault area and spot-welded all the entrance and exit and stairwell doors, closing all access. We also spot-welded forty vendors doors that opened onto the loading platform. Only the door opposite the vault elevator could be used.

To bring the Brink's trucks down to the underground loading platform we planned to use the J ramp, one of more than a dozen single-lane tunnels to locations underneath the WTC such as parking garages and vendor docks. The Brink's trucks would be screened by PAPD officers in the security booth at the ramp entrance on Barclay Street, one block from the WTC, then drive directly to the Scotiabank loading platform under Building 4.

There was a snag as soon as we tried it. The J ramp itself was undamaged, but there was a steep downhill grade with a sharp left turn at the bottom where so much water and sludge had accumulated that the ramp was impassable. The Brink's trucks couldn't get to the loading platform till the sludge and water were removed. If the J ramp wasn't cleared or was blocked again, we wouldn't be able to get the trucks out, leaving us worse off than before. In the vault, at least the gold was safe. Trucks trapped outside the vault, loaded with gold, would be a security nightmare. Far better to leave the gold where it was.

Somebody not so bright decided we couldn't just have the construction guys get the sludge out from the J ramp. We had to get the Department of Environmental Protection to remove it because it might be contaminated. A DEP team arrived and suited up. They took all the precautions a DEP team takes. There was nothing we could do to speed them up. We could only wait.

After the J ramp, electrical power was our greatest concern. Without it, the mission would have to be scrubbed. But by the morning of October 30, the electrical engineers were still working to drop a cable down to the vault to tap into its circuit box.

Welding the doors and access points had been completed hours earlier, but the DEP operation didn't remove enough sludge for us to get the trucks in and out until late afternoon. I was in command. My number two was Sergeant Frank Giaramita, who would videotape the opening of the vault, the initial entry, and any problems that emerged. I wanted a tape so there wouldn't be any doubt what had been done.

I went down to the loading dock to look things over. The glare of the Daisy lights, and the heat and stale air made the place very uncomfortable. This would be our home for four days. A few minutes into my inspection Peter Harris from Kroll came out on the loading dock. He waved me over and we moved out of the glare into the shadows by the loading bay.

"Bill, I wanted you to know I'm here but this is your show. We hired electricians. They are *your* electricians. They'll be here as long as you need them."

"Is there any flexibility on the time frame, Mr. Harris?"

"Four days is it. After that, the buildings come down."

"We'll make it," I said.

"You seem so certain. May I ask why?"

"Peter, this operation is costing me a lot of manpower. I've had to scramble like hell to make sure I didn't have to reduce our recovery teams by even one man. But at that first meeting you said not moving the gold and silver could hurt the global economy. I don't know the COMEX market from the supermarket, but if that's true, the terrorists would win something if we failed to move it. Well, that isn't going to happen. The economy is not going to be hit again. Nobody's going to lose one more dollar. I want them to know that."

Even in the dim light I could see him smiling.

"One last thing," I said. "OEM figures we'll need over a hundred Brink's trucks. I want to add that we'll be loading them night and day. Can you get that many?"

"Brink's says yes."

I had work clothes and boots on. Incongruously, it struck me that Harris had on some of the finest clothing I had ever seen. He wore tan slacks and a melon-colored cashmere sweater over a white button-down shirt. I could tell that his shoes were worth more than probably all my suits put together. Just beautiful shoes.

Harris stopped for a moment. "Bill, I'm depending on you and John Moran to get this job done. Any problems, I'm here to help. If I'm not here, one of my associates will know how to reach me anytime, day or night."

I should have said something reassuring, or even inspirational. What I did say was "Excuse me, Peter, but do you know what you're doing to those shoes standing in that water?"

He looked down and grinned and swished the water. "Bill, for what they are paying me, I can get new shoes. Believe me."

I just laughed.

We climbed onto the loading dock and went to the vault. The noise of the engineers' drilling was constant. They were still trying to drop the wire to the circuit box. Several of my guys were in tactical clothing, heavily armed, standing guard. A little Italian man in his sixties in a suit and a trench coat was waiting. Harris seemed relieved to see him.

"Bill, I brought this gentleman in case we have trouble tonight. Let me introduce you."

He didn't have to. The man walked right over and stuck out his hand to me with a big smile.

"Hello, Lieutenant Keegan, I'm Mr. Rea. My son, Mike, is one of your cops. He speaks very highly of you."

"Mike Rea? You're his father? I worked with Mike for years. Mr. Rea, it's a pleasure to meet you, sir. What are you doing here?"

He slid a thin black leather case out of his inside jacket pocket. It was a little bigger than a wallet, more the size of a passport case. "If they can't open the door, I will." He hefted the leather case. "I have my tools right here."

I didn't want to insult Mr. Rea, but unless he had a howitzer in that case, I didn't think he could open that vault. What was he going to use, a credit card?

Harris saw that I was dubious. "Bill, Mr. Rea is one of a dying breed. He is a master locksmith and knows every lock ever made. If he says he can open it, I absolutely believe he can."

"Mr. Rea," I joked, "I might not have reported the vault so fast if I had known you existed."

Harris laughed. "You couldn't carry a whole lot out of here on your own. The gold is too heavy."

Right around that time, the electricians notified us that they had been able to drop the wire that would connect the circuit box to the power truck upstairs.

The initial entry team was led by PAPD Emergency Service Unit sergeant John Flynn. The FDNY wanted a representative to take the air readings and check any fire issues in the vault, so I had agreed to take FDNY member John McConnell.

Sergeant Flynn and his team were suited up and looked ready to go. They wore full tactical gear—ballistic helmets, full vests, safety glasses—and carried heavy weapons.

"Sergeant?"

"All set, Boss."

"Sergeant Giaramita?"

He popped in a videocassette and hefted the video camera to his shoulder. "Ready to roll, Loo."

I did a mental roll call. Glenn Vey, the extremely calm and competent director of worldwide security for Scotiabank was there. Peter Harris and Jimmy Spratt, the other Kroll executive, were there. Joe Gilhooley and the other vault officer, a trim man with glasses and a ponytail, were ready at the vault locks.

"We're good to go," I told Peter Harris. "For the record, vault entry at nineteen thirty-five." I keyed in the NYPD radio. "John?"

"Moran here," he responded.

"John, we're going in."

"Roger that."

"I'm anxious to see what half a billion in gold really looks like." I flipped a channel and sent, "All units, tighten it down." I turned to the vault. "Mr. Gilhooley?"

"Yes?"

"Let's try that door."

Personally, I would have liked to see Mr. Rea open the vault with whatever he carried in that little leather wallet, but it wasn't to be. There were two locks on the vault door. Mr. Gilhooley and Matt Ledbetter, assistant to the day manager, each with half of the entry code, engaged the tumblers, spun the locking wheel, and pulled the door open as if no disaster had ever happened in the world above it. However, that ease was not proof conditions inside were okay. The vault door was opened just a crack, and Flynn had air monitors placed against it to check if there was anything dangerous. The air appeared okay, so they opened the door wider and checked again.

While the air testing continued, I made a radio call to my command post to make sure we were maintaining the number of men we needed to continue operations on the pile. From the start, I had made it clear I wouldn't allow this mission to lessen our effort at the recovery operation in any way.

I positioned myself by the vault door like a nightclub doorman. No one was going in unless he had a job to do. A number of issues had to be addressed before any operation concerning the contents of the vault could take place. We had to begin with a complete search of the entire vault. Number one, was anyone inside? Any survivors would be injured and possibly unconscious and need immediate medical attention; there might be deceased. Number two, was the air quality good in every area, not just near the vault door? Number three, was there any breach of the vault walls or floors or ceilings that would indicate someone had attempted to get in or had gotten in? That was why we needed the tactical gear. If somebody had broken in, they might still be there.

I ordered Sergeant Flynn to take his team into the vault. Flynn was about six one, with a marine's "high and tight" haircut—shaved but for a strip down the middle—blue-eyed, Irish, about forty-five. John's ESU unit had been the most heavily hit on 9-11, losing thirteen members. John was in charge of those men and had trained them all. He must have been totally torn up inside. But he never showed it. John was a "squared away" guy—all corners creased, all bases covered. He ran the vault search like the total professional he was.

With Flynn were highly trained ESU guys including Charlie Bardzydlo, Rich Depietro, Mike Kuligowski, and Eddy McQuade. I still could not let the electricians in to connect the circuit box and power the vault lights, so the ESU guys used flashlights and small floodlights. Flynn reported by radio that the air was okay in the vault. He also reported the presence of several inches of water on the vault floor and a musty odor resulting from it. With the vault secured, I sent in PAPD detectives Lou Maciocia and Joe Stitz under the command of Detective Sergeant Richard Brazicki to conduct the investigation to make sure that there had been no breach and no crime. After a thorough search, the detectives declared that everything was intact physically; apparently no crime had been committed.

I sent in the electricians Kroll had hired from a company called Adco. We needed light but had no estimate yet of when we might have it. I still hadn't looked inside the vault. It seemed an important measure of self-discipline and set a good example for the rest of the guys—reminding them we weren't thrill-seeking tourists.

Fifteen minutes later the electricians finished connecting the cable to the circuit box and the vault lights suddenly came on. For me it was a symbolic moment. For the first time since 9-11, lights were on in the World Trade Center. It was only one tiny, isolated spot deep underground beneath a million tons of debris, but for four days and four nights, the WTC was again doing business on a global scale.

That's when I looked into the vault for the first time.

The whole vault was lit up, and as far as I could see it was packed from the floor to the ceiling with stacks of gold ingots gleaming in the light. I was blown away. The vault covered more than ten thousand square feet, with enough room left over in front of the mountain of precious metal to operate the electric pallet jacks used to move the bars.

I could never have imagined anything like this—thousands of gold bars stacked all the way to the fifteen-foot ceiling, six or seven rows deep, all the way across the room. I kept thinking, *This can't all be gold. This is just incredible. How much is here?* I didn't think there could be this much gold anywhere.

Actually, I was right.

I didn't learn until an hour or so later that these were silver bars. The gold was on the floor below. The silver bars, and I still don't know why, had such an actual gold tone that I thought they were gold. I am eternally grateful I kept my mouth shut about how beautiful the gold looked so I was spared being the butt of a joke that could have followed me for a long, long time. *Hey, Keegan, what color are silver bars?*

With the lights on and the vault secure, the mission could proceed. I allowed in Joe Gilhooley, Harris from Kroll, and the two Scotiabank executives, all escorted by Port Authority Police officers. The protocol was that no one would be allowed into the vault unless escorted by a Port Authority Police Officer.

The bank executives began an inventory of the vault contents. Gilhooley examined the electric pallet jacks—low, rubber-wheeled, battery-powered, hydraulic lifts—for moving the gold and silver. They hadn't been used in almost two months, so the electricians had to run cables to them to charge the batteries. When Joe and I talked about other possible problems, every one centered on the elevator. If it worked and he was able to get the pallet jacks powered up, he said we would be okay getting the gold and silver out. If not, they would never leave the vault.

The bank executives had gotten to their books and records and inspected them for water damage. There was none. In a remarkably short time, they conducted a complete inventory of the gold and silver in the vault. It was a relief when they reported, "It's all here." That left only getting the elevator to work standing between half a billion dollars in gold and silver and the trucks that would take it to a new home.

I started coordinating the Brink's trucks. I wanted firm plans for how we were going to stage them before I would bring them down to the loading platform. Where were we going to put the loaded ones while others were waiting to be loaded? What security did we need?

The Brink's guards were going to be armed. I had asked for a list of the drivers, which Brinks had provided. Before we allowed a Brink's truck to come through the J ramp, the driver had to provide his license and Brink's identification card so we could check them against the list and against the picture that Brink's had given us. We had to make sure that somebody hadn't slipped into a Brink's truck or inserted a bogus truck into the line.

I was talking to Joe Gilhooley about the composition of the first load—how much silver, how much gold—when he said, "Have you seen the gold, Lieutenant?"

I pointed to what I still thought was silver. "I already saw this—"

Thankfully, Joe waved away whatever he thought I was about to say. "The silver's fine—nice yellow color they put in it—but you gotta see the gold. It's in the room downstairs. Come down. I'll show you."

When I followed Joe to the lower level, I saw another room even bigger than the one upstairs—and I saw the gold. It was stacked bar upon bar in stall-like lockers carrying the names of the biggest banks and brokerage houses in the world. It was wealth unimaginable. The silver upstairs, even with its golden sheen, couldn't compare to the gold in front of me. This was yellow-brick-road gold—deeper, richer, warmer to the touch.

Joe smiled when we saw a couple of our guys taking pictures holding the gold bars, with their heavy weapons still around them and their helmets on. He took one from a locker, cradled it in his arms, and passed it to me. I almost dropped it because I had had no idea how heavy it was—maybe sixty or seventy pounds.

I had never seen anything like the gold, but I had other things on my mind. This mission was important; I truly felt that. We were protecting the very economy that the terrorists had tried to destroy. But I wanted to get things going smoothly enough to turn it all over to Sergeant Giaramita. I wanted to get back up onto the pile.

Fortunately, the arrival of Sergeant Kevin Murphy two weeks prior had given me just the leader I needed to handle sections of the pile in my absence. He stayed with me to the very end of mission and did exceptional work the entire time. Of special importance to me was the great depth of his knowledge in all facets of ESU work, and his excellence as a leader; he was strong, clear, and always to the point. Maybe because Kevin seemed to know exactly who he was, the guys respected him from the start. I think he typified the very best of his position—the guy you can count on to make the decision you'd make if you were there. Kevin Murphy had my total confidence. He was *my* sergeant, and he holds a special place in my memory.

At 10 p.m., two and a half hours after we opened the vault, the engineers got the elevator working and the last phase of the PAPD's part in the operation began. I ordered the first Brink's trucks to be security-checked and sent down the J ramp to the loading platform. We began to move the first load of all that gold and silver out of the vault.

Joe Gilhooley switched the fully charged electric pallet jacks over to battery power, and his crew began loading them with silver bars. Each bar had a serial number on it; bank workers in the vault documented each bar as it left. At the loading platform, Brink's people documented those same numbers as the bars were put in their trucks. My people in turn documented the Brink's trucks' numbers as they were loaded. We decided to load the first truck with silver to get started. When that was done, we closed and locked the truck's storage doors. The driver and guards got in. The next time they would get out would be at the Brink's facility in the Brooklyn Navy Yard.

It took a while for us to coordinate everything, and no trucks were leaving till we had it all straightened out. The second truck and the third went a little faster, but we were still only loading silver. It was not until the fourth truck that we decided to load gold. NYPD lieutenant John Moran—in command of the convoy from here to Brooklyn—had asked me to make the first convoy small. He didn't want to be guarding a monster line of trucks the first time his security teams would be getting a feel for the route and what the traffic was like. John was happy we weren't ready to roll until late because traffic was lighter at that hour.

The NYPD had a black armored van full of SWAT cops and heavy weapons. John Moran drove it down to the loading zone and overlooked the operation with me. He left a minute or two before we were ready to move the convoy. He would be waiting for the Brink's trucks at the top of the J ramp.

Five hours after we opened the vault, the first Brink's truck loaded with precious metal got the signal to pull out of the loading platform. One by one, the four trucks headed up the J ramp to where the NYPD waited to escort them to Brooklyn. I had worked forty-eight of the previous seventy-two hours, but my fatigue vanished when that first convoy rolled out with horns blasting and echoing off the underground walls.

During the next five hours we loaded five more Brink's trucks, two with gold, and sent them to the Brink's facility in Brooklyn. The next day and night went even more smoothly, till one o'clock in the morning on Halloween night when the elevator stopped working.

The electricians weren't sure how to fix an elevator. The only Kroll associate left could not find his boss, nor did he know how to fix an elevator. I did the only thing I could think of: I picked up the yellow pages and called an elevator company, the only one whose name came to mind—Otis Elevators. Otis said they might be able to fix it but couldn't come over at what was now two in the morning. I wanted to arrest the Otis guy, but the only crime he was guilty of was failing to fix an elevator, assuming elevator repairmen didn't take an oath to serve.

The Kroll associate was feeling the pressure. The electricians were taking a last shot at fixing the elevator, but it didn't look good. The Kroll associate said Kroll would pay whatever it took to get it going, so I got back to Otis and offered them a huge amount of money, but that still didn't get them to come over. Around 5 a.m. I finally got a PA PATH mechanic named Mark Nawosky to come down. Without any special tools he isolated the problem so that when I got an elevator mechanic to show up, the mechanic was was able to fix the elevator in under an hour, replacing what he later told me was a simple burned relay. The elevator was operational again by 6 a.m. and the loading recommenced.

The man who was responsible for so much of the success of the mission was my number two, Sergeant Frank Giaramita. Frank did an amazing job. He was the kind of guy who made you feel cared about as an individual, made you feel that even in this kind of setting he was talking to you personally. He made sure the guys took in enough food and water. He instilled in the workers down there a sense of doing more all the time, doing better with each load. He urged them on. *Let's see how many trucks we can get tonight, right?* His attitude was contagious; everybody was trying to do their best so that each night we moved more trucks than the night before, and the night before that.

Frank got that kind of spirit going on down there, even though the conditions were growing more uncomfortable by the minute. There was no sunlight and no fresh air. We couldn't escape the incessant drone and noxious fumes from the Daisy light generators. The ESU cops in their tactical gear were so hot and sweaty they needed water constantly. Inside the vault it was so hot, and the air so stagnant without ventilation, that by the second night the vault employees were working in T-shirts.

Despite the heat, Joe Gilhooley never slowed his pace. His face was red. Sweat was pouring off him. His hair was plastered to his head. The pressure on him to move all of this treasure was incredible, and downstairs, where all the records were, was the hottest place. He was physically and mentally exhausted but he never lost control or raised his voice.

Along with everything else we did in that four-day period, the PAPD also made eleven partial body recoveries up on the pile, and the next day we made nine more. As I look back now, I see what I did not see then, that there was more than one mountain to conquer at Ground Zero. The first was the two-million-ton mountain of debris and victims' remains from the Towers' collapse. The second was the mountain of gold and silver.

It took four days to conquer that mountain. By the close of the operation, we had filled 133 trucks with gold and silver and gotten them out from the World Trade Center. There were no accidents and no injuries. Every single cargo was delivered without incident. The markets were not disrupted, our economy did not get a second shock, and we had the satisfaction of knowing we had beaten the terrorists who wanted it otherwise.

The members of the PAPD Late Tour: (standing L to R) Officers Mike Kostelnik, Larry Ayers, Ray Devito, Ed MacNamara, Bill Gutch, Brian Verardi, Kevin Murphy, Tony Perzichilli, Shawn Murphy, Derek Yuengling, Bob Essex, Rudy Fernandez, (kneeling L to R) Nick Yum, Joe McCloskey, Bill Keegan, Steve Butler, Rich Steneck, Terry Meaney, Bill Barry.

Talking about ongoing operations with (L to R) PAPD Officers Ray Devito, Ed McNamara, Steve Divino, and Sergeant Bill Gutch in the PAPD Command Post at Ground Zero.

I'm on top of a grappler in the area of 1 World Trade Center directing Operating Engineer Frank Lavery in the search for remains using the "first two looks" to examine debris removed from the pile. The height of the recovery operation saw upwards of twenty of these huge machines at the site. (PHOTO COURTESY OF MARK GRACE.)

NYPD Lieutenant Owen McCaffrey (front left) and I (front right) conduct the carry-out of a civilian casualty with a full honor guard of three police officers and three civilians and with the clergyman who conducted the prayer service. The steel bridge was lined on both sides all the way up to the street with cops, firefighters, and construction workers. Every one came to attention and saluted as the honor guard passed.

The thirty-seven Port Authority Police Department officers killed on 9-11 in the line of duty—the largest loss of police officers in a single incident in U.S. history.

The command supervisors of the Port Authority Police Department WTC Late Tour
Rescue/Recovery Unit at Ground Zero.

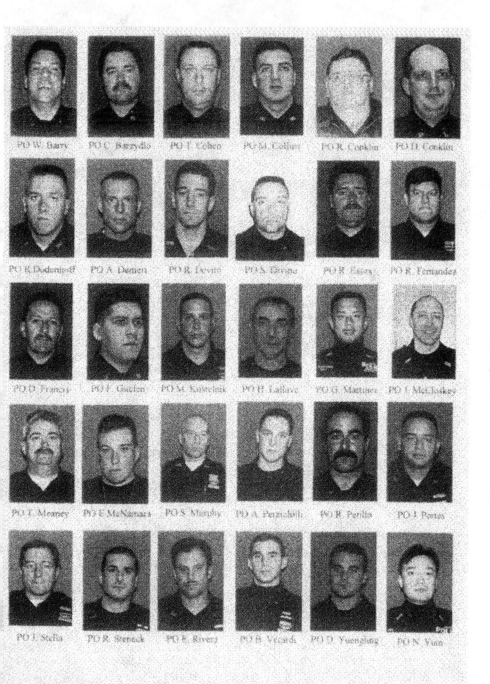

PORT AUTHORITY POLICE
Pride   Service   Distinction

My guys—the members of the Port Authority Police Department WTC Late Tour
Rescue/Recovery Unit at Ground Zero.

(L to R) PAPD Lieutenant John Kassimatis and PAPD Lieutenant John Ryan with me and Inspector Larry Fields at my Port Authority promotion ceremony. (PHOTO COURTESY OF PAT AND LARRY WISNIEWSKI.)

Karen and I were proud Irish parents when our eleven-year-old Kristine was selected Miss Colleen in the 2002 Jersey City St. Patrick's Day parade; here with her sisters Tara (eight) and Rory (one) at a family lunch at Jack Miller's Pub on March 10, 2002. (PHOTO COURTESY OF ALICE, CURT, AND CHRIS MILLER.)

My friend Jean Andrucki in 1999 at a dinner in Jersey City when I was promoted to lieutenant.

The twenty-foot-high section of crossbeam from the top of the North Tower that formed a perfect cross was discovered standing straight up in the debris by recovery worker Frankie Silecchia. (PHOTO COURTESY OF ©FRANK SILECCHIA.)

Somber pallbearers for the coffin of Christopher Amoroso: (L to R) PAPD Officers Ray Devito, Derek Yuengling, Brian Verardi, Dan DePrimo, Don Scala, Donny Conklin, and John Sloan.

The honor guard carry-out of PAPD Officer Christopher Amoroso at Ground Zero the night of November 30, 2001.

My visit to the White House on
December 11, 2001, where
President George Bush signed
photo of PAPD Officer Christopher
Amoroso for the Amoroso family.

This is the photo of PAPD Officer
Christopher Amoroso rescuing a
WTC victim that was signed by
President Bush for the Amoroso
family. Chris continued to go back
into 2 World Trade Center to help
others and was killed when it
collapsed.

For eight brutal months,
Bill Keegan and his crew of
Port Authority Police searched
for 37 of their own, lost in
the World Trade Center attack.
In that crucible of horror...

They Became A Fa

BY GAIL SHEEHY

Parade Magazine cover, July 21, 2002, highlighting Gail Sheehy's article on the PAPD rescue and recovery mission at Ground Zero: "They Became a Family." (CREDIT © *Parade* Magazine.)

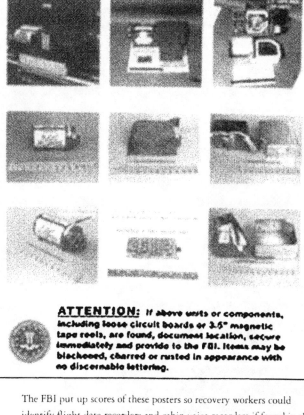

MISSING FLIGHT RECORDERS (BLACK BOXES)

ATTENTION: If above units or components, including loose circuit boards or 3.5" magnetic tape reels, are found, document location, secure immediately and provide to the FBI. Items may be blackened, charred or rusted in appearance with no discernable lettering.

The FBI put up scores of these posters so recovery workers could identify flight data recorders and cabin voice recorders if found in the debris. We thought the object we recovered sufficiently matched the pictures to call in the FBI.

Moving half a billion dollars in gold and silver from a vault underneath the WTC required a four-day caravan of 133 Brink's trucks. (R to L kneeling) PAPD Officers Bill Keegan, Joaquin Portes; Vault Manager Joe Gilhooley; Assistant Vault Manager Matt Ledbetter. The people standing in back are Brink's and Scotiabank employees bracketed by PAPD Officers Derek Yuengling and Shawn Murphy carrying shotguns.

Inside the Scotiabank vault, PAPD Sergeant Frank Giaramita holds a gold bar from one of the "goldlockers" used to secure large financial transactions. At his feet is a "pallet" of gold bars.

In front of seemingly endless rows of silver bars is the first team to enter the Scotiabank vault: (L to R) PAPD ESU Officer Ed McQuade, PAPD Sergeant Frank Giaramita, FDNY Firefighter John McConnell, PAPD ESU Sergeant John Flynn, and PAPD ESU Officer Rich DiPietro.

This is the last piece of steel before ironworkers cut it free from the foundation of what had been WTC Tower 2. Two PAPD officers added "PAPD" and "37"—the number of officers killed in the line of duty on 9-11. Behind it, you can see the slurry walls of the "bathtub," dotted with tiebacks.

The members of Team Romeo in front of PATH subway cars recovered from the World Trade Center PATH station: (L to R) Larry Ayers, Tyrone McCall, Bill Haubert, Joe Audino, Tony Zeoli, Chester Weekes, John Soltes, Gene Smith, and Dom Ricigliano. Not shown: Jim O'Hanlon, Ken Cordo, Rich Radoian, and Pat McLoughlin. (PHOTO COURTESY OF BILL HAUBERT.)

Comrades in arms—an informal moment for me on the floor of Ground Zero awaiting the procession for the Last Piece of Steel with NYPD ESU Lieutenant John Moran and a group of NYPD and PAPD ESU officers.

The Closing Ceremony, May 30, 2002. (First row, L to R) PAPD Lieutenant John Ryan, PAPD Lieutenant Bill Keegan, NYPD ESU Lieutenant John Moran, and PAPD ESU Sergeant Kevin Murphy lead the honor guard accompanying the Last Piece of Steel out of Ground Zero, the members of the NYPD and PAPD night tours following proudly. (CREDIT: SUSAN WATTS/NEW YORK *DAILY NEWS*.)

Chapter Eight

Sometime before 9 a.m. on September 11, 2001, a Brink's armored car driven by sixty-eight-year-old Joseph Trombino of Clifton, New Jersey, rolled down the J ramp at the World Trade Center and pulled into the underground receiving platform of Tower 1. The armored car was carrying millions of dollars in cash and negotiable bonds and a fortune in diamonds. The WTC was the first stop of the day, and Trombino remained with the truck while his fellow guards off-loaded $14 million in cash to waiting Scotiabank bank guards, who put the money into laundry-type canvas carts for transport to a vault.

Joseph Trombino was no stranger to terrorist attacks. Twenty years earlier, on October 20, 1981, he and fellow Brink's guard Peter Paige were ambushed by members of the Weather Underground and the Black Panthers as they left the Nanuet National Bank with bags containing almost a million dollars. Paige was killed. Trombino's arm was nearly cut off. More than a decade later, he narrowly missed being killed in the 1993 attack on the World Trade Center because he left after completing a delivery only minutes before the blast.

On 9-11, the Brink's truck's schedule called for the delivery of the diamonds next. It never took place. Trombino was in the armored car when the hijacked jetliner hit Tower 1 eighty stories overhead. Rather than leaving, he parked near the loading platform in an underground exit tunnel. Whether the thirty-year veteran

employee was heroically waiting for his fellow guards to return—
unaware they had already been evacuated from Tower 1—or stead-
fastly protecting his cargo, the choice cost him his life. When the
building collapsed, Trombino and the armored car were crushed by
falling debris and buried under tons of rubble.

On the night of December 21, 2001, I was called at the Command Post by Sergeant Kevin Murphy and told that a recovery
team had exposed a portion of the roof of a Brink's armored car
buried under the debris by Tower 1. I immediately notified the
Brink's Company. They said they would send someone as soon as
possible.

"Is there anything of value inside that requires us to search inside it?" I asked the Brink's supervisor.

The answer was yes. "The armored car contains over a million
dollars—two hundred fifty thousand in diamonds and seven hundred fifty thousand in negotiable bonds, and the driver is still missing," he told me.

I radioed Kevin Murphy to post officers and establish a crime
scene. This would allow us to keep the area cordoned off and secure—and if I was now responsible for a million dollars in bonds
and diamonds, that was the way I wanted it. I also called in the
PAPD detectives to augment the investigation.

I hastened over to the location. The Brink's supervisor, when
he arrived, turned out to be the same man who had worked with me
when we moved the gold and silver from the Scotiabank vault to
the Navy Yard in Brooklyn. The recovery team was using hand
tools to remove dirt and rocks to get into the front cab. The first
priority was always people. We had to know if the driver was still
inside. When we had the top of the cab exposed, we called in a
grappler to remove the heavier debris and clear an entry path.

When we were able to clear away enough rubble to see inside,
we found the cab was empty. Possibly the driver had sought refuge
under the truck or had left it altogether to get past the debris
blocking his way and get up to the street. The other possibility was

that he had gone into the back of the armored car for safety or had been in there when the building collapsed.

I also wanted to get into the back of the armored car to remove the valuables. I didn't have a lot of manpower to spare, and removing them would render the site worthless and posting officers unnecessary.

At first we thought we could enter the back of the armored car from the front cab, but we found that Brink's trucks are built without access that way. That meant we had to cut our way in. Using a circular-bladed K-saw, we began to cut away enough of the roof to "peel" it back with the "jaws of life." That tool wedged two prongs between two pieces of metal and the hydraulics separated them like jaws opening.

When the hole in the roof was large enough to permit entry, I chose Officer Tony Demeri, who was both thin and muscular, to go in. We lowered him down with flashlights and shined more lights inside. Tony did a complete inspection of the truck. There was nothing there.

No bonds. No diamonds. Nothing.

Oddly enough, on February 8, 2002, laundry carts filled with the $14 million that the Brink's truck had delivered on 9-11 were found in the rubble near where the loading dock had been. It was a moment reminiscent of the movies. A grappler accidentally uncovered one cart as it pulled out debris. The cart ripped open, sending money flying all over the site.

The money was collected and secured. A noncriminal investigation report—NCIR #05-02—was prepared and filed.

Neither the bonds nor the diamonds have ever been recovered.

Looking back, I realize that immediately after 9-11 we were working on adrenaline, and by mid-November we were on empty. The dust was a constant irritant. We breathed it into our lungs; we wore it on our clothes; we scratched it off our skin. We crawled through debris containing twenty-six miles of mercury lighting, 43,600 windows, 6 million square feet of masonry walls, and 200,000 lighting fixtures. We worked our way through openings in piles of concrete and steel while 1,500-degree fires burned above and below us. Steel loses half its strength at 1,018 degrees Fahrenheit. It melts at around 2,500 degrees. Inside the pile, we'd watch steel beams bend and buckle too close for comfort while we harvested body parts from the debris.

The departure of my PATH cops who were sent back to their prior command by the top brass, and the city's decision to downsize to twenty-five each the number of NYPD, PAPD, and FDNY workers allowed on site, radically changed the composition of the force under my command. Now I had three distinct PAPD groups with very different ways—ESU-trained officers from the JFK Airport command, ESU cops from the LaGuardia Airport command, and a group of high-spirited young cops from the Special Operations Division (SOD) who came to be known as the Out-to-Lunch Bunch.

The SOD was a pool of cops the PA commands could bring in to beef up a high-security event—like a president's landing at JFK or a strike at Port Newark—or to temporarily replace cops who got sick or were on vacation or in court. SOD cops were the new kids on the block; most had less than two years on the job. The idea was to let them see it all and do it all before assignment to a specific command.

The SOD cops posed very different leadership challenges than the JFK or LaGuardia groups. The upside was they were all young and strong and enthusiastic, with boundless energy. They were all talented and some had real leadership ability. I didn't need a carrot to encourage them or a stick to prod them. I needed reins to hold them back for their own safety. Excluding the one veteran in the group, the oldest was twenty-seven; the youngest was twenty-two. Inexperience was their downside. They had a growing sense of police work but had not yet gained the wisdom of older cops. The problem was they were working in the same hell as everybody else, and it had no mercy.

The Out-to-Lunch Bunch had no leader, no one everybody looked up to. My first insight about them was they functioned best as a group. They didn't need a leader; they needed each other. In action, they were a surprisingly well-coordinated team communicating through a network only they were on. The closest thing they had to a leader was kind of an older brother—Officer Bill Barry, a forty-year-old veteran who ended up changed by them as much as they were changed by him.

Bill Barry had a big grin and an easy manner. He was only five nine but thick and solid as a tree trunk. Bill never loved police work and had few attachments to it. He never worked overtime. He never went to PAPD functions. SOD seemed to suit him, as if filling other cops' spots was good enough; he had no real desire to have his own. I thought Bill could become a good cop, if he had the right motivation to step up to the plate. He found it on 9-11.

The destruction of the World Trade Center broke Bill's heart. The recovery mission at Ground Zero restored it. Suddenly the lethargy was gone. His commitment and purpose were so strong that not only did he step up to the plate, he hit a home run while he was there. Bill and the young guys knew each other from SOD but not very well. Now Bill took a real interest in them. His influence was calming. He got a kick out of how funny they could be. The young guys liked his veteran status. Soon they were coming to Bill if they had a problem. He was the one who named the group the Out-to-Lunch Bunch.

I assigned the SOD cops to security details at the site. Within days, they got to know the site and the people in and around it and rotated into the recovery operation.

It was axiomatic of Ground Zero that nothing could prepare you for it. But that axiom hadn't anticipated anything like the Out-to-Lunch Bunch. They thought they were invulnerable. Nothing could hurt them. No one could convince them that the dangers at

the site were real, unless one got injured—something I was determined to prevent. Yet I'd still find them working their way into a
hole without full regard for the potential danger.

"Hey, guys, where are you going?"

"C'mon, there's a big void here, Loo."

Void was short for an opening or a tunnel into the debris.
"Guys, who did you tell you were going into it?"

"Nobody, but we were just going to go in a little way . . ."

My face got harder. "Guys, you gotta let a supervisor know
where you're gonna be and where you're going. If something goes
wrong, we gotta know who's in there."

When you're caught, you don't make lame excuses. I called
Kevin Murphy over. "Murph, I just saw these guys going inside
this void. I didn't know about it. Did you know about it?"

Murph understood when I said it that I hadn't known about
it, and I felt that was wrong. Murph's expression told the guys that
Murph was even more pissed that *he* hadn't known about it.

Murphy frowned. "You knuckleheads were in the void and
you didn't tell anybody?"

They respected Murphy. He had a way of saying things that
took the sting out but still got the message across. Same with
Sergeant Bill Gutch, just recently promoted from police officer,
who commanded so much respect that he could supervise guys who
just a short while ago he had worked with shoulder to shoulder.
ESU protocol was clear: everyone got notified when you went into
an area that was unexplored or unstable.

Operationally, I was out there looking over everything.
Murph was responsible for the men—but he was responsible to me.
I wanted the men to adhere to the protocols; it was his job to see
that they did. He saw to it the protocols were adhered to—and my
wishes were the protocols. I didn't have to explain all that or dress
anyone down. Murph would do whatever was necessary after I left.

Instead, I said, "Guys, have I ever told you no when you asked
me to do something?"

They all looked down and away.

"No, Loo. You never did."

"All I want is for a supervisor to be aware."

"Okay, Loo."

I respected them. They knew I wasn't going to carry on. But their safety was my responsibility and there was no compromise on that. No apologies were necessary, but sometime later that night I knew that one of them would find me and say, "Loo, I swear we were going to call you if we found something, and let Murph know, but we figured why call you until we found something to tell you about?"

Right now, however, they didn't know how hot Murph was going to get over this and they didn't want to provoke him, so they looked especially attentive as he spoke.

"C'mon, guys, I told you we gotta have enough people and equipment on the scene in case there's trouble. If something goes wrong, you got to have one guy outside for each guy inside in case you need to pull him out. One guy can't pull two."

I left as Murph reiterated the importance of radio contact and how to advance as a team: one pair goes in and looks around, calls in a second pair to go past them and explore further, that pair calls for a third pair to advance past them, and so on. The team penetrates slowly and carefully, leapfrogging secure positions like climbers securing pitons before moving up the cliff face.

I took a last look at the guys as Murph continued his instructions. Each was interesting in his own right. Officer Brian Verardi was a former EMS worker and NYPD cop. Brian was six one, thin as a rail, with a long face, dark hair, and bushy eyebrows that were the only part of him not in constant motion. He was a chain-smoker who had so much nervous energy, his foot never stopped tapping even when he was standing.

Officer Derek Yuengling was the youngest of the bunch, but two factors had given him the aura of a much older man: he came from a cop family—his father was a member of the Suffolk County

SWAT team—and despite his age he had the unmistakable confidence that came from working the Bus Terminal Command and Times Square.

Officer Richard Steneck probably had a decade in age on Derek, but he was a classmate because he came late to the job. He was a sincere man who appreciated others and was a good friend to us all. Rich, always sensitive to the emotions around him, was able to defuse worry or tension with humor. Imagine how valuable that was at Ground Zero.

Officer Shawn Murphy had fierce blue eyes, a shaved head, and an intense stare. Shawn was perhaps the strongest man at the site. He would carry a generator in one hand, and in the other was enough fuel to keep it running for the next twenty-four hours. Officer Mike Kostelnik was so good-looking and in such great shape that the DA's office was afraid arrested prostitutes would claim entrapment. I had posted the officers at a critical spot in the vault's inner security perimeter—and had absolute faith it would remain secure.

Officer Ray Devito was a twenty-three-year-old St. John's University graduate. Ray had talent but his impatience with authority led to some minor trouble with other bosses. I was quick to make it right because I appreciated Ray and did not want to break up the group. One thing about the Out-to-Lunch Bunch—their camaraderie and support for each other was key in their identifying with the mission.

By contrast, my guys from the JFK and LaGuardia Commands were all highly trained ESU cops. There was Officer Terry Meaney from the JFK Command—as Irish as they come, with a quiet voice and a wicked wit. From the LaGuardia Command, Officer Tony Demeri had the rough good looks that women love. He could always be found at a tanning salon, the gym, or at a club. He also made everybody laugh.

Officer Joe McCloskey was an expert biker and camper who used those talents in his ESU work. Joe always talked about how after this was over he was just going to get on his bike and head west. Officer Richard Petillo was a big six-two, 215-pounder with a full mustache. He was a dedicated parent with three sons and he loved to coach lacrosse. Officer Danny Francis was a lightly built guy in his mid-forties. Danny was sharp, a PBA delegate very involved with the union but always an independent thinker.

They were all solid pros, highly trained, steady as rocks, including the independent Officer Steve Divino, a crusty former Rikers Island corrections officer. When the worst offenders had to be dragged out of their cells, the authorities sent for Steve. On the pile, he was a bloodhound who found body parts with eerie skill.

Youth and maturity; experience and energy—the combined qualities of these guys who were with me to the end provided just the right balance to create an amazing team. Rather than taking away from each other, they added to each other, strengths canceling out weaknesses, and judgment tempering enthusiasm. The JFK and LaGuardia cops willingly gave their knowledge to the Out-to-Lunch Bunch. The Out-to-Lunch Bunch gave them back the kind of youthful exuberance that older men find refreshing and that fosters a healthy competition: for example, the young cops called forty-five-year-old Danny Francis "Grandpa."

Rather than dwell on differences, they embraced what they had in common—their dedication to the mission. It was because the mission required them to be a team that they became one. When the mission required me to let them act independently, they exhibited sound judgment. When there were conflicts, they put the mission first and applied the prime rule of family: no matter what, you're family.

Simply, what we were doing was too important to let anything get in the way, and with that understanding we entered November at Ground Zero a force to be reckoned with, our esprit second to none. The NYPD and the FDNY acknowledged the PAPD and our participation. Ironically, as soon as we made peace, the relationship between the PAPD and the NYPD and FDNY changed yet again. A new danger emerged and threatened all the uniformed services. Instead of a tenuous truce, we became allies.

It came as no surprise that a recovery operation as thorough as ours slowed the removal of debris. The construction companies were used to working where there was no one except their own workers; now they had to work with thousands of people in their way. The conflict intensified. We told them they had to recover remains. The city told them their priority was a fast cleanup. More and more grapplers were brought in to move debris without regard for the recovery operation or the narrow confines we worked in. On-site traffic almost doubled over roads that were only barely carved out.

We got help from the operating engineers who ran the grapplers. They worked with us. They said that they bonded with the PAPD because we gave a 200 percent effort and because we respected them from the beginning. The operating engineers and the PAPD swapped Nextel phone numbers so we could talk directly. They kept us informed about when and where they were being moved.

When a construction supervisor reported he was sending a grappler off-site because of a fuel problem, we'd more often than not get a call from the operating engineer saying, "They told me they're moving my rig 'cause of a fuel problem, but somebody better follow me because there's no fucking fuel problem here."

The gap between where the grapplers were supposed to be and where they were began growing. The resulting confusion put my guys in harm's way, something I couldn't allow. It was only a matter of time till someone got hurt.

The conflict came to a head when one of the Out-to-Lunch Bunch was almost killed. Officer Brian Verardi was on the pile watching a 750 grappler remove debris when a construction manager decided to move the grappler without approval or warning. Brian was close in and didn't see the operating engineer unexpectedly swing his grappler around 180 degrees, sending the counterbalance on the rear of the machine heading straight at him. If the driver of the dump truck waiting to receive the grappler's load hadn't spotted the danger and blasted his big air horn, Brian would have been killed. Luckily, he spun around when he heard the horn, saw the counterbalance coming straight at him, and ducked just in time. It missed him by inches.

The construction supervisor instantly fired off a report to the DDC citing the incident as proof that it was too dangerous for my men to work so close to the grapplers. The construction supervisor had the city and the DDC behind him. I could even be removed from command over this kind of incident. But they made a mistake. They had almost killed one of my cops—and nothing that could possibly happen to me mattered a damn compared to my making sure it would never happen again.

I called Brian Verardi. "Brian, make your way over here. We got a meeting to go to."

"Is this about what happened today?"

There was a funny sound. It took me a second. "Brian, stop tapping and get the hell over here."

"Right, Boss."

The meetings of the highest officials on the site were held in the American Express building in a huge conference room. Wearing a DDC orange coat, the commissioner of the New York City Department of Design and Construction, Ken Holden, was at the podium in the front of the room. The site's construction superintendent and two city officials were seated behind him. The guys in the audience were supervisors and executives from every construction company on site, and each subcontractor had two or three representatives. There were also a lot of guys from the NYPD, mostly lieutenants and sergeants, and firemen of all ranks up to a two-star chief. I recognized some of the remaining people as engineers, including Port Authority engineers. The rest were from OEM.

By the time I arrived, most everybody was seated. The PAPD guys there included the day commander John Ryan and a PAPD lieutenant named Mark Winslow. They usually attended these meetings. I rarely did.

I went and sat with them. Mark Winslow grabbed me on the shoulder. "Listen, Billy, we gotta run this just right. I know you and Brian are hot about what happened last night, but these meetings are a little different. They're run by the head honchos. There's a representative from the mayor's office here. It's gotta be handled tactfully. So try to calm down."

"Mark, I'm gonna get this straightened out here and now."

"Look, Bill, what I'll do is at some point I'll get up and introduce you and say what the problem is. Depending on how it goes, if they need the particulars of what happened, then maybe you can get up and talk. But I don't think Brian should talk, okay?"

I knew what Mark was talking about. People on this level could make one phone call to the right ear and I'd be out of here once and for all. But if this problem didn't stop, the next guy might not be as lucky as Brian—and that wasn't going to happen on my watch.

I was four rows from the back and every seat was filled. There were people standing against the walls. Holden called the meeting to order. He told us we had to have safer working conditions and there would be more regulation at the site because we'd had a serious problem during the night tour.

"Last night something happened that I swore would never happen here. We almost had a cop killed. One of the police officers almost got his head taken off because these guys don't know how to work around the equipment at a construction site. It's not gonna happen again."

I stood up. "Excuse me, that's me and my guys you're talking about, and that's not what happened."

If he had started talking about the slurry wall or when we were going to get into Building 6, I would have stayed in my seat. But it was the DDC and the construction companies that had created the conditions that almost killed Brian, and not only were they completely indifferent to his almost getting killed, but they were going to use it against us.

Holden waved me down. "I'll give you a chance to talk later. Sit down."

"There's no way I'm sitting for this. You're gonna hear me out right now."

Every head in the whole place was turning to me. All the firemen turned around to watch. So did the cops and the engineers.

"This isn't about 'some' cop getting hurt," I said. "This is *my* cop. He's sitting right here. And you're right he almost died last night, but it wasn't his fault."

"That's not the way I heard it," said Holden. "But you'll get your chance. Just not now."

"Right now," I insisted. "I'll tell you what happened last night and I'll tell you what's been going on down here."

Holden tried to talk, but it was obvious he wasn't gonna shut me up. Nobody in the room was gonna shut me up.

I jabbed a finger at him. "The guy who was walking the grappler from one area to another was supposed to warn everybody before he brought it over. He didn't do that. He moved the grappler right into where we were already working. That's why my guy almost got hit."

"My point exactly," Holden said. "You're in the way and you're going to get hurt. You don't know how to work in a construction site."

"You know what? Maybe what you just said would make sense if this *was* a construction site, but let me tell you, it is *not* a construction site, and I'm sick and tired of you or anybody else calling it that. We are not here to help you remove steel. This is a *recovery* site, and *you* are here to help *us* find bodies."

Some of the firemen nodded. So did the NYPD cops. I had touched a nerve. I went on.

"There are hundreds of cops and firemen buried here and

thousands of civilians. We're gonna find all of them. This site is about recovering bodies, and we are in charge of it. So, if this is *not* a recovery site, you better tell me now, because I think everybody ought to know about it. Let's make it public, so we can let the families of the victims know what our new jobs are."

Adverse public reaction was what they feared most. Holden shot an uncomfortable glance at the guys sitting behind him. They looked uncomfortable too. Suddenly his tone got conciliatory.

"What I meant was that it is a construction site in part, not *only* a construction site."

"One more thing," I said. "You got too many goddamned grapplers down here and they're working too goddamned fast. That's why my guy almost got hurt. And it's only a matter of time before someone else is, if you keep this up."

The audience was audibly angry. The firemen were starting to shake their heads, and I heard grunts of assent from the cops.

"There *aren't* too many grapplers, and they're not working too fast," Holden said. "Although it's possible I didn't get a full report or one operator made a mistake."

The cops in the audience had heard too many stories not to recognize one that was falling apart.

"This isn't gonna continue," I said to Holden, and there was a grunt of agreement from almost everyone in that room. "I will shut down this site if I have to, for as long as I have to, and if you think a single truck is gonna move in or out of Manhattan, you better think again. My Commercial Vehicle Inspection team and my boys from the Holland Tunnel will inspect every truck that tries to roll in or out, and if there is so much as a single equipment violation, I'm impounding them."

"We're all here to work together safely." Holden was sweating. "We're very proud of the safety record established by the protocols we've instituted."

This time I didn't have to look around to know what every cop and fireman in the place was thinking. Cops and firemen are used to working around danger. We have a sense of what to do and how to keep ourselves unharmed. That's what was keeping this site so safe. Having Holden claim that it was some protocol keeping us safe was insulting.

One of the firemen called out, "It seems to *me* like there are more grapplers down there."

"I'm telling you right now there are no additional grapplers," Holden insisted. "We'll go out and we'll count them."

An NYPD cop yelled, "And if there's not more grapplers here, there are sure more in certain areas."

Holden gave up. I had the firemen and the cops talking to each other, and they were both mad. Brian gave me a thumbs-up.

As a result of that meeting all site commanders started getting daily maps of where each grappler would be working. We could easily count the number of rigs and know how many workers we needed to assign to cover them.

The construction workers were on board from minute one. They understood the safety issues and had also seen the PAPD giving what they called "200 percent." When the last building skins were being cut, ironworkers like Willy Quinlin were able to tell me not only which direction they were going to fall but how many revolutions they were going to make before they hit. It was like he was flipping baseball cards when we were kids and calling heads or tails. Jack Daly was a supervisor from Koch Construction who ceremoniously handed me the air horn to warn everybody that the last piece of building skin from the North Tower was coming down.

The operating engineers were instrumental to the success of our mission. It's ironic that the machines we thought would destroy the human remains and ruin the site for recovery became our most useful tools, and the men who operated them became our closest friends. They were so totally committed to the mission they wouldn't leave their rig no matter how harsh the conditions. It was with Martin Reilly and his sidekick Frank Lavery that we celebrated the birth of Frank's twins. Crane operators Bill and Dan

Nescas, Maurice Wardlaw, and Todd Gleason faced the hardships of recovery and reminded us that nobody was used to these conditions and they were going to finish the job no matter what it cost them. Our friends Tommy Barberi, Iggy Panepinto, Mark Dolan, Bill Huser, "Colorado Mike" Del Prete, and Bo (everyone knew him only as "Bo on the 1200" [grappler]) could massage a piece of steel out of tangled pile smoother than a pickpocket could lift a wallet. We had grappler operators who could lift a quarter off the sidewalk with a two-ton claw and drop it in your hand.

No matter what problems we may have had from time to time with the construction companies, we never had any problems at all with the construction workers. They understood our mission and gave us their unqualified support. They were the very best, and I am proud to this day I still call so many of them my friends.

Chapter Nine

I will never forget Veterans Day at Ground Zero for two reasons: the site was going to be shut down for the first time, to give us our first day off since 9-11, and it was the second time I met Rocco Scarpi.

The first time I met Rocco had been in late September. He was a supervisor for Turner Construction, the company doing the demolition of Building 7. While that was ongoing, the PAPD received orders from the Port Authority superintendent in charge of risk management, Nelson Chanfrell, to search for victims in and around the World Trade Center's air conditioning plant. The "chiller plant," as we called it, was a fortified structure that had withstood the '93 blast. Chanfrell remembered that the people who took shelter there had survived. In fact, the plant's fortifications and its location in the basement of Tower 1 enabled parts of it to survive the total collapse on 9-11 as well.

Additionally, Chanfrell wanted to ascertain the condition of the tanks of Freon gas used by the plant. Freon could explode under certain conditions. Because it was heavier than air, there was a danger of its sinking to the bottom of the debris, where there was both water and air, which could cause it to be ignited by a welder's torch or the fires still burning there.

Although the likelihood that anyone was still alive in the plant was small, I put a crew together and went over to where the Turner company was working. I had an idea I could reach the chiller plant by going through Building 6 and ultimately into Building 1.

I introduced myself to the supervisor running the operation where Building 7 had collapsed into Vesey Street.

"We think there could be people alive in the chiller plant," I told him. "I want to try getting to it through Six."

"If that's what you want, Lieutenant," he said, "the guy you definitely want with you is Rocco."

The way he said it, it was like one name was all the guy needed. He was just Rocco. I was impressed even before I saw him. Maybe five minutes after the Vesey Street supervisor made the call, Rocco came striding around the corner. He had a big black mustache and a white construction helmet turned backwards so the peak was on the back of his neck. Around his neck he wore a cowboy's red kerchief that could be pulled up over his mouth like an outlaw's mask, and a surgical mask dangled beside it. He was of average height but solid as a concrete slab, dressed in jeans and work boots and a flannel shirt over a thermal undershirt, with sleeves rolled to his forearms.

Rocco looked me over as we shook hands. "What do you guys need?"

"To get to the chiller plant. You know how?"

"I can get you as close as I can. Did you know the garage down in Building 6 is partially open?"

"I didn't."

"It will take us partway, but after that we'll have to crawl through. It's tight. Only one at a time, and it's a long crawl. All these guys you got, it'll take too long. Why not just you and me?"

"Fine. Let's do it."

I notified the Command Post that I was going in to inspect Building 6 with a Turner Construction supervisor and to send backup units. I wanted them to stay streetside in case I needed help. I followed Rocco through a partially collapsed doorway into the debris pile. We walked down a few steps and had to squeeze in between the dirt, mud, and steel beams to get into an alcove where the only way to move forward was to get down on the ground and crawl. With the pile overhead and sunlight flashing beyond, crawling under that maze of broken concrete and steel beams was like being in one of those tunnels where the fish swim overhead. The difference was that this passage was unsafe and unstable, and if it collapsed, we were finished.

"Not to worry," Rocco assured me. "I went through here three times already."

We crawled about thirty feet to where we could stand up again. It was dark, and we were using the heavy-duty flashlights with the square bottoms and round lenses. We went through a tunnel to an area where there was just a concrete floor, and steel beams still standing with nothing around them but rubble, and the flashlights making it all hazy as the dust rose. We got into the parking level. All the cars were covered with dust, and there was sediment and water on the floor.

"This is as close as I've gotten to Building 1 going through Basement 6. If the chiller plant is intact, we gotta look for a way to get there from here."

We looked for over an hour, but there was no going any farther. We even went back out and got Officer Stella and tried to make our way into the chiller plant from topside. We had no luck that way either.

Outside, Rocco stood with a bottle of water in each hand, drinking one and pouring the other over his head.

"Sorry, Lieutenant. I thought I could help,"

"Hey, I appreciate what you did. You gonna be here long?"

"Nah. Turner is doing number 7 and I'm only here for that. We'll be the first ones gone."

I liked this guy. He had a pair. There was only one reason he'd been through that debris before today—trying to help find victims. He didn't have a thing to do with the recovery operation, but he was looking to help us make recoveries just the same. In addition,

Rocco was a stand-up guy like most of the construction workers on the pile, but he took it up one more level. Nobody else seemed as all business, or as unaffected by the devastation, as Rocco. He was almost cheery in his work. *Solid,* I thought again. I didn't think anything could disturb his equanimity.

I was wrong, but I didn't find that out till I met Rocco a second time. That came on November 11, Veterans Day. Rumor had it that the site was going to be closed for the first time since 9-11, and although everybody had to report in, most workers would be leaving early. I got to the site at 5 p.m. and went to the construction meeting, where it became official. The site would be closed at 7 p.m. and all the machines shut down. We would mount security, do some preventive maintenance, and maintain some ESU presence for an emergency or a fire, but it was a skeleton crew that night.

Around 9 p.m. I took a walk around. It was intensely quiet. Most of the lights were out. There was steam coming off the pile but no noise from the grapplers, no noise from the Daisy lights, and no noise from people. It suddenly wasn't an active recovery site. It was a ghost town all bombed out and empty. For the first time, it looked like a cemetery to me, as quiet as a graveyard.

I walked into St. Paul's Chapel. They kept the door open 24/7. The church was small but beautiful, slightly damaged by the collapse but all cleaned up. There were volunteers at tables with throat lozenges, eyewash, lip balm, gloves, hats, and T-shirts. Past the third or fourth table there was a piano being played by a nun. The music was classical, subdued and melodic, very soothing. The nun smiled when I walked past. All I could think to do was say, "Thank you."

The church always touched me. Right across the street from the devastation, it was an oasis, spared on 9-11 as it had been spared a hundred years before in the huge downtown fire. As I walked down the aisle, I saw rescue workers lying in the pews or kneeling or holding their heads in their hands.

I prayed.

They had hot food in back, and I ate some before I walked back out to Church Street. It was around 11 p.m. A PAPD pickup truck driven by one of my cops was going by. He stopped when he saw me.

"Where you going, Boss?"

"Just walking."

He leaned over and pushed open the passenger-side door. "C'mon, driving's better."

I got in and we talked a bit as he drove down Church Street— quiet and empty except for two guys walking, one wearing a construction helmet and the other a baseball cap. They weren't so steady, kind of leaning on each other like they'd maybe had a few drinks. If they had, the drinks were the first since 9-11.

We pulled up and I yelled, "Everybody okay?"

The guy in the baseball cap turned around, and I saw it was Peter Vincent. I hadn't seen him except in passing since the day with Fellini and Ryan when we worked out the truck routes. Peter came to the truck's open window. The guy wearing the construction helmet had on a black ski jacket with a diamond pattern sewn in. He just stayed where he was, swaying a little, his back to us.

"Hey, Peter, how ya doing?" I didn't like the way he looked; a lot of stress showed.

He shrugged. "Okay. We went out for cocktails." He looked back at the site and shook his head. "It's really unbelievable."

"Yeah. I never saw it like this before. Eerie-like."

"I know."

"Who's with you?" I asked, gesturing to the other guy.

"That's Rocco."

"Wait a minute. Rocco from Turner?"

He looked surprised. "You know him?"

"Sure, I know Rocco. I worked with him over by Seven. Really good guy." I yelled over, "Hey, Rocco," and got out of the truck.

Rocco had his back to the site. I came up alongside him and put a hand on his shoulder. He didn't turn or acknowledge me.

"Hey, Rocco, what's the matter with—?"

I stopped in midsentence. There were tears streaming down his face.

Peter came up behind me. "It's been a tough night, Bill."

I was unprepared for it when Rocco suddenly turned and threw his arms around me in a huge bear hug.

I managed, "Bro, what's up? You okay?"

Rocco started to sob, big heaving sobs that racked his whole body and made his words come out harsh and pained.

"Look what they did," he cried. "It's unfuckingbelievable. Look what they did to my town. Those motherfuckers . . ."

"Easy, Rocco. C'mon." Peter said to him, trying to pry his arms apart.

Rocco pushed me aside and stood there weaving. He was angry now and his rage was growing, stoked by the grief within him. "No, look what they fucking did. They killed them. They killed the workers and the women going to work. They killed them. They *killed* them."

Staring at the empty space where the towers used to be, he threw both his arms straight up like they could replace the buildings and shouted defiantly at the top of his lungs. "Come on, motherfuckers. Come on when *I'm* here. Fuck with us now, mother-fuckers. C'mon out here *now* . . ."

Peter grabbed Rocco, who was still yelling. "Easy," he soothed. "Calm down."

I had never seen anger like that, the fury of it and the way his whole soul poured out. I had seen a lot, but never that. I had never felt so pulled into someone's grief before, till I was in the middle of it too and was trapped and could not get out.

Peter saw and put a hand on my shoulder. "Bill, I'll take care of him. He'll be okay. I'll take care of him."

His words snapped me out of it. Rocco was still yelling at the night, but his anger let me be.

"You sure you'll be okay?" I asked Peter.

"Sure. Thanks."

He took Rocco's arm and the shouting stopped. They walked away from me, but about ten feet away Rocco suddenly turned and came back. The furies hadn't left him. His face twisted up as he gave me another big hug.

"I'm outta here, man," he said, releasing me, and went back to Peter, and they walked off.

I never saw him again.

Ground Zero came back to life the following day, and I went back out on the pile barely ten minutes after I signed in. The night was cold but not frigid. The fires were beginning to burn out by that point and the sky was clear. We were operating in an area around Building 1. I was watching the grapplers remove debris, making sure we got our first two looks and talking to the guys and making sure they were okay, when FDNY battalion chief Steve Rossweiller called me on the radio. Rossweiller was the FDNY day commander at Ground Zero. He and I always met at the 5:30 p.m. meeting. We always talked afterward, and if we had any concerns, we'd share them. We tried to outthink the construction companies and what they told us: what were they trying to do now, where did we think they were heading, why were they doing what they were doing?

Of all the FDNY guys, I think Steve was the least parochial with us, a good man.

"Where are you, Bill?" Rossweiller asked.

"Over by Building 1."

"Good. Stay there. I'm coming over."

"No problem, Steve," I radioed back.

Not long after, two green Gators—4x4 all-terrain vehicles the size of a golf cart but much sturdier—rolled up on their small tires with the thick tread. Rossweiller got out, but his passenger stayed.

Steve was in bunker gear and wore the elite FDNY Rescue Squad's helmet, which was closer to a construction helmet than to the huge FDNY helmet with the insignia on the front.

Steve came over and put his hand out. "How you doing, Bill?"

"Good, Steve. You?"

"All good. Listen, Bill, that guy sitting in my Gator is a retired fireman. His name is Lee Ielpi. He lost his son here on nine-eleven, a fireman too."

"I'm sorry."

"He's been here every day, and I was wondering if it would be all right—I mean, I know you're working this section tonight—but Lee, well, he has this feeling his son's remains are here. It's a real strong gut feeling."

Lee was in his late forties or early fifties, medium height, in good shape, with a chiseled chin, clear dark eyes, and short graying hair. He was wearing his FDNY bunker coat and helmet, and he had a tool like a hoe or rake with him. He sat unmoving, his two hands wrapped around it. He was too proud to look at us while Steve was asking me for something on his behalf.

"How can we help?"

"I know the area's PAPD, but do you think it would be okay if he dug with you guys?"

I turned to Steve, surprised. "You seriously think you have to ask me?"

"Wouldn't be right to barge in, Bill. This is your ground."

"Not mine, Steve. His. Absolutely he can dig with us. All night tonight and any other time he wants to. Can I meet him?"

Steve smiled. "Sure, c'mon."

We walked to the Gator and Steve introduced me. "Lee, this is Lieutenant Keegan. He runs the night tour for the Port Authority."

We looked at each other eye to eye as we shook hands.

"Lee," I said. "You can dig anywhere you want with my guys, any time you want."

"Thank you, Lieutenant."

Lee got out of the Gator and went onto the pile with his hoe. He dug with us till dawn. He didn't find his son that night, but he never stopped searching for him.

On December 11, 2001, I was ordered to Washington, D.C., as one of several officers sent to meet President Bush. I had a special reason for going to Washington, one that had less to do with the president than with Christopher Amoroso, age twenty-nine, assigned to the Tactical Response Unit, a PAPD officer for only two years when he died at the World Trade Center on 9-11. Chris was a bear of a man, and his friends say his heart was bear-sized too. On 9-11 he responded from the PA Bus Terminal to the WTC. He led numerous people out of the burning Towers, going back in again and again. He was killed during a rescue, still on the job when the building collapsed.

Chris's body was uncovered while we were digging east of Building 1. We had only begun removing debris when one of the younger guys said with grim certainty, "Loo, it's Chris Amoroso."

"How can you be sure?" I asked.

"The tattoo on his arm—Coffin."

"But others could have that—"

"No, it's not what you think. Coffin was his mother's maiden name."

The cops who found him were roughly the same age as Chris. Some of the guys had been Chris's classmates or were close friends of Chris and his wife, Jamie, and their newborn baby girl, Sophia. Their emotions almost overwhelmed them, but they held themselves together. It was best for me to leave them be, to let them do the job they had done so many times before.

We called for a body bag, an American flag, a member of the clergy, a GPS fix on the body to record the exact location of recovery, and more lights to improve visibility as we took him out of the ground. After calling for a PAPD ESU truck to transport the body to the temporary morgue, I notified my officers there that a PAPD officer was being brought in. Then I radioed NYPD lieutenant John Moran and asked his help setting up the honor guard. It had become established practice with the NYPD and PAPD that whichever service's cop was found, the other service set up the ceremony so it could be ready when the recovery was completed.

Emotions threatened to overwhelm many of the guys as Chris Amoroso was placed in a body bag and laid gently on a Stokes basket. He was covered with an American flag. As always, the stars were placed over the heart. Six of his classmates and best friends curled their hands around the grips of the Stokes basket and lifted it up. They paused as the honor guard was called to attention and to present arms by Police Officer Rudy Fernandez.

While everyone was at attention, I saw Ray Devito reach his left hand into the pocket of his dark Carhartt work coat and remove what looked to me like a piece of paper and place it on the stars of the flag covering the body. I moved closer and saw that it was actually a photograph of Chris taken from an ID badge maybe, or a yearbook, but bigger, at least five by seven. It struck me that Ray had been carrying the picture for two and a half months since 9-11 waiting to put it on his friend's body. I had the feeling he never doubted that he would.

There was no reaction from the others at all. I thought, *But they had to all see it.* Ray glanced at it only once, as they began to move, and then stared straight ahead as the friends of Christopher Amoroso walked him out between the twin columns of the honor guard.

To this day, I cannot say for certain if the others carrying the Stokes basket knew Ray had the photograph or would place it on the body, and I have never asked them. That is how certain I am that they were all part of the moment together.

•   •   •

Chris had acted bravely on 9-11, but the true extent of his courage wasn't revealed till once more Ground Zero saw events come to pass that seemed to reflect something greater than ourselves. When Chris's body was returned to his family, they held a memorial service at their church. Before the service began, I was standing outside talking with the other PAPD officers when a man in a sport jacket walked up to me.

"Excuse me, Lieutenant."

"Yes."

He handed me a press card. "Forgive me for intruding. The *Daily News* sent me to take pictures of this service. Can you please tell me if that would be permitted, and if so, what would be the most respectful way to do it?"

Put that way, the request was one I agreed to carry to Chris's family.

"Thanks. Just one more thing. I was one of the first photographers at the World Trade Center on 9-11. I took a lot of pictures. There's one of a Port Authority police officer I'd like to show you, if it won't upset you, to see if you recognize the guy."

The eight-by-ten black-and-white photo he slid out of a manila envelope was of Chris Amoroso, wearing black gloves and his short-sleeved PAPD uniform shirt, injured from what must have been several previous rescues, carrying a woman in his arms out of the burning Towers. The picture also told us that saving the woman in his arms was not his last rescue. His body had been found wearing a Scott air pack that was not present in the picture— meaning he had gone back into the building despite the fire's being so bad that he needed a breathing apparatus to keep going.

When I was asked by my chief to go to Washington, the reason I said okay was to get that picture of Chris signed by President Bush for Chris's family. My guys made four copies—one each for his wife, daughter, mother, and father—and put them in a red manila envelope.

At the White House I realized I was not going to meet the president personally. He was going to give a televised address, and the cops and firemen invited were going to be the audience. Later, after it was over, we were all ushered out into a corridor and led toward a large room for refreshment. I had been in the front of the audience, so I was at the end of the line as we left. Being a police officer, I know how well the president is protected, so I was surprised because the odds on winning the lottery are better than the odds I would see him standing in an open doorway not ten yards away with his back to me because the Secret Service agents flanking him had forgotten to close the door behind him.

I have gotten reactions before but few like when I walked up to President Bush and touched his elbow. Agents from everywhere started to move in before I was halfway through, "Excuse me, Mr. President," but President Bush saw my uniform and the pictures I had taken from the red envelope, and he stopped the Secret Service agents from coming between us.

"What are those?" he asked me.

"Mr. President, I brought some pictures of Port Authority police officer Chris Amoroso taken the morning of September eleventh as he saved lives prior to the collapse."

He took one of the photographs. "It looks to me like he was already injured."

"It does."

"Tell me what I can do for him."

"Would you sign these for his family, sir?"

The president didn't hesitate. He signed all four, asking for each person's name. "Please, be sure you tell his family how much America appreciates what he did for us. We'll never forget that sacrifice."

President Bush took one long, last look at the photograph of Officer Christopher Amoroso, and from the way his jaw tightened and his eyes filled, I knew that he understood and appreciated what he had just seen—a rare but unmistakable portrait of courage.

•   •   •

As the weeks rolled toward Christmas at Ground Zero, for the first time since I was married I didn't feel part of the holiday. My mind and body were not home; they were at the site. No matter how hard I tried to find joy in the season, the spirit eluded me. The feeling would come soon, I told myself. Maybe tomorrow, or the next day. While I waited, I made plans to take a day off to help Karen but I kept postponing it.

I took the family to buy the tree. I didn't even put it in the stand; I just left it leaning against a wall. While Nigel Joseph put up the outside lights, Tommy Coohill helped Karen get the tree up—something I had always done. I wasn't home to decorate it. I didn't go with Karen to buy presents or help her with preparations for Christmas dinner for the family—over thirty people. Dinner was always at our house because we had the youngest kids.

I wasn't home for Christmas Eve because I held a gathering at the Command Post and invited the families of the victims to come to the site. The invitation was made through headquarters and the unit of detectives and retired volunteers who were liaisons to the families. They were all under the direction of Captain Christopher Trucillo, who is now the four-star chief of the Port Authority Police Department. There would be food, and the Port Authority chaplains Father Dave Baratelli and Rabbi Ichi Heschel would lead us in prayer. It was a rare appearance by Rabbi Heschel without Rabbi Jack Meyer. Together, they always brought great food and a pat on the back for everyone that made us all feel good.

I put newly arrived Sergeant Rich Ruiz in charge of getting the new Command Post ready. We had just moved into two double-wide trailers with their own generators for heat and lighting. We were now located on the southwest corner of Warren Street and West Street and the FDNY Command Post was on the southeast corner. The NYPD had taken over the AFSCME District Council 37 union hall, one block away on Chambers Street.

The PAPD Command trailers had four nine by twelve-foot offices—one for the tour commander, one for the sergeant handling administrative matters, one for us to change in, and one for secure storage. The trailers sat in a fenced-in compound containing storage sheds, a tent where ESU units stored equipment and changed clothing, and a parking area for the vehicles we used. The mobile Command Post was moved from North Moore Street and parked outside the compound to serve as our communications center.

We put a memorial in the open area between the offices, with objects from the site and pictures of the officers we lost. They were mostly personal photos, some taken at a party or a department function or the St. Patrick's Day parade. A big green chalkboard on the wall had the names of the deceased in alphabetical order. When John Moran accepted our invitation to the NYPD to join us on Christmas Eve, we hung the NYPD memorial poster there too.

The Port Authority provided food. Nothing fancy—sandwiches, soft drinks, and coffee. With both PAPD and NYPD night tour officers and the families, we had fifty or sixty people inside the trailer, so it was packed. Across the room I saw Janice and Ken Tietjen Sr., whose son Ken had been a PATH Command officer. He liked the more traditional police work in the subways and out on the streets. He was an excellent cop with a sterling reputation, always looking to learn more about the job.

Janice Tietjen was a small blond woman wearing a coat and scarf against the chill, with soft eyes that told you at once of her great capacity for compassion and understanding. Ken Sr. was in his late fifties, with light-colored hair and eyes, wearing a brown overcoat over a sweater and shirt with dark slacks. We had grown up in the same section of Jersey City and, the first time we met, had talked affectionately about the German bakeries and ethnic food stores we remembered.

I kissed Janice on the cheek and shook Ken's hand. "I am so happy you came tonight. Thank you."

"Bill, we wouldn't want to be anywhere else tonight," Janice said, taking my hand. For a few seconds she looked at all the people around us. "You can't believe what this does for us, to be able to be so close to where Kenny was, on Christmas Eve."

I was struck by the air of serenity about both Janice and Ken Sr. despite their loss. I had seen a lot of people grappling with sorrow and pain before and after 9-11. I had never seen the kind of peacefulness I saw in them.

"I appreciate that, Janice."

She patted my hand. "Remember, you have to stay strong."

After what had happened to them, how was she still able to care about me? How could you care about anything?

"I just want you to know how sorry I am for your loss," I said. "He was a good cop and a great guy."

Janice patted my hand again as if to console me, not the other way around. "Bill, Kenny is in a better place. It's okay. Our faith tells us that he's okay. It allows us to live with this."

I had heard a lot of people say that. Up till that moment, there wasn't one whom I believed, but I believed her.

Ken put his arm around his wife's shoulders. "Bill, I'd give anything in this world to have my son here with us. Having faith that he's in a better place helps make some sense of all this. It gives us a reason. That's what he'd want."

Looking back, I think what moved me most was that the body of their son had not yet been recovered.

I talked to the Tietjens a little while longer, then a Port Authority chaplain led us in prayer. I remember the moment. It was one of the few we were all together—PAPD cops, NYPD cops, and the families, all jammed together shoulder to shoulder as Christmas Eve became Christmas Day.

I couldn't leave the site for home till the end of the tour. I drove fast so I could get there before the kids woke up and came downstairs for their presents under the tree. I told myself driving home that it was going to be great when Karen and the kids opened their presents; it would make up for things. That Christmas I had shopped in stores I never shopped in before. I hit three stores in one hour before going to work. I went to Neiman Marcus in the Short Hills Mall and spent money like a drunken sailor. I bought jewelry for my wife. I even bought jewelry for Kristine, who had absolutely no use for it, being eleven at the time.

I just bought things to fill the void. I bought things so I could drive home thinking about how great it would be when they opened their presents. I thought about how great a holiday Christmas was going to be. I had the day off. I was going to enjoy myself. At the time, I didn't know all the excess was to make up for my not being there. In a very real way, I was buying time.

I couldn't get it off my mind that so many of my friends' families were waking up to their saddest Christmas. Daddy or Mommy wasn't going to be there this morning or any morning. They couldn't open presents the way my family opened them. The thought was always reoccurring, and I was frustrated that I couldn't let go of it.

I slept for a few hours and woke up to the house bustling, filled with people. I was still tired. I couldn't believe it was Christmas. The problem was I started out feeling happy and excited when I watched the kids and Karen open their presents on Christmas morning, but all of a sudden I felt exactly the reverse. To enjoy Christmas morning without remorse felt selfish. I had a kind of survivor's guilt: what right did I have to sit here and watch Karen happily open up a diamond necklace, and Kristine diamond studs, and everyone loving the expensive clothing from Saks Fifth Avenue or the latest DVD players, and put all the suffering conveniently out of my mind?

The excess continued. I usually have a bottle of wine—one bottle—on Christmas day, but I started drinking eggnog laced with vodka and crème de cacao. More excess: we usually serve pinwheel steaks for dinner; this year we had filet mignon and lobsters.

One glass of eggnog felt good, two better, and another and another until I was drunk. I was okay with everybody and laughed with them, but I wound up on the downstairs couch and fell asleep to the Christmas music on the stereo.

I woke just before midnight, alone. I began to be afraid of my own thoughts. I wondered if I would ever be able to feel good again, ever stop thinking about what 9-11 had done to us all. As I struggled with the pain, it was memories of the Tietjens and Chris Amoroso and Lee Ielpi that came to me and helped me find peace that Christmas Day.

Who knows why certain things occur to you, but suddenly I was able to resolve the conflicts that had been going on inside me for weeks and had peaked this day. I remembered when the President of the United States had looked at a picture of Chris Amoroso and recognized a man's true courage—and it helped me to remember mine. I remembered Lee Ielpi, a man who never lost hope, who had found the remains of his son buried in the rubble by Building 1, the area where he had never stopped looking for him—and it renewed my hope. I remembered that the Tietjens had never stopped believing there was good in people and a reason for what happened to them, and despite their pain they were certain that God was here and could pull us back from despair—and that renewed my faith.

I was blessed to meet people like the Tietjens, and Lee Ielpi, and Chris Amoroso, and also Rocco, whose wounds I pray have healed. They all belong to a special group I have never forgotten, for most often it was in their presence I learned something of lasting value or witnessed the best examples of faith, hope, and courage: these ideals being not only what I found at the end of my journey, but what I found was the reason for it.

Chapter Ten

Winter coated Ground Zero with ice and made it glisten, then froze the muddy ground into hard swirls whose edges were so sharp we could feel them through our boots. The city vanished beyond the hazy snowfall and within a perimeter of Daisy lights we looked very much like an army camp in the Arctic.

We wore wool ski masks under our helmets to protect our faces from the icy wind slicing off the rivers to our east and west. Along with the heavy thermal wear and thick coats and gloves and scarves wrapped around our necks, winter made us a group of featureless forms roaming the pile, hunting remains in the snow, blowing plumes of breath like car exhaust.

When the temperature rose above freezing, the snow and ice melted and turned the ground into six inches of slippery mud. The mud replaced the dust that had previously coated us, with one addition: when the temperature dropped back below freezing, the mud coating our arms and legs hardened like plaster casts.

We were physically and mentally exhausted. We had worked from six o'clock at night till six o'clock in the morning—seven days a week at first, six days a week thereafter—for almost six months. During that time we had also attended the memorial services for all our fallen comrades. The city officials and Port Authority officers who were automatically dispatched to the services as representatives must not have known we went to all of them. They delivered the exact same eulogies at every one, till we could quote them by heart.

We could not all go to every service. Priority was given to men who were closest to the deceased—a classmate, a best friend, someone who had worked closely with the deceased. I let the guys attending a service go home two hours early by giving them "last blow"—their last relief—at the end of the shift. It was no gift. Instead of going home and sleeping until late afternoon, they were up at 8 a.m. to put on their class A uniform and drive to a nine o'clock service at the church or synagogue. Services, which were held any day of the week except Sunday, ended at 11 a.m. If they got home by noon, they could maybe sleep until four before heading back to work.

There were thirty-seven PAPD memorial services. None was ever taken lightly. There were pipes and drums, and an honor guard. My guys and their peers saluted the remains, the partial remains, or sometimes only a picture. They listened to the bagpipes and the eulogies and the people crying. Afterward they talked for a while before going home to get some sleep; then it was back to the site to find human remains.

To this day I am still fiercely proud of my guys and the job they did. Not only did they stay together, they stayed focused on the mission. Even under such duress and trauma, my guys performed at levels that set new standards in their professional and personal lives. They raised the bar on the goodness and resilience of the human spirit. Not only for a few days but time after time.

By the time they fought traffic, took the patrol car back to the Command Post, got into their private cars and drove home, their kids were up and getting ready for school. *Hey Dad, how's it going?* Depending on the kids' ages, maybe they recognized the difficulty of what he was doing. Later, even if he wanted to talk to his wife, he was too exhausted to do anything other than hit the sack.

He woke up six hours later. It was three o'clock in the afternoon. The kids were coming home. He kisses them, has a little something to eat. Then he has to get showered and changed and drive to work by 6 p.m. They did that for nine months—seven days a week for the first two months, six days a week for the rest. That's what was heroic—their resilience. These guys were sent in to run a marathon every day for nine months. It never stopped, and neither did they. They never quit or failed to do what I asked of them, every single time I asked.

The recovery operation at Ground Zero was an extraordinarily harsh mission. As stress-related problems increased over the winter, the Federal Emergency Management Agency responded to the trauma of the attack on the World Trade Center by bringing in a horde of critical incident stress management (CISM) teams. According to FEMA, "A Critical Incident Stress Management Team is responsible for the prevention and mitigation of disabling stress among emergency responders in accordance with the standards of the International Critical Incident Stress Foundation (ICISF). Team composition, management, membership, and governance vary, but can include psychologists, psychiatrists, social workers, and licensed professional counselors."

Help is a dangerous weapon in the wrong hands. The CISM people had their hearts in the right place trying to deal with the mental and emotional health of the workers, but they were just too eager and intrusive. They seemed to assume that if someone refused help, he was screwed up for not knowing he needed it. On the other hand, accepting help meant he was definitely screwed up. Somehow the *help* got lost. It was not unusual for someone to wander off alone for a while to rest, think, or pull himself back together. Private communion was important to an individual's balance. The CISM workers didn't understand that. Being alone meant you had a problem.

If they saw anyone alone, they descended like locusts with questions: "Are you okay?" "What's the matter?" "Would you like to talk?" "Want to discuss it?" Their demand to be allowed to help was just more pressure.

At one point there were so many CISM people trying to find someone to cure, we couldn't take a leak without running into one. Their approach was almost always the same.

"You okay? Something the matter?" asked the CISM member.

"Nothing's the matter," the worker insisted.

"But you're over here alone, and you have your head down."

That made the worker angry. "Listen, Jack. Take a look at what we've been doing these last six hours. I *feel* like being alone and putting my head down."

"Being alone can be a sign of—"

"Of being alone. Go away, please?"

We dubbed them the "therapy dogs." FEMA brought in hundreds, and I wound up having to get between them and the men because of their intrusiveness. Finally I called the team leader aside.

"Listen, you can't treat these guys like there's a sign on their back that says Emergency and if you don't help them at once they're going to fall apart. They're tougher than that. You can't corral them. It makes them afraid you think they're really fucked up. If they need help, and some do, you're scaring them off. Don't go into their tents. Don't seek them out. If they come to you, fine. You can talk to them if they come to you. Other than that, I want them left alone."

I could tell that didn't sit very well with him, but I was in charge and that was the way it had to be. I was about to learn that therapy dogs have a term for someone in charge who gives an order they don't like or don't agree with. It's called "denial," and unbeknownst to me, they decided I was in it.

A few days after my meeting with the CISM leader, I went down to the supply tent over by Liberty Street that supported our guys working in that area. I was talking to the supply officer about what we needed when one of the CISM workers, a woman, walked in. She looked around, asked what the supplies were for, and I told her. She was pleasant and I responded the same way.

"You're Lieutenant Keegan, right?"

"I am."

"This job isn't easy, is it?"

"No, ma'am. Important things usually aren't."

"How long have you been here, Lieutenant?"

"Since September eleventh. Why?"

"Well, if it's so difficult here, and I agree that it is, maybe you could use some time away from here, you know? I mean, with the stress and all."

This was nonsense I didn't need. "I'll leave when we pull the last body out of here—and not one minute before."

Maybe I could have been more diplomatic, but I thought it was a tactless question. She left without saying anything, so I was surprised when she returned with four other people.

"Wow, you found four friends? And there are only three coffees."

"Lieutenant, can we talk to you for a minute?" one of the women asked.

"Sure, what can I do for you?"

The woman whom I had spoken to before said, "Maybe we could step outside the supply area. Lieutenant, we're a CISM team."

Alarm bells rang in my head. I could have kicked myself. The therapy dogs were hot on my trail. The first one had set the trap and I had walked right into it by giving her a response that was a little too flip and maybe a shade arrogant.

"Lieutenant Keegan," one of the two men asked, "what did you mean when you said, 'I'll leave when we pull the last body out of here'?"

I had to be very careful what I said. These people could make real trouble for me. If they filed a report with FEMA, it wouldn't take long for FEMA to be calling the PA and speaking to my chief. The next thing I'd be taking time off to talk to the PA psychologists about what I said to the CISM people.

It was the only time at Ground Zero I remember backing down. I couldn't give them anything they could use as ammunition, especially anger. I had to treat them like serious people. If I told them to get out or acted dismissively, I'd only reinforce their perceptions. It took me half an hour to explain to them why I wanted to stay with the mission, and should be allowed to stay. I spoke like I'd had a lobotomy. No emotion, no passion; just simple stuff and smiles. Whether I convinced them, or they just sensed I couldn't be made their prey, I'll never know. I was never so relieved as when they left.

An NYPD psychologist later said about the CISM workers, "You know, Bill, the problem with those therapists is they pathologized everything." If I correctly interpreted her to mean they made us feel fucked up, she was absolutely right.

Although many of the CISM therapists were more obstructive than constructive, there were some like Donna Lamonaco who were among the absolute best we had. I met Donna a few weeks into the mission, a petite blonde with bright blue eyes who usually wore a New Jersey State Police windbreaker. Donna's husband, Philip, was shot and killed on Route 80 in New Jersey by a domestic terrorist group. She and her daughter Sarah and their colleagues Diane and Roland came down every midnight to visit and work with a different command. She was a cop's wife. She was there to solve problems. She knew how to help. She became somebody I trusted. I often went to her with questions about the issues that were coming up with my own guys or what I should be anticipating.

Donna said something that's always stuck with me. "Billy, here at Ground Zero the abnormal is now normal. So the abnormal feelings you're feeling are normal too. Don't think that it's crazy. Don't think *you're* going crazy. This is what you have to do to deal with conditions like these. It's okay."

She was right. You know you survived something when you accept it, when you stop fighting it and you're not angry at it anymore. It was one of the lessons we all had to learn. Those who did transitioned from being victims to survivors.

During that winter we fought what I see now was the last battle to preserve the recovery operation. It was one of the warmer winters on record, so any snow melted rapidly and made the ground so muddy it was difficult to walk without sliding. A constant flow of groundwater from where the tiebacks were being installed in the slurry wall made the mud even deeper and slicker. It became difficult for the grapplers to find safe purchase. The construction companies decided to deal with the water deepening at the bottom of the site by laying down heavy wooden pontoons as a dry subfloor. The pontoons looked like railroad ties but much bigger and longer. Maybe they weren't such a bad idea from the construction point of view. From the recovery standpoint, they were a disaster.

The pontoons would have made it impossible to find any remains that washed in between them. Much of what we recovered was just pieces of people. Those remains could easily stick to the big ties or be crushed between them. Remains would be lost if somebody abruptly decided one or more of the ties was no longer needed and had it trucked out without our being on hand to watch the process. I was adamant; anything that left the site had to be looked at. A load of railroad ties or anything else had to be taken to the shakeout area, where it would be sifted through using the grapplers, then raked out by my men. That protocol had been agreed to at meetings. It was supposed to be law—until I got a call from Sergeant Kevin Murphy that I'd better get down to the pile without delay.

The Bovis Construction Company was now the lead construction company and in charge of the site. It had ordered cranes and trucks to move a whole section of ties. Any that broke or were otherwise damaged were going to be loaded onto trucks and sent off-site. They were proceeding without notifying me or my people. The loads had not been checked for remains. I was about as hot as I could get. Their action was an insult to the recovery, to the workers, and to the families. What made me maddest was that this removal was taking place at 8 p.m., contradicting agreements we had reaffirmed just hours before at the evening meeting of the site commanders with the construction superintendent—a meeting that had been devoted precisely to this issue.

"Murph," I radioed back. "No way in hell do those trucks leave here before we look at them."

"I'm not letting anything go, but you better get down here Boss."

I hopped in a red Port Authority pickup truck and came down the steel bridge fast enough to fishtail to a stop near where Kevin and some of my guys were waiting. Murph had a half smile on his face when he saw me pull up that fast and get out leaving the pickup running and the door wide open.

I headed for three trucks lined up with their motors idling and headlights on. The drivers were standing with Big Tony. You couldn't miss Big Tony. He was a supervisor for Bovis Construction, and he wore the Bovis white helmet. No coat, no scarf or gloves, nothing thermal. Even in winter Big Tony never wore heavy clothing. It was rumored heat could not escape a body that size.

I walked over to Big Tony and said angrily, "You guys gotta be fucking kidding me."

"Good evening, Lieutenant," Tony said calmly.

"Good evening?"

"And how are you?" Tony asked with a big smile.

"How am I?" I looked at him. "Is this a fucking joke?"

"No, no joke, Lieutenant. I was told to take these pontoons to the other side of the site. If any of them broke, and you can see some did, I was told to get rid of them."

"Tony, it wasn't two hours ago we agreed that pontoons

weren't leaving this way, and they weren't going to be moved from one spot to another unless we could take a look at them and check them here first."

"Okay."

"What do you mean, okay? That's the way it was." Was I missing something? How come he was so calm and cooperative? "Tony, every time I turn my back, whatever you told me changes and you're doing something else."

"Lieutenant—"

"I'm getting sick and tired of this. When a man gives his word, it should stick."

He held up his hands. "Let's not make this personal. I keep my word."

"Tony, we've been talking about this for two weeks, talking about these pontoons and how we're gonna look at them. This isn't what we said."

"I know."

"You know? Well, here's what I know. I'm too damn tired to run around checking on you guys anymore. I'm going to close this place down. The trucks upstairs are gonna stay upstairs. You know the shape of the trucks you've been running? I'll bet I get at least five or six knocked out of service just to start. Maybe you also wanna figure out how much time can be taken up when we do a really thorough inspection. Shit, when I stop and think about it, Tony, it could take fucking forever."

Tony shrugged. "Probably."

"And that's not to say anything about the drivers. You think their licenses are all okay? You think if I run them, I'm not gonna find a few guys with outstanding warrants? What if I start taking guys out of here in handcuffs? What do you think the unions are going to say when their members are collared down at work?"

Tony let out a sigh big enough for me to feel the wind. "Keegan, you know what your problem is?"

"Tell me, Tony. Tell me what my problem is."

"Your problem is you remember what people tell you."

It stopped me.

"Just listen for a minute," he said. "I promise this'll all be done the way that way you want it to be done—"

"Fine."

"Lieutenant, I remember the meetings just the way you remember them. Exactly the way you remember them, but I was told to do this. I was ordered to. I needed you to come down here, you understand"?

I realized Tony had been trying to help me all along. He couldn't ignore a direct order to move the pontoons, so he had set up a situation where he knew I'd step in and countermand it.

Tony pointed to the trucks. "You're in charge. Where do you want these loads?"

"Murph will handle it. I'm calling in the CVI team," I said, referring to the PA's Commercial Vehicle Inspection unit.

He frowned, but an inspection was unavoidable. If I said I would do something, I had to do it, or sooner or later someone would start thinking I was only bluffing.

"Okay, Keegan, that's it," Tony said.

"That's it," I agreed.

"You still got a problem?"

"Nope," I said. "You?"

He smiled. "Nope."

We shook hands and I headed for the PA pickup truck. It was snowing lightly. I felt the flakes melt on my skin.

Sometimes, you don't see the end till you're past it. The war at Ground Zero wasn't lost or won.

It simply came to an end.

Chapter Eleven

The first days of spring brought us soft weather and hard truth: we were running out of virgin areas for recovery; the mission was coming to an end. Ground Zero was nearly empty from its concrete floor to the slurry walls. The crucial sites—elevator banks, stairwells, and lobbies—had all been located and searched. We had gone over the building footings and underground shopping areas twice. We couldn't recover any more people because there was almost no one left to recover.

Our effort resulted in 1,588 of the 2,749 people who died at the World Trade Center being identified on the basis of recovered physical remains. We had to face the fact that a collapse of this magnitude had pulverized flesh and bone so completely that some of the bodies had disintegrated; four months of twelve-hundred-degree fires had burned the rest.

The recovery mission had changed us. The irony was that in the beginning we thought we would do anything to get to the end; now—and it may be hard to understand—we dreaded the end. We were about to lose the certainty of purpose and place we had found here. We felt a growing emptiness as we thought about what would replace it. It didn't matter anymore if you were a PAPD officer or a construction worker, NYPD or FDNY: we had all become reflections of Ground Zero itself; somewhere in the rubble contrasting values and competing interests had become selflessness and personal heroism. It was a good measure of that selflessness that a mission begun in chaos would end with grace. With few remains left to recover, we maintained our dignity and devotion and committed ourselves to clearing the last of the debris from this sacred ground.

At the end of all that struggle, it would have been easy to see the mayor as evil, the city fathers as indifferent, and the construction companies and unions as wicked underlings. It would also have been naïve. The ironworkers and operating engineers were among the finest people I have ever known. The construction companies invented new methods and procedures to accommodate the recovery mission on a daily basis. It would have been equally easy to blame every politician from the Battery to the Bronx for Ground Zero's uncertain future, but *I* didn't have to figure out how to repair the damaged economy of a traumatized city lacking confidence in its ability to recover.

Looking back, I see that the impact of nine months at Ground Zero on those of us who worked there was much greater than I realized. The people around us had for the most part moved on in the nine months after the collapse of the Trade Center; we had never left Ground Zero. It was still 9-11 for us, and we weren't prepared to let it go. One incident in particular brought that home to me.

We were told by the OEM to move the PAPD Command Post to the other side of West Street. Neighborhood groups had requested our space so they could build a baseball field. Our response was "Are you kidding? We're doing incredibly important work here and they expect us to waste all that time and effort moving the Command Post so they can have a goddamned baseball field? Where are their priorities?"

We had tipped the scale of values a little bit too much in the other direction. The people who lived here had a right to restore the neighborhood, and if the first thing they wanted to build was a baseball field, what could be better or more American? Of course we acquiesced, but we shouldn't have needed reminding that it was *their* neighborhood, and everything we did was to make it safe for *them.* The people here had suffered grievously. They needed to move on, and we should have cheered their building a baseball field where kids and parents could play ball and eat hot dogs and burgers and fries and drink sodas on a thousand summer nights to come.

All around us the city was coming back to life. Inside Ground Zero we were a group of cops and firemen and construction workers and others who weren't sure what life we were coming back to. We suddenly faced a void in our personal and professional lives equal in size only to the mountain of debris we had removed to create it. For a while our situation got worse rather than better. The more the recovery slowed, the more tension increased. My guys were coming to me with problems about feeling empty when the mission that had given meaning to our lives was so abruptly ending.

Conditions were deteriorating. A fight broke out for the first time, and not just a little pushing and shoving—two guys hitting each other with broom handles. There were guys with sleeping problems, guys sick from the dust and the asbestos, guys showing signs of post-traumatic stress disorder, some guys who just lost contact with themselves. Even the escape valve, humor, that always existed among us, the making fun of each other, now led to bruised feelings and anger. The level of intensity was too high; the emotions were too fierce.

I needed strong medicine, so I brought in Tony Senft and his group. There's nothing as pointless as a civilian saying to an injured cop, "I know exactly how you feel." What made Tony and his group so special was that every one of them had experienced significant police-related traumas.

Tony's own story started on New Year's Eve in 1982 when he responded to a call that would change his life. There had been an explosion at 26 Federal Plaza—the Federal Building in downtown Manhattan. When NYPD officer Tony Senft and his partner Officer Rich Pastorella arrived, they saw that four stories had been devastated. While they conducted an investigation for a second device in the building, a second explosion occurred, this one at NYPD headquarters at One Police Plaza. Rushing to the scene, Tony and his partner rendered aid to a bomb squad detective who had received severe facial injuries from the explosion.

In a moment of extraordinary courage, the injured bomb squad detective was able to put aside his pain and tell Tony and his partner that the bomb had been composed of sticks of dynamite housed in a Kentucky Fried Chicken container. Tony called that information in.

Meanwhile, a third bomb went off at Cadman Plaza in Brooklyn Heights, less than a mile away. Tony and his partner would have responded there but they were called to the Federal Building where a possible second device had been located. Upon arrival, they saw what seemed to be just a box of food, but based on what the other detective had told them, it aroused their suspicions. But when Tony and his partner approached, it went off.

It was determined later that the bomb in the food box had a "hang timer." It was supposed to have gone off earlier—most likely with the first bomb—but the timer had gotten "hung up." Tony remembers only a loud boom, but he was thrown eighteen feet through the air, his body on fire. He woke up ten days later to learn his partner had been blinded; Tony himself has never fully recovered from his injuries. The FALN, a terrorist group out to make Puerto Rico independent from the United States, was responsible for all the bombs.

What led Tony to start his therapy group was an invitation to NYPD headquarters to help the NYPD form a support group for injured cops. During the conference, Tony met Angel Poggi who, on very his first tour as a cop out of the academy, had been lured to an empty tenement and maimed and blinded by a booby-trap explosive device planted by the FALN. Tony embraced Poggi on the spot and both cried; they knew they had a special bond, both the victims of terrible disaster. Tony and Angel knew the hard truth: one day you're alive and vibrant, the next day you're a quadriplegic. They realized a support group of men who had been through the same or similar circumstances as they had could help others. That is still the spine of their group—being able to say to someone who has suffered a trauma, "I know what you're going through; I went through it."

Tony loved being a part of the NYPD, loved to help, and knew that the carnage never goes away inside or outside, and the pain and the memory can be triggered by anything. For him, it was fireworks on a beach that once forced him to leave a festival because they brought him right back to the explosion.

Tony brought three people with him to our command trailer to talk to my guys. Ed Carroll, a New Rochelle Police Department motorcycle cop whose crash in the line of duty left him in a wheelchair for life; Donald Rios, who was shot with a .45 in the line of duty; and Kathy Burke, whose partner was shot and killed in front of her after she was also shot.

Tony and his group talked to my guys twice. Tony was blunt: "Okay, who has not had sex with their girlfriend in the last month?" The guys didn't like being confronted. They didn't want to deal with something that revealing, or mess with the rationalizations they had invented around it. They especially didn't want to think their sexual behavior was a symptom of something bigger.

"Hey, who wouldn't rather sleep, after what we've been doing?"

"It doesn't matter to me. I like to go out with my friends, have a couple of beers. What's the big deal?"

Tony's group was able to get past the resistance because they had suffered enough that we could accept their saying, "I know exactly how you feel." Yet even as I brought in Tony and other counselors, and FEMA sent CISM teams until waves of therapists were hitting Ground Zero like the marines on D-day, *not one of them knew exactly how I felt.* No one knew how much I was hurting.

I didn't understand how much pain I was in until a well-known writer I had never heard of came to the site late in the spring. She wanted to interview me. I tried to get someone else to talk to her, but she kept coming back. We were standing at the edge of the pit, and she kept asking me about what it all meant and what I was going to do now that it was almost over. She annoyed me. She wouldn't stop. Question after question. It was like she just kept jabbing me, jabbing me, jabbing me, and I finally blew.

"Look down," I said. "What do you see?"

The pile was gone. The pit was empty. From its slurry walls to the dirt floor scored with tread tracks, the debris that had once filled it had been carted away to Staten Island. The last viable place we had hoped to make significant recoveries was barren.

"What am I supposed to see?" she asked. "There's nothing left."

"Right. Nothing. Same as here." I pointed to my chest. "I'm empty. My cops are empty. The families are empty. No more rescues. No more recoveries. No more giving. It's over."

If she hadn't gotten to me, it would have been someone else. She had just been scratching. She didn't know she would scratch me open.

"What the people here did was nothing short of amazing," I said to her. "You know how this job was done? It was done with heart. There's no way something like this could have been done with anything *other* than heart. The people here wore their hearts on the outside and got beat up every day. But they put themselves back together again and came back the next day."

Another problem was my cops were going to go back to their commands in the real world, where no one else had taken part. Not only would they be misunderstood, they would face animosity. A lot of cops had wanted to come here but couldn't, for one reason or another. There was still a certain amount of *How come* you *got to go? Why* you *and not me?* The term "Ground Zero heroes" wasn't one of appreciation; it was a term of derision and envy.

To many, it might seem crazy that anyone could be envious of nine months in hell—and most of the time Ground Zero was certainly that—but I understood it. I understood it perfectly. Combat veterans told me the workers at Ground Zero acted the same way as soldiers under fire. There was so much no one else shared. We had camaraderie and relationships. Everybody else was outside.

The cops who weren't part of the mission at Ground Zero knew they had missed something that had inspired us, something we'd never forget, a mission that made even all the pain and suffering worth it.

In the midst of hell, we found the face of God.

In the last weeks of the mission, the installation of the 460-foot-long, 30-foot-wide steel bridge from Liberty Street down to the bottom of the pit—a structure perfect for the job because it was fast to erect and required a minimal amount of labor—enabled us to start removing debris from the area around Tully Road, so named because it came in off Greenwich Street, which was in the Tully quadrant. Tully Road became the last area of virgin material to give us recoveries. It was also where the idea for a closing ceremony walking the "Last Piece of Steel" out of Ground Zero was conceived.

As we moved the recovery toward the east slurry wall, we had to remove the steel beams of the WTC that ironworkers call "candlesticks"—the big box beams that were set directly into the cement at the base of the World Trade Center. The tradition among construction workers who finish a building is to hold a "topping-off" party, in which an American flag and a tree are erected on the apex of the new structure to top it off. It is a ceremony of great importance signifying the end of the project. When we reached the candlesticks, one construction worker suggested, "Why don't we use one of those big steel beams, because we really should have a last piece, like at the top of a building." The last piece of steel that goes up in a building is momentous; the last piece of steel to come out of Ground Zero would be momentous too.

One candlestick was left standing. It was a huge piece of steel, extremely thick and heavy. The next night, my guys on the night tour, led by Sergeant Kevin Murphy and Sergeant Steve Butler, painted the top of the steel white on both sides. They wrote *PAPD* in blue spray paint, and the number 37 in memory of the officers we lost. Immediately the NYPD and FDNY painted their names on it, along with the number of people they lost, 23 and 343 respectively.

Workers came from all over the site, and soon the steel beam was covered with writing and emblems and stickers—a PAPD ESU patch, memorials to lost friends, prayers, sayings, names. The NYPD and FDNY added "We will never forget" and shield and precinct numbers and firehouse emblems till every inch was covered.

At the next 5:30 p.m. meeting, a Bovis supervisor named Terry Sullivan brought us together with a grace and resolution that I will never forget. Terry always wore a shirt and tie, no matter how cold it was, a big blue down coat that went all the way down to his calves, and a white Bovis helmet that was always clean.

Terry was well respected. He was out there with us, not calling plays from some office. He stood up to address the meeting, and his Irish brogue was heavy with emotion.

"Gentlemen, I have a request and a question. My request is that on a date to be determined, the Last Piece of Steel be taken out of the site on a flatbed truck draped in black. It will start at the bottom of the pit and go up the steel bridge to the street. I would like there to be an honor guard of all the representative companies, agencies, uniforms, and others that have been part of this rescue recovery mission.

"I would like, without one spoken word, as that piece of steel goes up the bridge, for everyone to fall in behind it without rank or rancor, and we will follow that piece of steel out to its final resting place accompanied by the single beat of a single drum."

It was a fine speech. For a moment, Terry looked us over.

"Gentlemen, my question is, do you want to do this?"

We all stood in agreement. It was a good way for the piece of steel to go out. There wasn't going to be a single spoken word—not a single politician's speech.

A few nights later, in a ceremony presided over largely by the construction workers, torches were used to sever the Last Piece of Steel from the ground. It was then lifted by a crane onto a flatbed truck, where it was draped in black bunting and a large floral arrangement was placed on it along with an American flag. To protect it from the elements, we parked it under a garage till the walk-out on the last day.

It should have been simple. Then the mayor's office and OEM got involved. They held a meeting to discuss the last day. There was a woman in charge who announced their plans. She told us the mayor and OEM had decided on the number fifteen, there would be fifteen members of each uniformed service on the bridge, fifteen from different construction companies, fifteen from OEM, fifteen from this and that, and they would also have some family members on the bridge, but we didn't know who or how they were picked, or whether they would be fifteen families or fifteen individuals, and so on.

What sense this made we did not know, but I was damned if I was going to get into endless discussions about how to do what those of us in charge of the site had already agreed on and knew to be the way we wanted to do it.

Ground Zero had taught me a consistent lesson from the first days to the last: you could only control what you owned.

"Excuse me," I said to the woman in charge, "I just wanted to let you know that the Port Authority police will make sure the beam stays safe and secure, and we will certainly maintain a twenty-four-hour guard on that piece of steel."

It was such a simple statement she didn't even think about it.

She said, "Okay, that would be good," and moved on to another point.

Some people in the FDNY or NYPD probably understood what had just taken place. A few heads leaned together to talk. I don't think anyone would have opposed my action, but it didn't matter. One move did it. It was all over.

Effectively, the PAPD now owned the Last Piece of Steel.

Chapter Twelve

My last tour of duty at Ground Zero began at 6 p.m. on May 29, 2002. I assembled the entire night tour in the center room of the PAPD Command Post for the final roll call. The faces of the fifty case-hardened rescue and recovery workers seated before me at the big table in the double-wide trailer were a mix of emotions. They were different men, but they had all been through the same struggle. There was always that under-standing, that bond.

There was sense of satisfaction in having made it to the end of the mission. I could see the shared pride of my PAPD cops: they had come together as a team I could depend on. The retired vets of Team Romeo—guys who were still larger than life for me—looked as if they were ready for round two whenever the bell rang. Part of my attention was on a very nice woman standing off to the side with her arms wrapped around herself as if warding off the cold. Her name was Mrs. Lisa Luckett and she had lost her husband Ted on 9-11 when the North Tower fell. I had only met her that day, but she was obviously in pain and fighting hard for control. When I asked her if there was anything I could do, she began to cry.

"Lieutenant Keegan, I can't come to the closing ceremony to-morrow. I just can't handle the crowds. It's too much . . ."

I understood that and suggested she might come to the PAPD Command Post for the last roll call. It was the last time we would all be together and I had a few things to say. It was our closing ceremony, and she understood that. She would still be taking part. She was extremely grateful. Later, when she asked to speak to the guys, her sincerity was evident: "I just want to thank you from the bottom of my heart for letting me be here. I'll tell all the other widows I know what you have done here."

I wanted to treat the roll call as the normal administrative function it was, but I couldn't escape the finality of it. None of us could. I was performing the last incantation, the last spell, the last rite. After this, our connection to the sacred ground that had been such a wellspring of spirit, despite its dangers, would be severed. It would end some of the most important relationships of our lives. I had come to think of most of the guys facing me as brothers, some of the younger men almost as sons. With the end not just near, but here, I wished I could give them the answers to the questions plaguing us. I couldn't.

The first order of business was to give them the protocols established for removing the Last Piece of Steel from the site—the who, what, where, why, and how that constituted a good cop's mantra. I peered at them over the glasses I needed to read the papers in my hands. One by one the various cellular phones and radios were silenced.

"Gentlemen, we have come to the end. This is the last night we will be together as a team to do the work none of us thought we could ever do. In the beginning, hundreds of us stayed. We few will be the last to leave.

"Tonight, our regular crews will be down in the pit. Our first focus is what it has always been—the recovery. However, we will also sit security on the Last Piece of Steel until it leaves the site tomorrow morning. Those are two very important jobs. We will need to start thinking logistics and getting supplies down to the pit, because in preparation for the ceremony tomorrow, this site will be secured from all entry after eight p.m. The steel bridge—the only way to get down there—will be closed to all traffic and secured by us at top and bottom. We will be the only people down there until

tomorrow morning, so we need to have everything staged at this location."

I didn't want anger seeping into my voice, but it was hard to
stay neutral. "I know how all of you felt about only being able to
pick fifteen guys for the honor guard. The NYPD felt the same way.
But tonight I can tell you that every guy from our night tour is
going to be part of the honor guard when that steel leaves here; so
are a good number of the day tour, and the NYPD tours.

"I fought for that," I said, and had to turn away for a moment
before I went on. "That's *ours*."

Ceremonies mark birth and death, beginnings and endings,
openings and closings. The idea for a closing ceremony and the
planning and execution of it came from us in the pit. The way I figured it, that meant no one else had the right to tell us how few or
how many of our guys were going to be on the bridge or in that
honor guard. Not even the people from the mayor's office who ran
the meetings in preparation for this day. None of them had sweat
here, or had their lungs scorched, or their hearts torn out. The men
before me had been the real honor guard for the better part of nine
months. If anyone doubted it, they should know that when it was
announced that we could only have fifteen men in the honor guard,
by unanimous vote, they decided to give their places to the members of Team Romeo to honor them.

I wasn't going to see that kind of honor and sacrifice overlooked. No one was going to repeat the kind of incident we had
with the banner across the street, where we were forgotten. No one
was going make me pick a handful of guys to be "representative" of
the rest. Every one of my guys was going to take part in the walk
out—and so was every one of the cops, operating engineers, construction workers, and volunteers who had broken their backs to do
the impossible like it was all in a day's work. My last act as commander of the night tour was to honor each and every one of them,
their service to the families of the victims, the victims themselves,
and the entire Port Authority Police Department.

Looking back, five years later, if the incident with the ID cards was the PATH cops' finest hour; and the longest recovery was John Moran's; and defending the bodies of the men was Owen McCaffrey's; and if for the Out-to-Lunch Bunch it was the photograph they carried and placed on Christopher Amoroso's body as it was carried out; and if crawling into that burning hole with the bucket brigade was Chief Esposito's—then maybe this was mine.

Five years later, I have no trouble admitting what I did, and why. I had already taken charge of the Last Piece of Steel. That day, I took part of the closing ceremony and gave it to my men. I did it because they deserved it. I knew exactly how to do it because in the nine months since I'd taken over the PAPD rescue and recovery operation at Ground Zero, I'd become the commander I set out to be. I had the map *and* the territory.

That was the beauty of controlling security for the Last Piece of Steel. Closing the steel bridge to keep everybody out would also keep everybody in—and if the city officials thought that the PAPD didn't know more ways into the pit than the steel bridge, they hadn't seen what had transpired here in the last nine months. With the bridge closed, I had a free hand right up to when the ceremony began, when Andy Infante, the driver, who was a Port Authority civilian who had lost his brother, Tony, a PAPD inspector, on 9-11, started up the truck carrying the steel and headed slowly up the bridge to the street and out of Ground Zero.

John Ryan and I had already worked things out with John Moran and all the construction workers. Everyone agreed. It was going to be *our* day.

"Listen up. The city has ordered the ramp closed and the pit emptied of all personnel except the PAPD security force. We will be maintaining a security cordon around the truck carrying the Last Piece of Steel through the night, and will continue that cordon when we escort it to the bottom of the ramp, where it will begin its ascent.

"We will be on both sides of that truck until it reaches the bottom of the bridge. At that moment, we will send up an honor guard of workers from every agency, union, department, and construction company that has been involved in this incredible site. They will come up from the pit ahead of the truck and line both sides of the bridge. They are not here yet. They will be arriving during the night. We have identified several routes they will use to get down here. Some, I might add, are rather creative. None, however, will violate our compliance with the order closing the steel bridge."

I smiled. "Security is paramount."

They brightened visibly. Most of the Team Romeo guys looked like they had already figured out the scope of what I was doing that last day at Ground Zero. The younger guys had questions, but I wasn't ready to answer them.

"As the truck goes up, those of us in the pit will fall in behind it. The honor guard on the bridge will fold in behind us as the truck reaches them. They will form two columns and follow it out. The families will merge in from Hall Road, Liberty Street, and West Street. The procession will go southbound to Albany Street and make a U-turn and go into the southbound lanes of West Street at about five miles per hour. A Port Authority Police Department vehicle will pick up the escort at Vesey Street and take it north to Canal Street, where the procession will end. The truck carrying the steel will drive onto the Manhattan Bridge on its way to JFK airport.

"We will have our people on that bridge—the late tour of the Port Authority Police Department. As everybody here knows, the night tour elected to withdraw themselves from standing on the bridge so that we could give the places to Team Romeo. They have given us their support. We gave them ours by asking them to stand in our place. The only change is that now we will be standing beside them.

"Captain Whittaker, our incident commander, is going to stand with them, and so is Andy Rivers, Sergeant Andy, from the Passaic County Sheriff's Department. We all know how many important jobs the sheriff's department did for us in the first few months of the mission. We want to repay those guys.

"We're also going to have the honor of one of our own on the detail carrying the empty Stokes basket draped in the American flag that represents all the people we could not recover. You all know that Sergeant Butler lost his brother, Thomas, a member of the FDNY, on 9-11. Sergeant Butler will be our representative on that Stokes basket . . ."

I had enormous respect for Steve's staying with the mission despite his pain. His brother Tom meant so much to him. Tom was the guy who played sports ahead of him, who joined the uniformed services ahead of him, and Steve had followed in his big brother's footsteps. I had watched him every night at Ground Zero, hoping it was the night he would find his brother. Tom was never found, which was why Steve was one of the people carrying the Stokes basket for the unrecovered. Getting to know Steve over the past months, and knowing the man *he* was . . . God, I wish I had known his brother.

For what seemed like the hundredth time that night, I tried to keep my voice from breaking. This time I couldn't.

When I could go on, I spoke about my team's bravery and commitment. I told them all what they had accomplished and how proud they should be. I told them how much they had done for the families. I told them that their sacrifice and pain would become legend, and that I was prouder of them than I had ever been of any men in my career, and in my life. I told them we were going to walk out of Ground Zero with heads high.

"When we leave here in the morning, we will not show pain or loss; not because we have none, but because we were here for the families. They were the reason for all we have done. This sacred ground is theirs.

"You all know that at every point in this process we've talked together. I always tried to keep you up on what was going on.

We've progressed from the confusion of September to where we came together as a close unit in the weeks after. This is just about over. It may seem like it's taken a long time, but it's incredible what we've accomplished in less time than anyone imagined. I remember the first estimates. They said it would take years. We did it in nine months—and if you think God hasn't been on our side, check the temperatures we had. Check the amount of snow and rain that fell on us. It was one of the best winters on record.

"If you still have any doubts, ask yourself how many people we lost in what was the biggest construction project ever. Zero. We lost no one. Check major injuries. There were none. Everybody who came into this site, to do God's work basically, came out all right. Remember that."

I paused. I had never heard the room so quiet.

"So, we've come to the end . . . and I couldn't have worked with a better bunch of guys and women. I can tell you it's been easy to supervise you, and I will never forget you, and I hope you never forget me, because as I told you before, we're not quite done, right?

"When we leave here, we're going to experience the pain and the problems other people have been experiencing and trying to work through since September. We've been too busy to stop and do that. We were doing important work. But a lot of things may hit us now that it's over and we're going home. Maybe some us aren't so sure we're comfortable at home. We've been so isolated, some of us haven't even *been* home. It's a burden we carry, one more added. Give yourselves time to adjust.

"It is very important to make sure we maintain contact amongst ourselves, keep watching out for each other. I want a phone call from anyone who thinks their buddy's not doing so well—because if there's one thing I think you guys know, it's that you guys come first with me and I would never do anything that would hurt you personally or professionally, or hurt your families. So I want to be the clearinghouse, because I'm the one who cares about you. I want that from you. Trust me, and if we come out of this a year from now just as we are now, then maybe we're done, but not till then."

I had already turned away twice to keep the tears back. Now I had to force my throat to let go of my voice.

"A lot of people talk about closure like it's something you're supposed to have—like pain just stops because you want it to. Like if you don't move on, you're selfish or screwed up, right? Let me tell you, closure just means someone else is tired of dealing with your pain. But life isn't about forgetting what hurt you; it's learning to live with it. It's getting up when you're at the bottom and you got nothing left. It's believing there's still a reason to try and make things better. If you forget that . . . you call me."

I didn't know that night that months later, I would again be facing many of these same men and women, and members of the families, and fellow workers. This time it was from the stage of New York's Beacon Theater, at a special concert that was one widow's gift of thanks to the Ground Zero rescue and recovery teams. The widow was Lisa Luckett, who hadn't forgotten us. She was, and is, responsible for kindness in abundance. I was called to the stage, where I was flanked by John Ryan and John Moran; Larry and Danny from Ironworkers 40; Jules Lizner of the Medical Examiner's Office, Bovis supervisor Charlie Vitchers; Fire Chiefs Harden and Werner; the giant operating engineer Martin Reilly; and others. I wrote no speech. I just spoke from the heart.

"To all of you gathered here today, I must tell you this: there are no heroes here. The heroes are the two thousand eight hundred twenty-three people who went to work that day and didn't come back . . ." I could barely see from the glare of the lights on the water in my eyes. "And the heroes are their families and their loved ones, their children and wives and mothers and fathers and brothers and sisters. We are not heroes.

"These people up here worked very hard together, and we

went through a lot of emotions together. We still don't understand all of what happened to us. We called it a lot of things and we searched for a word that might describe what it was we were doing down there. Was it a crusade? A mission? Was it a tour of duty and we can compare it to a war? We were most alive when we found the dead for the living—what sense does that make? Well, I recently heard a sermon given by Reverend Phillipa Turner, who was a chaplain who gave many blessings down at Ground Zero, including over Lee Ielpi's son, Jonathan. Everyone who worked there knows her. She's a little bit of a thing. Pippa, as we called her, quoted a definition of the word "vocation." It was when your deepest desires met the world's deepest needs. It's when you turn your reverence for God into a mission for the world. That's where we were. The world's greatest needs were met by our greatest desire to fulfill them.

"It was our deepest desire to rescue every single person, and that transitioned into the reality that we needed to *recover* every single person, and those were the goals we set, and those were the goals we aspired to, and every single person here did everything they could to meet that goal.

"We did not attain our goal, but we did not fail. Each and every one of us can go home and look in the mirror and feel comfortable and know that we did the best we could, and be proud of what we did. And now that we are removed from that circumstance and from doing the job we were sent to do, we now can look at the families, look them in the eye, and say we did our best to do what they asked us to do; we did the best we possibly could."

Five years after 9-11, I remain certain. We did our best, every one of us.

At midnight, May 30, 2002, arrived: the last day. We maintained security all night. Anyone trying to come down the steel bridge had been turned back. A little after sunrise, NYPD cops, construction workers, and union workers began arriving in the pit by various routes. When guys couldn't get through, they called us on their Nextels and we guided them in.

An hour later, city officials and VIPs from the mayor's office started to arrive up on street level. John Ryan was there assisting with the logistics of the upper part of the bridge, securing special sections for the families, local politicians, the press, and so on, and clearing a path for the truck carrying the steel to take. We stayed in touch using our radios. John was a sharp guy. He spotted trouble coming and moved to intercept it even as he was calling me.

"Billy? Got a problem about to happen up here."

"What kind?" I asked.

"The lady from the mayor's office who spoke at all the meetings we were at. She's in charge here."

"So?"

"So I think she's noticed the number of guys you got down in the pit. She's coming at me and she doesn't look happy."

"She's no match for you."

John barely had time to acknowledge that before I heard a strident female voice come over the open frequency and lash out at him.

"Lieutenant Ryan, who are those people down there?"

"Port Authority police, Commissioner."

"Why are there so many of them?"

"They're doing security," John responded.

"On what?"

"The steel beam. You gave us the assignment, remember?"

"They don't need all those people for that. You think someone's going to walk off with a fifty-ton steel beam?"

"Not with us on the job."

"That's not what I meant. Go tell them they have to come up here. Right now."

She had just assigned John the task of throwing us out. Of course, John accepted.

"You want me to go down?" he asked.

"No, Lieutenant. That's why the city bought you radios."

"Actually, Commissioner, we're not—"

"Just do it," she said coldly, followed by the dwindling sound of footsteps that meant she was walking away.

"You there, Billy?" John sent.

"Here, John."

"You're going to love this: she wants me to throw you out of the pit."

"What are you going to tell her?" I asked.

I could hear the grin in John's voice. "We're going to have to get you a new radio, Billy. Yours doesn't seem to be working. Hard to get through. I'll have to get back to you."

"Ten-four, John. See you on the bridge."

The ceremony began at 10:28 a.m., the time the second Tower had collapsed on 9-11. A bell sounded the fire code, four sets of five rings, in memory of 343 firefighters lost at Ground Zero.

First to ascend the steel bridge was the flag-draped Stokes basket, Sergeant Steve Butler carrying it for the Port Authority Police with members of the NYPD, EMS, FDNY, and construction workers. The pipers and drummers marched behind them, silent but for the cadence beat from a single drum.

The flatbed truck carrying the fifty-ton Last Piece of Steel circled the pit and lined up with the entrance to the steel bridge. As it reached the bottom, the honor guard from the pit flowed past it and lined the sides of the bridge as far as our numbers allowed. The first people marching behind the truck were the last in line; John Moran and I fell in and called to Kevin Murphy to come with us. We were now three; Kevin Murphy and John Moran were on the left, I was on the right. The three of us marched behind the truck. As it passed, all the Port Authority cops fell in behind us. PAPD Captain Whittaker, our commanding officer at the World Trade Center, stepped in too.

We reached John Ryan, standing tall on the bridge, saluting.

I saluted him, and he moved in to my right. Four abreast, Murph and Moran and Ryan and I walked up the steel bridge, a slow walk with everybody saluting us as we went by.

I have felt a lot of emotion in parades—pride, honor, solidarity—but nothing compared to what I felt now. We walked behind the Last Piece of Steel, the pipers, the drummers, and the Stokes basket. There was still complete silence but for the single drum beating cadence, left . . . left . . . left . . .

Up ahead, we saw the governor and the mayor. Joe Morris, now four-star chief of the PAPD, was there too. He gave me a big thumbs-up. We had done what he had asked us to do and he was acknowledging it. He was proud to see the PAPD leading everyone out. I was proud too. We started here as a department that was left out, a department no one even knew was here, with no voice and no role. On the way, we became a major force for every rescue and recovery worker.

We made the contribution we came here to make. Most important, we did it by dint of our work, our experience, and our talent, and an unswerving loyalty to the mission; we did it with our hearts. Yet, nearing the top of the bridge, I didn't know what to expect. None of us did. We had been at the bottom of the pit since the previous day. We didn't even know if there were people up there in the streets. We weren't sure anyone was watching or waiting—until we came off the top end of the bridge. The streets were packed eight and ten deep. It was awesome. John Ryan and I looked at each other. John shook his head in amazement. All he could say was, "This is unbelievable."

There were people hanging from windows; there were people on the roofs; there were signs on the buildings. It could have been a ticker tape parade—but every person in the honor guard, a column of hundreds stretching behind, was completely stone-cold silent, and so was every person in the crowd watching. NYPD cops put up dividers to hold the crowds back but they were unnecessary; the solemnity of the event did it. Respectfully silent, the people watched us approach. When we came up onto West Street, I felt uneasy. What do we do? What are we supposed to do?

The drum never stopped beating its single cadence for us. I didn't know what to feel. Looking back at that moment, maybe I just felt too much to understand it all. We were leaving Ground Zero. We were going back to the world. I wasn't sure how to relate to all these people.

Four abreast we followed the steel, all those who had given so much, so tired and unsure, deathly silent, yet so proud. And then it happened. One person in the crowd started clapping, clapping to the same slow cadence as the drum. And with that, a few more began to clap, then a few more, until everybody in the crowd was clapping and it got louder and louder and louder until it was a wave of sound all around us. My throat tightened and tears came to my eyes.

"My God" was all I could say as the sound swelled louder.

John Ryan looked at me and I could see his eyes were filled with tears, just like mine were.

"Billy, I can't make this. I'm not going to make it."

"Yes, you will," I assured him.

John Moran walked with his head up and his back straight, and I knew that everybody in the line felt the same way: we'd had no idea what to expect, no idea what to do, and now all of a sudden there was the clapping. It was not wild applause; it stayed always the same rhythmic beat, but it swelled into the loudest noise I have ever heard. Thousands of people clapping all at once while they looked at us so solemnly, so deeply. No waving or yelling out; just people looking. I saw they were crying too. People just crying. I didn't know if they were family members, people who lost people. Maybe at that moment it was just being there, knowing what had been done, and why.

As we walked, it came to me that this marked the end of one of the most horrific events in our history, and all of these people had turned out to recognize it. I believed some of them had come to say thank you for the job we had done. Others came to honor what the empty Stokes symbolized. And still others came to honor just being a New Yorker, for this was their moment too.

The outpouring of emotion toward us from the people all around was a statement, and we understood that. It was a thank-you. It was an honor. When those people broke the silence, it was like breaking the envelope that surrounded us. We were overwhelmed by the wave of sound washing over us, and the emotion that came pouring in with it.

We didn't think we had done all that much in light of the fact that so many people, so many friends, had lost their lives. I thought, *We're just bringing out this Last Piece of Steel; why are you clapping?* Years later, I know it was for the human spirit, and the piece of steel that was a symbol of our greatest resilience. I asked myself why I had wanted to be at Ground Zero. I knew in that moment it was because I could look at those nine months with the certainty that I had never rendered finer service.

Now we were being welcomed home.

The procession ended at Canal Street. The drummer stopped his beat. The truck carrying the Last Piece of Steel made a slow right turn onto Canal, then headed for the Manhattan Bridge and the Brooklyn-Queens Expressway and out to JFK. There were press and photographers. People were hugging us and shaking hands. The NYPD came over, and some firemen, and Port Authority people, and the Team Romeo guys, and operating engineers, and ironworkers, and construction workers, and Salvation Army and Red Cross workers and so many others, and we just hugged each other.

I turned around and there was FDNY chief Ron Spadafora right in front of me. We both had huge grins on our faces as we hugged. We were members of the same family. We had completed an honorable mission in service to others, and completed it with no fatalities and almost no major injuries. What we said to each other as we hugged was "Great job."

In all of us there was a core, an inner thing, a knowing. Surely nothing like this would ever happen to us again. Relationships and feelings would never be as intense or profound. I was happy to see the crane operators and shake their hands. They were great guys. One of the operating engineers, Martin Riley, an Irishman about six five and three hundred pounds, actually picked me up.

"Lieutenant, you're a fucking great man. It's been a pleasure working for you guys."

When I could breathe, I said, "Great working with you too, Martin."

My cops Terry Meaney and Steve Divino walked over and we shook hands and clapped each other on the back. Danny Francis came up and we shook hands too.

"Hey, Lieutenant, aren't you going to call this in?" Danny asked me.

"Call what in?"

Terry Meaney said, "Boss, we were thinking you're gonna call in that we're all nine-eight, right?" Nine-eight was radio code for "clear of site."

The last beam of WTC steel was gone. The thousands of who had worked so hard to come to this day, who had followed the black-shrouded truck, were now just individuals.

When Bill Barry walked over, he was one more voice for what they wanted me to do. "C'mon, Loo," he urged. "It's only right."

"Fair enough." I leaned toward the mike on my collar. "Central desk, this is Lieutenant Keegan."

"Go ahead, Lieutenant Keegan."

I was standing still and the crowd was swirling past. While I waited to get clear air, Shawn Murphy and Derek Yuengling saw us and came over. It felt good to have them all around me. So much sound; so many people there at the end. When the air cleared, I said, "Advising World Trade Center rescue and recovery mission has concluded. Last Piece of Steel is on its way of JFK. All units accounted for and are nine-eight."

"Ten-four, Lieutenant Keegan. Marking the World Trade Center rescue and recovery job final. All units accounted for and nine-eight. My time: eleven twenty-eight a.m. Great job."

I made my final report as night commander of the PAPD rescue and recovery operation at Ground Zero.

"Ten-four. Thanks, Central," I radioed back.

The last day was almost a duplicate of 9-11. A broad blue cloudless sky, sun shining; the sweet clear air of spring. I stayed for a while longer talking to friends, mostly about what we were going to do and how we wanted to try to stick together. Everybody was heading to the Borough of Manhattan Community College gym, where we had run our staging area. There was a gathering for the entire Port Authority, including the families of our lost police officers. All thirty-seven families would be there. We had recovered loved ones for twenty-three; I wish we could have done it for all of them.

Karen and the kids had come to the walkout. They had left the site but were somewhere nearby. She called to tell me she was going to get the car and park over by the Holland Tunnel; did I want to come home with them, or was I going out? I was torn. She knew that. She would wait.

I walked the six blocks to the gym. The noise of a hundred different conversations hit me as soon as I opened the door. I was unprepared for how many were here. The place was packed. There was everyone who had worked at the site, and the families of the thirty-seven PAPD officers and the thirty-eight PA civilians killed on 9-11. There were tables set up to seat people. There were people standing. I saw my friend Jean Andrucki's father and her sister. We shook hands and hugged, but it was a difficult moment. Jean was gone forever. I still feel the loss.

I hadn't been around this many people in months. I needed

time alone to work up to it. I didn't want people walking by, coming over to say, "Great job, Loo." I found John Ryan and looked for someplace we could get our feet under us, but someone came over to tell us they wanted the rescue and recovery team to come up to the front of the gym. There we saw every single family standing on kind of a receiving line for us.

Janice Tietjen, one of the leaders of the families, handed me a small box and a letter and said to me what she would say to each one of us in turn, "Bill, on behalf of all of the families I want to thank you for doing such a great job. Thank you, and we want you to have this small token that cannot tell you or repay you for what you've done. But please keep it near always, and think of us, and we will always keep you in our prayers."

Over the years, I have taken the silver key chain out to look at it countless times. The only thing I have looked at more often is the letter, dated May 30, 2002.

Dear Port Authority Police Officer,

Every day since September 11 the officers of the Port Authority Police Department have been a source of strength and comfort to our families. Even while working 12-hour shifts, 6 days a week and having your own family and emotions to deal with, you have found the time to call us, stop over at our houses, make us smile, take us to Liberty State Park, Pier 94, hold our hands down at Ground Zero, and cry with us at our memorial services all the while tirelessly continuing to work to complete the recovery efforts at Ground Zero.

Although the enclosed key chain is just a small token, we hope that each time you look at it you will truly understand the amazing impact you have had on our lives. Without the

encouragement and support of each one of you
we could not imagine dealing with the loss of
our loved ones. Please take solace in the fact
that you have made our former officers proud
with the dignity, strength, kindness you have
shown to our families and each other and in
the world. Although the media may not always
recognize the PAPD, our families will never
forget the kindness, concern and love that you
have shown us.

On behalf of our families, please be patient
with yourselves and your colleagues and know
that you're in our hearts, thoughts, and
prayers every day.

With eternal gratitude,
[signed by the 37 families]

I left the gym knowing we had the same lack of defenses here as we had in the site. Powerful emotions were painful. We needed time to close the distance between us.

I called Karen. "Where are you?"

"Parked by the Holland Tunnel, Bill. Do you know what you're doing yet?"

"I'm not sure."

"Okay. Call me."

"I will," I said.

As I turned to go, there was another of those little things can be so big—like the trees and the tents back on 9-11. I ran into one of the PA chiefs. He asked me a few questions, like when would my guys be back at their commands. He commented how different Ground Zero looked and praised our effort, and then it seemed just sort of thinking out loud, he added, "You know, Bill, we're gonna need your Nextel back soon."

He had already moved on; 9-11 was history. Thousands of

workers had taken part in the recovery operation compiling over 3.1 million man-hours. John Ryan told me he and I had personally worked well over three thousand hours each. Turning in my phone was a small request, but so big. There were new priorities. We were done here.

As I walked up West Street, I realized I was taking the same route back to the Holland Tunnel as I had taken to get here on 9-11. This was the street that was covered in dust and paper when we got out of the tunnel. Here was the corner where I was dropped off on 9-11. That day, West Street was closed. Nine months later, it was wide open. I looked down to Ground Zero and there was no mountain of steel anymore. In those nine months we had given it everything, and now we were totally spent, but look how we changed it.

Every step of the way I was conscious of the past. The tents were gone on West Street where the mobile Command Post once stood, but so were the trees. At Borough of Manhattan Community College, I had walked up the wide stairs where conga lines once moved supplies up from the street. The vast gym that had been our original staging area still echoed with John Kassimatis's sadness, "I lost guys."

I walked alone, except for the ghosts. They hovered nearby, the spirits of the fallen heroes we failed to recover. The area was still packed with people who had come to the closing ceremony and were now going home or to work. They filled the sidewalks and flowed into the street. No one left footprints; there was no more dust. It was odd to be back in the land of individuals. No one spoke to me. In the pit, we never passed a guy without eye contact or recognition. Among the living, I was a ghost too.

I walked through Tribeca, a neighborhood where people offered me food and water in those first critical days. These were the folks whose homes were covered in dust, who couldn't let their kids outside, who had their cars destroyed, their windows shattered.

They were changed, just as I was, but everywhere I walked I saw they were back now too.

What came back to me were the words of a close friend who had seen action in the Vietnam War. He had survived, come home, gone to Dartmouth, and lived a full and rich life. One time, I asked him, "Why do you think you went on to do all the great things you've done, and another guy hits the bottle or does drugs or just never makes it back to being whole again?"

"I made a decision," he told me. "I was going to take everything good that had happened to me in Vietnam and everything bad that happened to me in Vietnam and I was going to use it all in an effort to do good. I was going to look at what happened to me as an opportunity to become a much greater man than I ever could have been had I not been through it."

My friend's name is Ed O'Sullivan. He was a captain in Vietnam, awarded the Silver Star for action in combat. He answered the biggest question for me—what was I going to do now? The answer was simple; I was going to be a better man. I would see things differently. I would live differently; and at that moment, although my legs hurt so much I thought they might not carry me, I felt a little better, a little stronger, and I just kept walking until I saw Karen and the kids ahead of me.

"Let's go home," I said.

Karen was happily surprised. "Great, I thought you might want to go out with the guys."

I smiled. "Not today."

Then I did something that got me by far the strangest look from Karen she had given me in all the time I had been at Ground Zero; something that felt good and right, but that would take time for both of us to understand fully.

In our entire marriage I had never let anyone else drive. Never. Not once. But that morning when Karen handed me the car keys, I handed them back.

"You drive."

That's when I got the look. "Billy?"

"You drive today, hon."

I got into the car with the kids. They were happy I was coming with them. I was happy too.

I was going home.

Afterword

The legacy of the attack on the World Trade Center is far from over, and will never be complete until we recover the final remains we left behind. Neither will it be finished if we continue to let our workers and volunteers suffer and die. *There can be no closure without real answers; there can be no real answers without the truth.* The tragedy is that America knew it then, and is ignoring it now.

After the official closing ceremony, I was reassigned to another command on June 3, 2002. I refused to sign-off on the completion of the mission when asked to do so by the New York City Department of Design and Construction (DDC), the agency that managed the clean-up of the WTC site. Like many of the Ground Zero commanders, I maintained there were locations that might contain additional remains of the fallen that had not been properly searched. The holes in West Street caused by falling steel, and later just paved over, are just one example. It is clear that the DDC also knew that, but chose to end the mission for the sake of political expediency.

This serious charge is backed up by a May 24, 2002 memorandum from the Assistant Director of the DDC Environmental Health and Safety Service (EHSS) regarding the start of the EHSS team walkthroughs at Ground Zero. The memo states, in part:

> Previous to our Wednesday 05/22/02 meeting, DDC-EHSS requested FDNY to submit those areas where recovery operations were completed. . . . Lt. John Ryan of the PAPD raised issues

concerning the PAPD sign-off of the recovery areas of the EHSS
Transition meeting. . . . These new sign-off arrangements would
hamper the work of the EHSS Transition team, potentially de-
laying the sign-off by two weeks.

As you are aware, DDC and FDNY are the co-incident
Commanders for the WTC Emergency Project. FDNY has the
sole authority over issues concerning recovery. . . . [A]t this time
I am instructing the transition team to immediately begin the
walkthrough assessment so that we can avoid any further delay.

There are several problems with this memo. First, it is untrue
that, as the memo states, "FDNY ha(d) the sole authority over issues concerning recovery." Although the FDNY was given command of Ground Zero on 9–11 because of its control over all
"collapsed buildings" within New York City, shortly thereafter, the
Unified Command structure that was ultimately put into place at
the site gave equal authority over the recovery operation to the Port
Authority Police Department, the New York City Police Department (NYPD), and the New York City Fire Department (FDNY).

Second, the "issues concerning the PAPD sign-off" refer to,
and are a result of, a specific conversation I had with John Ryan that
there were areas at Ground Zero we felt had not yet been thor-
oughly searched for human remains. Clearly, if these improperly
searched areas were to reveal remains, it would take a lot longer
than two weeks to complete the mission. The DDC figured that if
the public knew there were still remains at Ground Zero, the site
would have to be kept open months longer. But not closing the site
would have put bonuses and new jobs for construction companies,
and promotions for members of the DDC, in jeopardy.

The Memorandum never said the PAPD was wrong—only
that we didn't have authority to delay the intentions of the DDC.
Such an obvious ploy by the DDC can only erode the victim family's
confidence in the very people they depend upon for their answers.
The families weren't given the truth about the extent of human re-

mains still at the site. *The New York Times* reports (Associated Press, December 7, 2006) over a thousand bones have been recovered during the past year, and the continued search for more remains will take at least another year. There are too many people who will never be able to move on as individuals or as a community because of it. Leonard Wong of the U.S. Army War College wrote, "While taking risks to recover the body of a fallen soldier may make no rational sense, it impacts significantly on the unit, the military profession, and US society." The creed is *Leave No Man Behind*. The victims of the World Trade Center attack deserve no less.

Those in charge of Ground Zero refused to do it the right way six years ago and still refuse to do it the right way today. I have had too many tearful phone calls from my former colleagues at the site saying simply, "Loo, how did we miss all this?" I can only tell them that, along with the families, our hearts were broken, too . . . and that we did our best but were prevented from doing all.

It is the same with the health and safety of the workers and volunteers at Ground Zero. Six years after 9–11, I have had to come to grips with the fact that my future is at best uncertain—and the terrible irony is that I am one of the lucky ones.

The Ground Zero environment contained debris contaminated by 26 miles of Mercury lighting, 6 million square feet of concrete dust, thousands of tons of plastic and asbestos. Wood, metal, plastic, jet fuel, and many other substances that were present in the debris at the site released toxic fumes as they burned. Mercury vapor is a neurotoxin. Yet workers who showed high levels of mercury in their blood were given only brief respite, and then reassigned to the site. Since November 2001 I have experienced sinus infections, headaches, and eye irritations. In August 2002, I developed a nerve weakness in my neck, back, and shoulder that left my right arm nearly powerless—and I am not alone.

According to the September 6, 2006, *New York Times* report on the results of the health study released by doctors at Mount Sinai Medical Center, the largest study yet of the thousands of workers who labored at ground zero (*Illness Persisting in 9/11 Workers, Big Study Finds*, by Anthony DePalma): "the impact of the rescue and recovery effort on their health has been more widespread and persistent than previously thought, and is likely to linger far into the future. . . . Roughly 70 percent of nearly 10,000 workers tested at Mount Sinai from 2002 to 2004 reported that they had new or substantially worsened respiratory problems while or after working at Ground Zero.

"The study is among the first to show that many of the respiratory ailments—like sinusitis and asthma, and gastrointestinal problems related to them—initially reported by Ground Zero workers persisted or grew worse in the years after 9/11.

"*The New York Times* reported that most of the Ground Zero workers in the study who reported trouble breathing while working there are still having those problems up to two and a half years later, an indication that the illnesses are becoming chronic and are not likely to improve over time." Some of the workers worked without face masks, or with bandannas, when what we needed were full-face sealed respirators, or the Bio-Hazmat suits which workers are using now.

"There should no longer be any doubt about the health effects of the World Trade Center disaster," said Dr. Robin Herbert, co-director of Mount Sinai's World Trade Center Worker and Volunteer Medical Screening Program. "Our patients are sick, and they will need ongoing care for the rest of their lives."

Beyond their physical ailments, many of the rescue workers and volunteers who were at Ground Zero remain isolated and disconnected from their families, alienated from former friends, and unable to reestablish their place in society. In short, countless thousands of men and women who gave "above and beyond" are suffering. Dr. Charles L. Robbins of the Stony Brook University School of Social Welfare states "former WTC workers are experiencing significant health problems manifesting in all body systems and organs, including stress disorders and emotional disturbances, caused by their exposure at Ground Zero." For some, the pain is unbearable because the immensity of their effort has been met by a public denial of their pain, creating an isolation which is the root cause of a rising rate of suicide. During the event, no sacrifice was too great. Now that ethic has set the scene for another disaster, unfolding today.

Dr. Spencer Eth, vice chairman of psychiatry at St. Vincent's Hospital and professor of psychiatry, New York Medical College reports:

> The St. Vincent's World Trade Center Healing Services have seen over 50,000 people who were psychologically affected by 9–11. Many victims have needed to remain in treatment for years. Our efforts continue because the suffering continues; and although fewer people are seeking help for the first time, those that are tend to be especially distressed and disabled, including uniformed service personnel, including firefighters and police officers. Tragically, almost all of the funding for these special programs has been terminated. That should not be allowed to happen—effective psychiatric treatment must be provided—or we may be forced to witness additional suicides and misfortune borne by the true heroes of the World Trade Center disaster.

On a daily basis I talk to my men who worked at the site and I bear witness to the number who are close to suicide, or who are simply going through the motions of life as shadows of the men they once were. Last week we buried a fine man, a husband and father, a former Marine, and a decorated veteran Port Authority police officer who jumped off the George Washington Bridge because the pressure building since the mission at Ground Zero finally proved too much to bear. There have been more than half a dozen PAPD suicides since the rescue and recovery mission at Ground Zero—and 25-year PAPD veterans can't remember a single suicide prior to it.

The recovery mission changed us; ending it changed us again. Life after has never been the same. Many still search for the certainty of purpose and place we found here. That emptiness was never properly addressed. When we left the site many of us were brought to an upstate hotel for a "debriefing." The intention was admirable but the result was woefully inadequate. I completed over 220 tours of duty at Ground Zero and I was interviewed by a volunteer for a private organization with less than 16 hours of "training" who had never even been to the site.

It doesn't matter who is to blame for the past. What matters is who is accountable for the present. We who worked at Ground Zero are still denied even the acknowledgement of our conditions. I am sick of hearing how complex the solution to our problems has to be; it isn't—not if we educate the public about the plight of those who served at Ground Zero concerning the isolation and denial which are the root causes of the stress disorders and suicides that have followed.

We must provide free medical screening and care for all those who worked at Ground Zero and their families. We must create a mechanism within a federal agency that immediately establishes a baseline medical data bank for all workers in mega-disaster situations, with blood and tissue samples taken on a regular basis. A coalition of federal and state officials must establish an independent commission for responders and recovery workers similar to the 9/11 Victim Compensation Fund. A no-fault alternative to lengthy tort litigation, the 9/11 Victim's Compensation Fund was initially received with skepticism but proved successful in allowing families to move on with their lives. If we do not allocate the time and resources needed, the ghosts of those who have died, and will die, because of it will haunt the building built on what became their graveyard.

The men and women who worked at Ground Zero rose to the greatest challenge of our lives. We fought the first part of the battle without a single fatality or serious injury to a worker and the startling fact is we have lost more workers *after* the rescue and recovery than during. The dust we cleaned up is still choking us. If we can sit back and watch that happening without taking action we are not the America we say we are. That America would not leave those who have sacrificed for their country in harm's way; would not leave them to fend for themselves; would not ignore compassion and look away pretending everything is okay. That America would not use accounting principles instead of medicine, for when the call comes again—and it surely will—who will respond if we teach our children that America turned its back on those who did what was asked of them?

Author's Note

By its nature, the rescue and recovery operation at Ground Zero invaded people's lives. Families delivered items as personal as toothbrushes, shaving razors, and combs in the hope that the DNA they held would match a body part recovered at Ground Zero and produce an identification. Establishing identity was paramount. We had to handle human remains with that in mind, always conscious our prime responsibility was to the recovered person's family.

In practical terms, that meant the codes of conduct we would normally expect to follow took a back seat to the magnitude of the task, the enormity of the loss, and the personal jeopardy of the mission. I know it is not an easy thing for you or anyone to look closely at what we went through. It was not easy for me to relive it, or relate these episodes in the kind of detail this book required.

Closure relates my experiences at Ground Zero and those of others who were there. I did not observe Ground Zero from the confines of a command trailer—I worked side by side with my men, a field commander whose tour of duty began on 9-11 and did not end until the closing of Ground Zero itself. I was never motivated by a desire to be sensational or lurid. In certain passages I chose to relate far less detail than what was available in order to protect the emotions of those involved. I tried to respect the sensitivities of the people I worked with, the families I worked for, the people that inspired me, the remarkable Port Authority Police Department, the NYPD, the FDNY, the construction workers, and all the people who taught and guided me. If sometimes the stories are hard, it is because the job and the place were hard too.

Closure is a term I placed in context several times in the book. Those who know me personally know that I also have wounds that will never heal, just as you do.

William Keegan

Acknowledgments

This book came about as the result of countless people who put their time, energy, and passion into helping me tell my story to the world.

I would like to give special thanks to the following people:

Thank you to Bart Davis for climbing into my skin, no matter how painful, and turning my thoughts into words.

Thanks to Bob Gottlieb, the CEO of Trident Media Group, for his wisdom and guidance.

Thanks to Paul Fedorko, my very patient and supportive agent.

Thank you to Mark Gompertz—every first author should have a publisher as professional as Mark, whose standards are reflected throughout Touchstone/ Fireside.

Thanks to Amanda Patten, my enthusiastic editor, who provided clear direction for me and for the book.

Thanks to Nicole Steen at Trident Media Group, and Betsy Haglage at Touchstone/Fireside.

Thank you to my friend Marc Gurvitz, who first suggested that I should make my story into a book.

I would like to acknowledge the support of Anthony Coscia, chairman of the Port Authority of New York and New Jersey and the entire Board of Commissioners.

I'd like to recognize Phil Clites of the Port Authority– the families of the 1993 WTC bombing victims should be proud of the way you protected the memorial honoring their loved ones.

I especially would like to recognize the men and women of the Port Authority Police Department who stood vigilant patrol, policing high-profile terrorist targets such as the Holland and Lincoln tunnels, the George Washington, Bayonne, and Goethels bridges and the Ouerbridge Crossing, Newark Liberty International, LaGuardia, and JFK airports, the Port Authority Bus Terminal, the PATH trains, and the Brooklyn, Elizabeth, and Newark Marine Terminals. These brave officers stood guard six days a week, twelve hours a day, for twenty-one months.

Thank you especially to my respected tour commander and friend Lt. Michael Carnevale (retired).

I would like to acknowledge my fellow officers on the Port Authority Police Department WTC Night Tour. It is impossible for me to name all of you, but please know that you each made a difference in my experience.

I'd like to thank my fellow Night Tour lieutenants: Bill Doubrawski, Senior Lieutenant, Command Post and Operations; Ed Moss, Site Security; Enzo Sangiorgi, Planning and Administrative; John Brant, Security and Logistics; and Ronald Willoughby, Staging. Thank you to the Inspectors—E. Ceccerelli, Captain A. Whitaker. Thanks to the Lieutenants—Sangiorgi, Brant, Fiore, Moss, Willoughby. Thanks to the Sergeants—Concepcion, Rodriguez, Whelan, Aquino, Vil, Korbul, Farrell, King, Devlin, Mania, Bryan, and Leary. Thank you to the police officers—R. Hill, E. Houston, L. Moronne, J. Morales, Doyle, Johnston, N. Rhem, E. Coleman, R. Conklin, Courtney, W. Gutch, F. Aresta, , V. Johnson, P. Hearty, S. Manning, N. Hardy, L. McRae, J. Hawkins, J. Confreda, B. Andrews, M. Koval, J. Frank, R. Challener, G. Fernandez, B. Essex, K. Ryan, R. Steneck, B. Verardi, M. Collins, R. Devito, E. Guclen, R. Singh, D. Yuengling, C. Cascante, A. Iadevaio, G. McDade, A. Marin, E. MacNamara, G. Georiadis,

T. Bongiovanni, R. Codner, S. Ahmad, K. Kostanoski, L. Mancuso, M. Ashton, T. Mastromonico, S. Farfalla, Hutzel, Salvador, Anatro, M. Fraone, C. Elliott, E. Rivera, A. Delara, R. Rodriguez, J. Saleh, D. Guriel, A. Perzichilli, K. Livelli, H. Holland, T. Paterson, M. Kostelinik, S. Murphy, J. Fredella, P. Duffy, R. Fernandez, A. Grant, Burgos, R. Mendyk, W. Fitzgibbons, Truglio, K. Jackson, J. Alvarez, J. Noble, J. Johnson, A. Blackman, D. Deprisco, J. Stella, P. Callahan, P. Nunziato, W. Piatti, D. McCabe, J. Giaguzzi, T. Mueller, G. Griffith, T. Reilly, Cohen, Wittman, Riiska, Gayson, Mueller, McDaniels, A. Burgos, Wallace, Chin, Caruti, B. Toohey, J. Gorman, M. Milne, W. Meyer, E. Cheatam, S. Rotolo, Smith, Lindenman, Placido, Eisenhardt, Militinovic, Way, Chalao, McCarthy, Cooper, Boye, Heinlein, Diluca, Howard, Hill, Farfalla, Hutzel, Salvador, Anatra, J. Rice, L. Lyans, M. Rabasca, S. Wilde, M. Prendergast, and E. Schmidt.

Thank you to the PAPD WTC Night Tour detectives, especially Chief R. Caron, Sgt. T. Bomengo, Sgt. A. Cooper, Sgt. B. Heim, Sgt. M. Palermo, and Detectives R. Chambliss, M. Dalton, C. Eng, W. Kehoe, C. King, D. McMahon, T. Ng, I. Pinckney, S. Poulos, B. Viania, J. Trotter, A. Gachette, Sgt. J. Mathieson, Vin Martino, Mike DeMello, Jim Wheeler, Al Gachette, and Ron Nafey.

Thank you to all of the men and women from the following forces, who gave their time and energy to help at the site day after day. The following names are just a sampling:

The Millburn PD, especially Lt. Dave Cuomo and Police Officers Bernie Neuhaus, Joe Johnson, Will Laverty, Mike Mulligan, Dave Benny, and Bob Lenihan.

The West Orange PD, especially Lt. Arezzi, Lt. Cali, Sgt. Racenello, Sgt. Philips, Sgt. Cali, Det. DeMars, Det. Spero, Det. Rugrero, and Police Officers Cullen and Verzi.

The Union/Essex County Auto Track Force, especially Lt. Vitellli, Sgt. Cassidy, Sgt. M. Mathis, Detectives Burke, Fag, and J. Deldyia, and Police Officers Schmidt, McCaffery,

E. Schmidt, Stallone, Mellilo, Andrews, Doherty, Sommese, Jones, Cureton, Corte, and Frank.

The Fairfield NJPD, especially L. Cammarata, T. McArdle, P. Pollack, and C. Zanpino.

The force from Fenton Twp, Michigan, especially R. Horrmann, C. Yonkers, and Thompson.

The Roxbury NJPD, especially Noll, Quinn, Smith, Winstock, Palanchi, Niemynski, Groff, Driscoll, Zarro, and Curtis.

The Wycoff NJPD, especially V. Portes, C. Cedano, D. Espinoza, McNamara, M. Grass, B. Plisich, P. Goodman, and M. Musto.

The Clifton PD, especially Chief Logioco, Sgt. Dara, Sgt. Camp, Sgt. Van Winkle, Sgt. Galvano, and Police Officers Skidmore, Frank, Napoleone, Cooke, Klein, Dvorak, Tuzzolino, Moreira, Little, Kosinski, Bracken, Centurione, McLaughlin, Petrone, Flanagan, Vassoler, Brancato, and Pereda.

Thank you to all of the Port Authority civilians, especially R. Kucks, R. Niemczyk, R. Oakes, M. Visceglie, F. Guariglio, E. Lombardo, D. Selle, B. Burneyko, S. Vuotto, G. McCann, and B. Reilly.

Thank you to SEMAC, especially F. Dantuono, S. Witas, S. Orgonas, B. Saccente, B. Beales, Lou Ambrosio, James Hineson, Frank Minervinni, Fred Grover, Roy Pechera, Robert Breault, Kevin McSweeney, Hudson Saintul, James Nazzaro, Willis Pagan, Ron Esposito, Luis Colon, Dean Baztellucci, Mike Krus, Todd Whitehill, Rick Ciprich, John Ruggiero, Mignoli, Slootsky, Marks, McGlynn, and Balbella.

Thanks to all of the Port Authority engineers, especially C. Bognacki, Dan Webber, Dennis Cooliere, Mark Wierzewski, Terry Ryan, Dilip Nisralyya, Aiman Abosharria, Tom Murphy, Angel Aviles, Jim Fenster, Antonio Miranda, D. Java, Ron

Vigdera, David Platt, Dave Potts, Herman Stapf, Ken Wright, Chris Cavalari, Ronald Shaw, Frank Wogelowski, Steve Weir, Mike Snure, Frank Petrullella, John Zarks, Misba Oladele, Lance Krakowitch, John Varrone, Carlos Perez, Mazen Oudeh, Armando Arcenal, John Bullard, N. Rao, Bill Baumann, John Tetar, Dorian Bailey, and Robert Gill.

I'd like to give a special thank-you to Lt. John Ryan, Operations Commander of the Port Authority Police Department WTC Day Tour—together we fought for our men and the families, day and night.

Thank you to all of the men and women on the PAPD WTC Day Tour, especially the following: Lieutenants J. Ryan, P. Fucci, D. Heffern, R. Caroleo, M. Brogan, M. Winslow, W. Burns, J. Collins, B. Tierney, and K. Walcot; Sergeants A. Devona, M. Florie, J. Flynn, K. Kohlmann, E. Spinelli, and J. Gilburn; Police Officers F. Accardi, R. Amott, A. Basic, E. Beneati, S. Booncome, G. Brady, M. Brown, J. Carrigan, C. Cascante, R. Cassella, A. Ciccone, G. Colligan, J. Collins, A. Croce, J. Cronin, B. Cubero, S. Ditomasso, C. Durham, B. Faustina, E. Finnegan, G. Fortaleza, J. Fosello, L. Gonzalez, R. Hartnett, J. Hawkins, J. Henkel, D. Henry, P. Hernandez, H. Jarratt, J. Jennings, K. Kaczka, T. Kennedy, M. Legiec, B. Lepre, E. Luongo, D. Maharaj, M. Mauceri, L. Mays, D. McCarthy, G. McDade Jr., R. Miller, E. Miranda Jr., M. Morin, R. Murawinski, R. Murray, A. Nazario, J. Noble, J. O'Connor, K. Olszewski, G. Page, M. Polito, N. Rawlins, E. Rodriguez, C. Roughan, J. Sanchez, D. Scala, M. Serrano, S. Skific, J. Sloan, E. Smith Jr., L. Solivan, P. Speciale, P. Tuite, P. Versage, J. Weir, J. White, W. Wilson, and V. Zappulla Jr.

Thank you to the following members of the Passaic County Sheriff's Department: Sheriff J. Speziale, Undersheriff E. Dornbroski, Chief J. Comperatto, Warden C. Meyers, Deputy Warden B. Bendle, Lieutenants J. Hearney, A. Manzo, S. Meyers, M. Loston, and K. Beamon, Sgt. A. Rivers, Detectives F. Ernst, J. Capizzi,

P. Torres, and M. Hoeft, Officers M. Skala, J. Messenger, K. Taylor, D. Cavallo, F. Lurato, M. Trella, E. Castellanos, D. Owen, D. Lemay, S. Sciuto, S. Pellington, K. Hill, N. Tejeda, F. Korsak, M. Kaylani, P. Statutto, N. Acarasquillo, and J. Arturi.

Thank you to the New York City Police Department/ESU, especially Commissioner Ray Kelly, Chief of Department Joe Esposito, First Deputy Commissioner John Dunn, Chief Purtell, Chief Bruce Smolka, Inspector Wasson, Deputy Inspector John Cadaglia, Captains McKeel, Charles Barbutti, and Barry Galfano, Lieutenants Cory Cuneo, Mark Porter, Sean Lawless, and Delia Mannix, Sergeants Mike Walsh, Otto Kroll, Gene McCarthy, John English, Pat Steffens, Patrick Golden, and Pete Smith, Detectives Patrick McGee, Tom Nerney, Steve Theofanous, Mike Oldmixon, Peter Moog, Ron Derosa, Glen Iannatto, and Ed Gardner, Police Officers John Gorman, Mark Whelan, Marge Sarlo, and Debbie Gossett.

Thank you to the members of the Fire Department of New York City, especially Chiefs Steve Rosswieller, Jim Harten, Ed Kilduff, Jim Ritchie, Ron Spadafora, Ron Werner, Patrick McNally, Frank Fellini, Jim Benson, Steve Rush, and Harold Meyers, and Lt. Mike Banker.

Thank you to New York City Emergency Medical Services.

Thank you to the New York City Corrections Department.

Thank you to the New York City Office of Emergency Management, especially Bob Wilson, John Mussina, and Andy Leonik.

Thank you to the New York City Office of the Chief Medical Examiner, especially Dr. Charles Hirsch, David Schomburg, Dr. Schaler, Dr. Emily Craig, Craig Angard, Jude Anglode, Esther Arrington, Allison Bederman, Barbara Butcher, Dennis Cavalli, Russell Czuekus, Frank DePaolo, Kenneth Dunn, Michael Vaivao, Gregory Williams, and Jules Lisner.

Thank you to all of the chaplains who volunteered at the

WTC temporary morgue, for the comfort you brought to the families of the victims.

Thank you to the following building trade unions: Local 3 Electricians (NY); Local 14 Operating Engineers (NY); Local 15 Operating Engineers (NY); Local 15 (A) Operating Engineers (NY); Local 15 (C) Operating Engineers (NY); Local 20 Cement & Concrete Workers; Local 40 Iron Workers (NY); Local 52 Motion Picture Studio Mechanics; Local 79 Laborers, Construction & General Building (NY); Local 147, Subway/Sewer/Tunnel; Local 282, Teamsters (NY); Local 361 Iron Workers; Local 608 Carpenters; Local 638 Steamfitters (NY); Local 731 Building, Concrete & Excavating Laborers; Local 817 Teamster Drivers for Theatrical Industry; Local 825, NJ Operating Engineers; Local 1010, Highway, Road & Street Construction (NY); Local 1456 Dock Builders (NY); Local 1536 Timbermen (NY).

Thank you to the following construction companies: Bovis Lend Lease, Tully, AMEC, Army Corps of Engineers, Turner, Mazzocchi, D.H. Griffin, Allcom, Angel Aerial, Atlantic Heydt, Atlas Concrete, Component Assembly, Eddington & Associates, Grace, Koch Skanska, LaStrada, LKB, Moretrench, Musco, NY Crane, Nicholson, OSS, ProSafety, Safeway Environmental Group, York, Cone Contracting, S.J. Electric, Semcor, Forest Edwards, Headway, Patrol and Guard, Weeks Marine, En-Tech, EROC, Gateway, Liro Construction Managers, and Yonkers.

A special thank-you to Augie Manzo, Ed Davis, Ed Segali, and Chris Raiz. I would also like to thank my friends from the Salt River Project in Arizona.

Thank you to the following health organizations that offered their resources to help the WTC workers: St. Vincent's Hospital, especially Dr. Spencer Eth, Linda Rizzotto, Don Thoms, and Bob Kupferman; CISM, especially Donna Lamonaco, Sarah Lamonaco, Diana Brunell, and Roland Kandle; Cedar Grove Family Chiropractic Services, especially Dr. John Bomhoff, Dr. Jeff Burrows,

Dr. Steve Bales, Steve Balestracci, Franklin Loeffler, Ann Marie Bomhoff, and Barbara Needham. Thanks also to Practitioners Linda Hazlett, Raven Keyes, Dola Rogers, Wendy Henry, Gail Moroso, Sharon Marchand, Mary Gillespie, and Kathy Prinz.

Thanks to everyone from WTC Ground Zero Relief, especially Rhonda Roland Sherer, Stephen Gould, London Allen, Denise Markey, and Valerie Ghent.

Thanks to all of the support groups at the WTC site, including Manhattan Community College, St. John's University, the Red Cross, and the Salvation Army. Thank you to those individuals who offered their expertise in service to the workers, especially Lisa Luckett, Tom Thees, Christine Spencer, Trish Strain, Karen Robertson, Barr Scott, Beth Neilson-Chapman, Phoebe Snow, Bobby Bandera, and Garry Talant. Thank you to everyone at Moving Pictures, especially Ron and Nan Hansa, and Jason Gillet.

I would like to take a moment to thank all of my friends and family. You were all my personal support system throughout the rescue and recovery mission, and I wouldn't have made it through without any of you. I want to particularly thank the Keegans, the Sloyans, the Jagos, the Wisniewskis, the Skinners, the O'Briens, the Murphys, the Cuttinghams, the Canzanos, the Marsellas, the Meyers, the McCormicks, the McConnells, Jack and Mary Ellen Cox, Richie and Bernie Massano, Dar and Rory Shelly, Tom Ruane, Jerome St. John, Steve Skrocki, Erach Screvalla, and Nancy Schade. I would also like to thank my friends from Oklahoma City, Diane Leonard and Reverend Jack Poe.

Most particularly, thank you again to my wife, Karen, and my daughters, Kristine, Tara, and Rory. Your support and love mean everything to me.

This book was written in remembrance of my great friend Jack Miller, who I miss and think of often, and in loving memory of my aunt Pat and uncle Larry Wisniewski, with gratitude for their generosity to me and my family, especially Tara.

Rett Syndrome (RS) is a neurological disorder seen primarily in females, although it also rarely occurs in males. It is usually caused by mutations of the MECP2 gene on the X chromosome. Early development milestones appear normal, but between six and eighteen months of age, there is a delay or regression in development, particularly affecting speech, hand skills, and coordination. Intellectual development appears to be severely delayed (although intelligence is difficult to measure).

I would like to thank the International Rett Syndrome Association for the support they have provided to me and my family. Thanks especially to Kathy Hunter, Barry Rinehart, and Mike and Leslie Greenfield. If you'd like to learn more about Rett Syndrome or if you'd like to find out how to help families who struggle with the disease, please visit the International Rett Syndrome Association website at www.rettsyndrome.org.

If you'd like to make donations or find ways to help the families affected by 9-11, you can contact the following people and organizations for information:

The Police Officer Kenneth Tietjen Memorial Foundation
Janice, Ken, Laurie, Cindy Tietjen
Laurie1653@verizon.net

The Fallen Heroes Fund
"Paying tribute to and supporting the men and women of our military who have sacrificed for our nation."
www.fallenheroesfund.org

If you are a WTC worker and you are in need of physical or mental health resources, you can contact the following people and organizations for help:

St. Vincent's Hospital:
www.svcmc.org/

Mount Sinai Hospital:
www.mountsinai.org/msh/msh-home.jsp

New York Rescue Workers Detoxification Program:
www.nydetox.org

Survivors of the Triangle (Donna Lamonaco):
www.survivorsofthetriangle.org

To the men and women of the United States of America Armed Forces who continue the fight that the above people began on September 11, 2001, at 10:29 a.m. God bless you, your family, and your loved ones. As we do the men and women who sacrificed on September 11, we honor your sacrifice and we will never forget.

Printed in the United States
By Bookmasters